Start SKETCHING & DRAWING now!

Future PLC Quay House, The Ambury, Bath, BA1 1UA

Editorial
Editor **Charles Ginger**
Senior Art Editor **Andy Downes**
Compiled by **Sarah Bankes & Andy Downes**
Head of Art & Design **Greg Whitaker**
Editorial Director **Jon White**

Cover images
Grant Fuller

Advertising
Media packs are available on request
Commercial Director **Clare Dove**

International
Head of Print Licensing **Rachel Shaw**
licensing@futurenet.com
www.futurecontenthub.com

Circulation
Head of Newstrade **Tim Mathers**

Production
Head of Production **Mark Constance**
Production Project Manager **Matthew Eglinton**
Advertising Production Manager **Joanne Crosby**
Digital Editions Controller **Jason Hudson**
Production Managers **Keely Miller, Nola Cokely, Vivienne Calvert, Fran Twentyman**

Printed by William Gibbons, 26 Planetary Road, Willenhall, West Midlands, WV13 3XT

Distributed by Marketforce, 5 Churchill Place, Canary Wharf, London, E14 5HU www.marketforce.co.uk Tel: 0203 787 9001

The content in this book was previously published in the Penguin Random House LLC book entitled: Start Sketching & Drawing Now

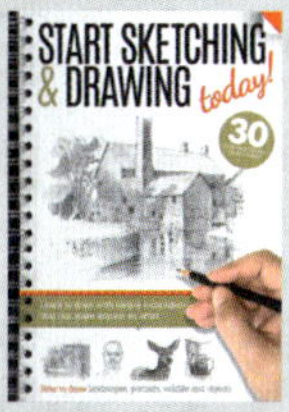

Start Sketching & Drawing Now Third Edition (CTB4115)

FUTURE Connectors. Creators. Experience Makers.

Future plc is a public company quoted on the London Stock Exchange (symbol: FUTR)
www.futureplc.com

Chief executive **Zillah Byng-Thorne**
Non-executive chairman **Richard Huntingford**
Chief financial officer **Penny Ladkin-Brand**
Tel +44 (0)1225 442 244

Widely Recycled

ipso. For press freedom with responsibility

CW01656159

Welcome

The bookazine you hold in your hands is designed to help get you creating art. Not tomorrow, or next week, but right now. This volume by Grant Fuller is dedicated to sketching and drawing and will teach you an array of different styles and techniques. If you're new to all this, then it will have you making art in minutes. And if you're already an artist, then you'll hopefully pick up a few fresh ideas. Whatever your skill level, we hope you enjoy the book. Now go and grab your pencils and paper and get down to business!

About the Author

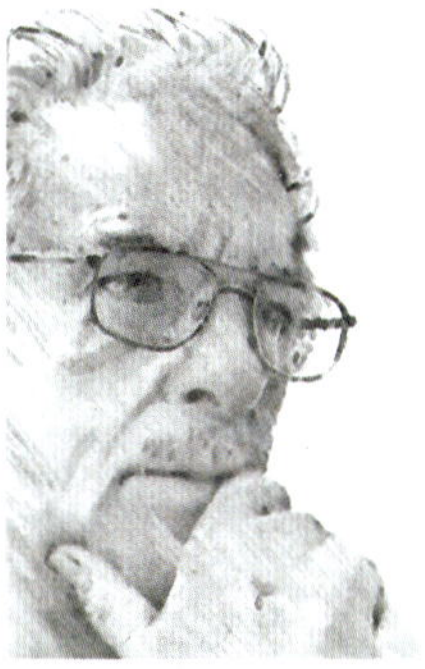

Grant Fuller was born in Winnipeg, Canada. During his early career as a commercial artist and an art director in broadcast production he worked throughout the United States, Canada and Puerto Rico.

From 1984 onwards Grant worked as a painter and teacher of watercolour art full time, travelling to teach workshops across the U.S., Canada and the UK. Grant's paintings won several jurors awards and have been featured in magazines and newspapers at local and international levels. He had numerous one-man shows and participated in various group shows. His subjects ranged from buildings and boats to figures and portraits. He sadly passed away in October 2016 at the age of 73, but his legacy lives on in the form of his stunning artwork and the many students he guided. By purchasing this bookazine you are helping to continue his work for years to come. Thank you, and good luck on your journey to becoming a better artist.

Contents

6 Introduction

8 Tools

11 Paper

CHAPTER 1

12 Graphite Techniques

Line Quality · Blind Contour Drawing · Hard Lines · Soft Lines · Learn to "See" · Demo: Transfer a Drawing

CHAPTER 2

24 Tone

Faking 3-D · Applying and Blending Tone · Demo: Create a 3-D Effect · Demo: Blend Tones With a Stump · Demo: Apply Tone Without Smudging · Demo: Blend Tone With a Pencil

CHAPTER 3

36 Proportion

Plotting Proportion · Foreshortening · Demo: Draw a Cat in Proportion · Demo: Draw a Coffeepot in Proportion · Demo: Scale a Drawing With a Grid

CHAPTER 4

50 Simple Perspective

One- and Two-Point Perspective · Cast Shadows in Perspective · Perspective and Shapes · Demo: Practice Two-Point Perspective · Demo: More Practice in Two-Point Perspective · Demo: Practice One-Point Perspective

CHAPTER 5

60 Outdoors

Drawing on Site · Demo: Explore Tone and Texture · Demo: More Tone and Texture · Demo: Practice Cast Shadows and Reflections · Demo: Explore Soft Lines on a Hard-Line Subject · Demo: Draw a Street Scene in One-Point Perspective · Demo: Draw a Street Scene With Multiple Vanishing Points · Demo: Estimate Vanishing Points

CHAPTER 6

78 Faces and Figures

Facial Anatomy · Sketching Facial Contours · Demo: Sketch a Character Study · Demo: Plan a Portrait · Figures · Gesture Drawing

CHAPTER 7

92 Other Mediums

Pen & Ink · Charcoal · Demo: Draw a Deer in Charcoal · Wash Drawing · Demo: Mix and Apply a Wash · Colored Pencils · Demo: Mix Colored Pencil Pigments · Demo: Draw Autumn Leaves · Demo: Draw Lily Pads · Water Soluble · Demo: Create Bold Sunflowers · Demo: Get Watercolor Effects With Wax Pastels · Demo: Create Painted China and Reflective Glass · Demo: Sketch on Location · Demo: Blend Pigments in a Seascape

124 Conclusion

126 Index

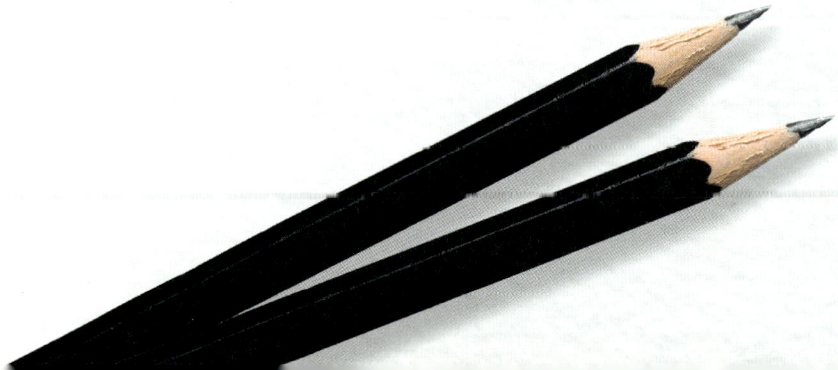

WHAT YOU NEED

Surfaces

200-lb. (425gsm) rag watercolor paper
acid-free art paper
medium-texture illustration board
tracing paper

Graphite

2H, HB, 2B graphite sticks
HB, B mechanical pencils
2H, HB, B, 2B wooden pencils

Other

ballpoint pen
blow dryer
colored pencils
charcoal pencil
electric pencil sharpener
kneaded eraser
masking tape
no. 8 synthetic round brush
paper towels
sandpaper
straightedge
stump
tissue
transparent sleeve
T-square
watercolor pencils
wax pastels

METRIC CONVERSION CHART

To convert	To	Multiply by
Inches	Centimeters	2.54
Centimeters	Inches	0.4
Feet	Centimeters	30.5
Centimeters	Feet	0.03
Yards	Meters	0.9
Meters	Yards	1.1

Introduction

Although I have had an affinity for drawing since the age of four, I did not become accomplished until much later in life. I never saw another person draw well until I reached art school and even then, it was limited to brief glances over someone's shoulder. Drawing instruction in those days was more verbal than visual.

After four years of art school, I was able to get work as a commercial artist. It was only then that I began to get the type of hands-on direction I needed to improve my drawing skills. Without proper instruction, natural talent will struggle and all too often fade, giving way to other pressures in life. But my opportunity to work closely with professional artists and receive personal demonstrations made all the difference in the quality of my own work.

I have documented the steps I took, based on the instruction of experts, in order to pass along this knowledge. Practice is important in developing good drawing skills, but professional instruction can save many hours of trial and error.

Most importantly, think of drawing as a pleasant pastime, a process of searching and exploring. If you view the drawing process as some sort of test, you will only increase the pressure and decrease the pleasure. Learn instead to think of the drawing process as a form of freedom. Grab a sketchbook, and don't be afraid to scribble and play.

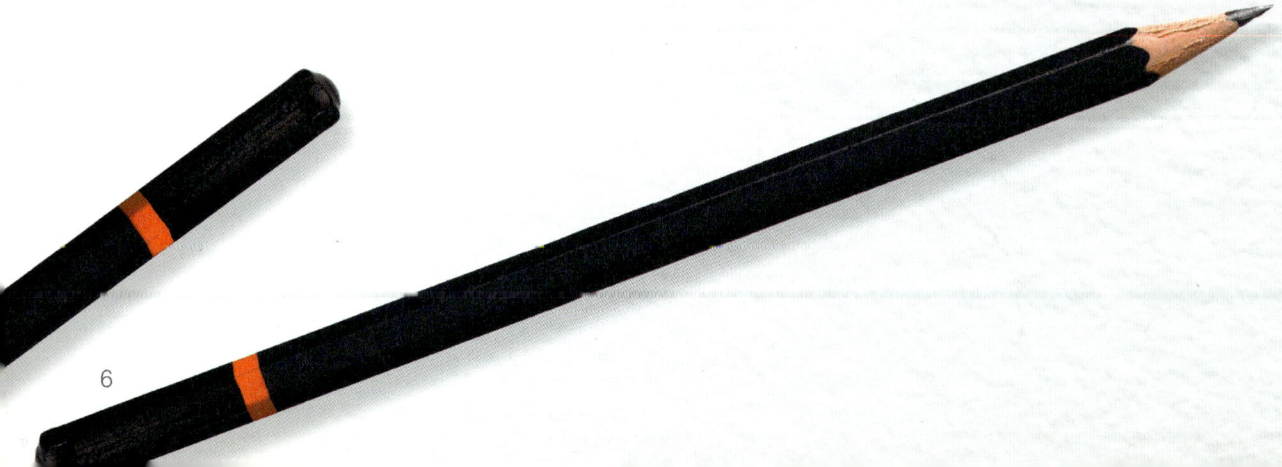

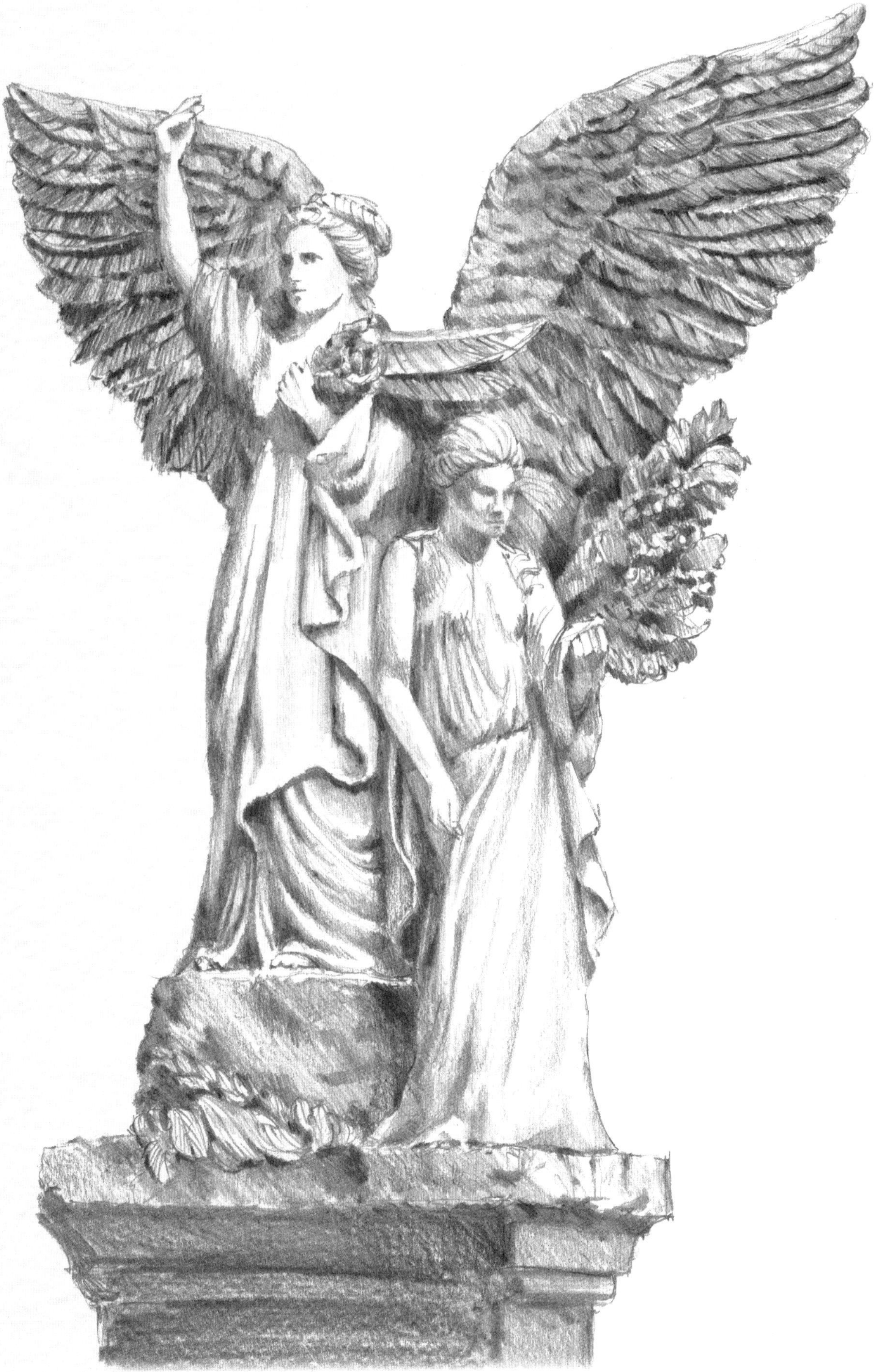

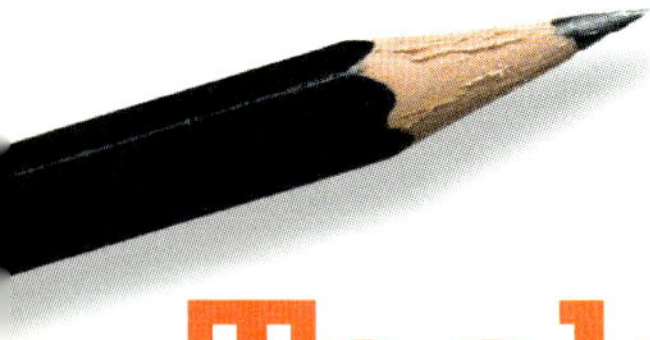

Tools

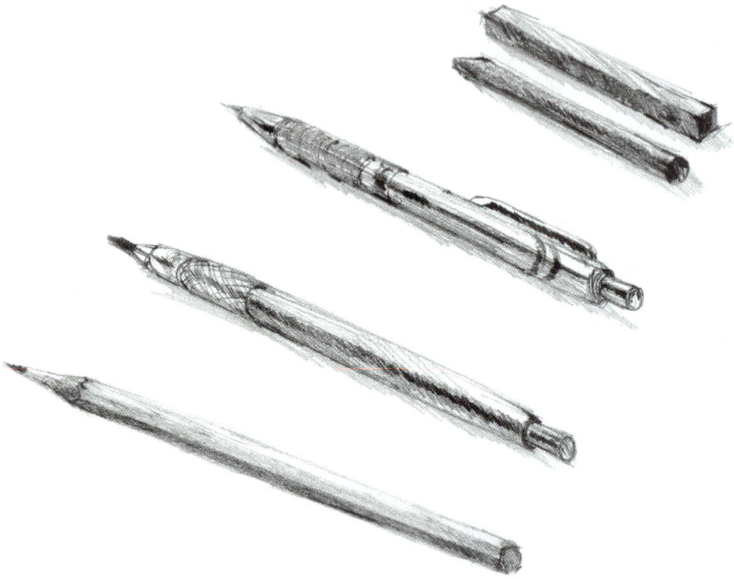

Graphite

Graphite is measured in degrees of hardness. The highest degree on the soft half of the scale is a 6B pencil – very soft; 5B is slightly harder, then 4B, 3B, 2B, B, all getting progressively harder until you reach the midpoint which is HB. On the hard side, the numbers progress from H up to 6H, which is the hardest in that series. Commonly called lead, graphite comes in various forms – wooden pencils, mechanical pencils and plain sticks.

Graphite sticks are useful for applying tone to large areas or making wide lines. They come in several degrees of softness but not the full range. Mechanical pencils are available in different diameter leads – sizes .05, .07, .09 – and can be found in office supply stores. They are good for finer work as well as everyday sketching. Larger gauge holders and leads can be found at art supply stores. Wooden 2B pencils can be found everywhere, but the full range from 6B to 6H is available through art suppliers.

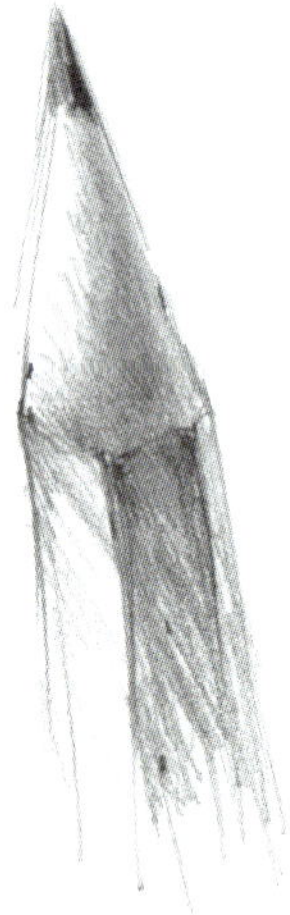

Keep It Simple

There are specialty leads which exceed the range discussed here, but this will be more than enough for our purpose. I rarely use any pencil harder than 2H or softer than 2B.

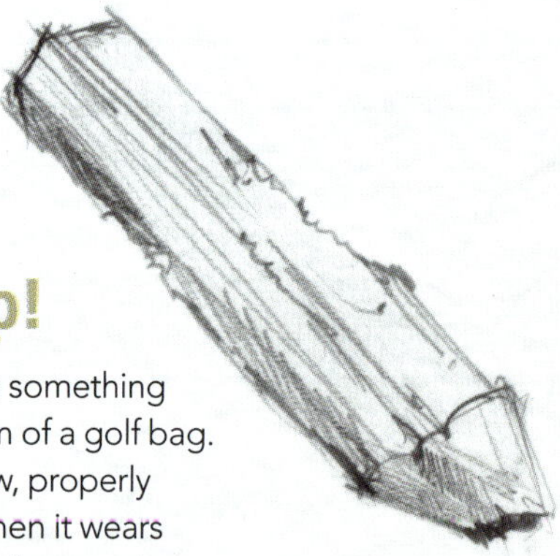

Stay Sharp!

Don't try to draw with something you find in the bottom of a golf bag. Start with a brand new, properly sharpened pencil. When it wears down about half way, then use it to keep golf scores!

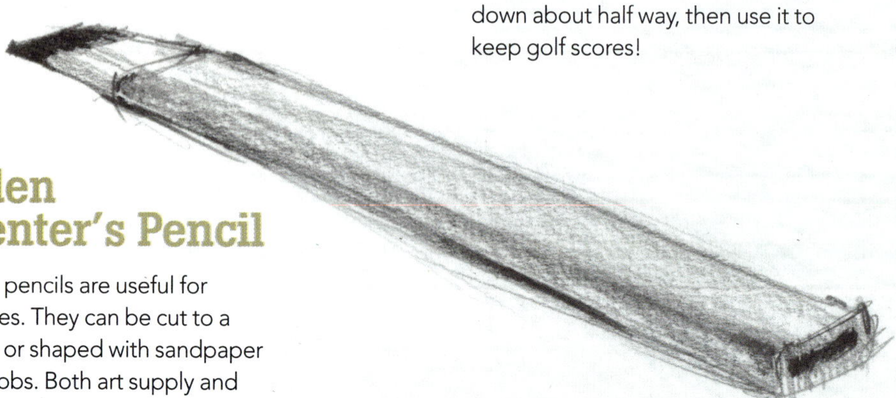

Wooden Carpenter's Pencil

Carpenter's pencils are useful for broad strokes. They can be cut to a chisel point or shaped with sandpaper for special jobs. Both art supply and hardware stores carry them.

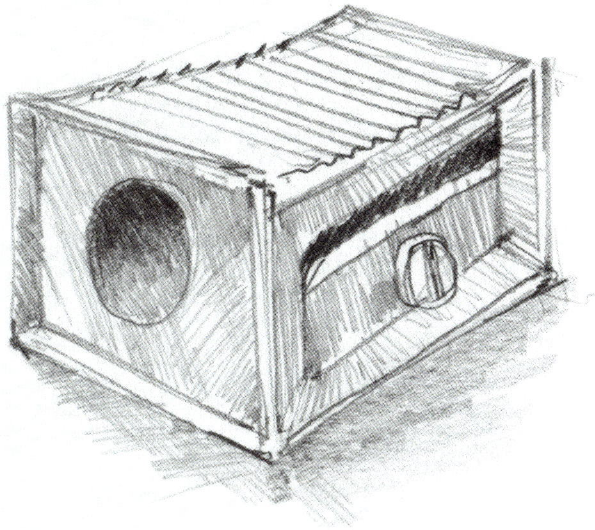

Pocket Sharpener

There's no excuse for using blunt pencils with the number of tools available for sharpening. Some are ancient collectibles like the pocket sharpener from elementary school days. They still work, though they can be a bit messy if you don't have a convenient place to dispose of the shavings and graphite powder.

Manual Sharpener

Who can forget the old manual school model? (It was usually wall-mounted and overflowing with shavings that never seemed to make it to the waste-paper basket without leaving a trail.) Use a paintbrush to clean the blades on a manual sharpener periodically. They also always seem to work better after a blast of spray oil (sold in hardware stores).

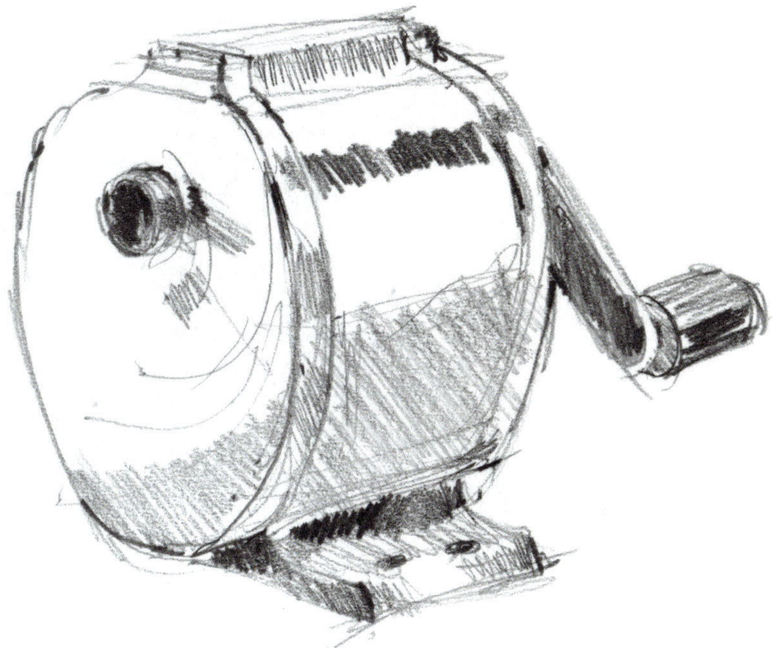

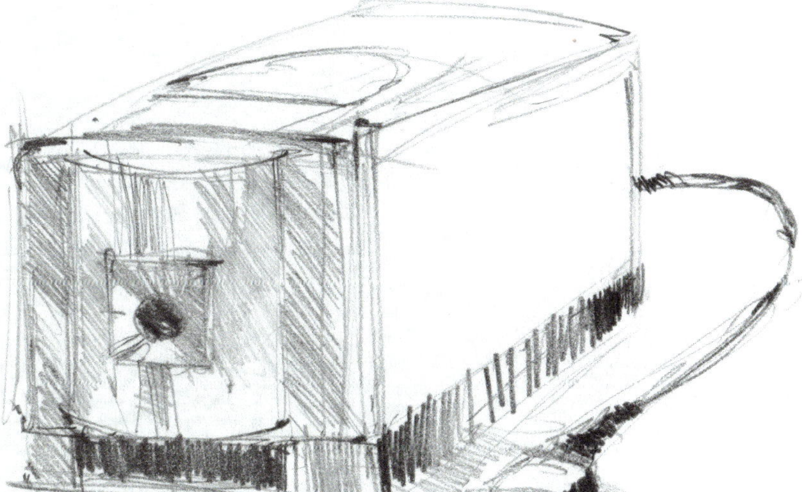

Electric Sharpener

The most popular sharpener in the studio is the electric sharpener. It also benefits from having the blades dusted out with a paintbrush and sprayed with a bit of oil every once in a while.

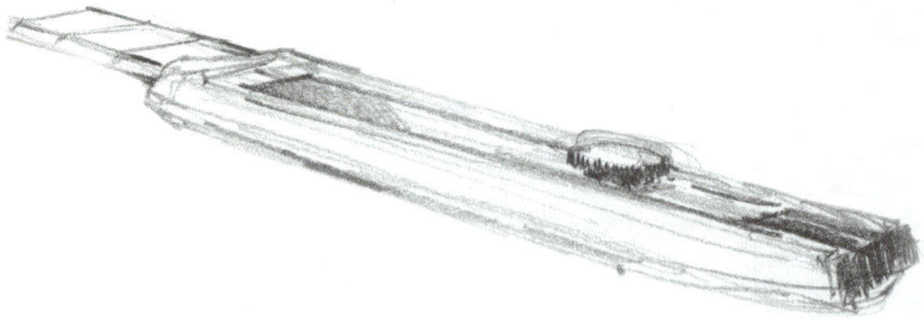

Utility Knife

There will be times when you want to draw with a tool that just won't fit in the hole provided by the sharpener. Whittling the wood away from the graphite without breaking the lead is a valuable skill to develop. The retractable snap-off blade is cheap and handy for this job and many others.

Erasers

Don't use the eraser on the end of a pencil. It will smear the graphite and tear the paper. Two types of good erasers are white plastic and kneaded. White plastic erasers are best for removing stubborn lines without damaging the paper. Kneaded erasers stretch and shape to suit the space you're working in. They can be pinched to remove even a single line. They can be cleaned easily, simply by stretching them to disperse the graphite particles.

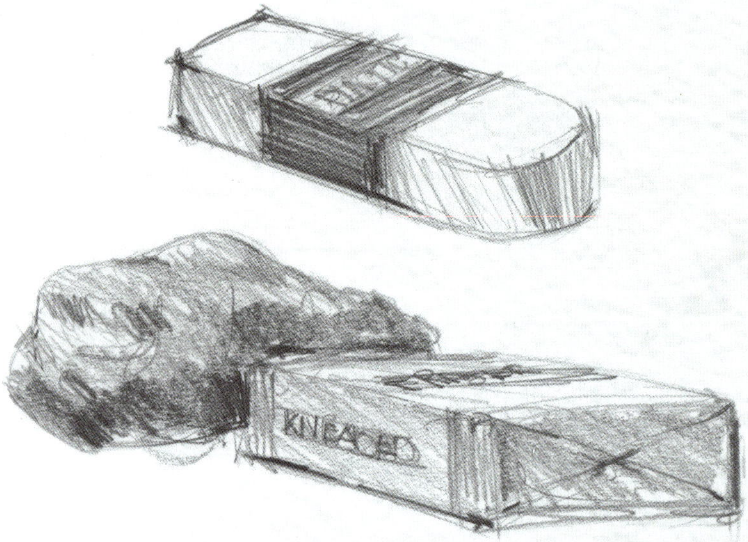

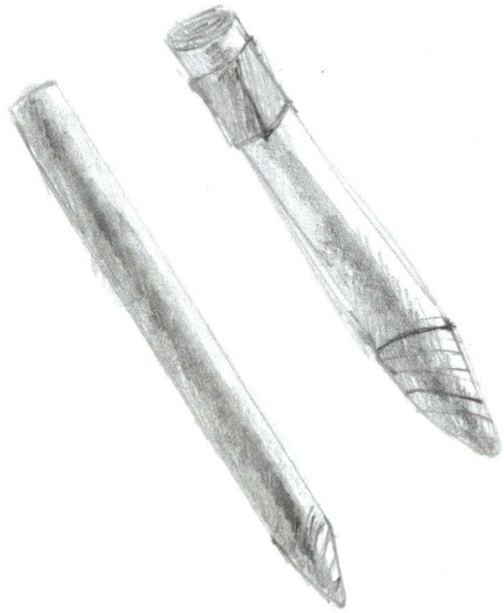

Stumps

A stump is a tightly rolled piece of paper that can be shaped to a point. It is used to smudge or blend graphite. Stumps can be bought or homemade. The machine-made version comes ready to use. The homemade version must be shaped with a piece of smooth sandpaper.

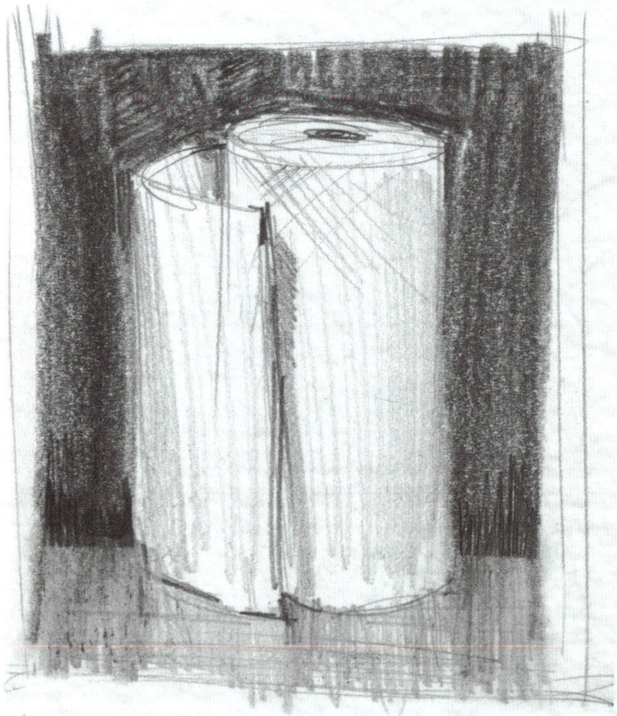

Paper Towels

Place a paper towel under your drawing hand when your work is in danger of being smudged.

Tools

How to Choose

You will find an overwhelming number of strange new names for paper when you first venture into the local art supply store.

- **Vellum** – originally made from animal skins, now made from plasticized cotton or wood pulp mixtures; used largely for plans or diagrams.
- **Bristol board** – named after the city, this board has two workable sides.
- **Illustration board** – very heavy stock with one workable side.
- **Cartridge paper** – commonly sold in loose sheets for pencil drawing.
- **Canson** – a French-made, acid-free paper designed to hold pastel chalk, charcoal and more.

As with many things, you get what you pay for. Don't make the mistake of thinking, "I'll wait till I'm good at this before I buy good materials."

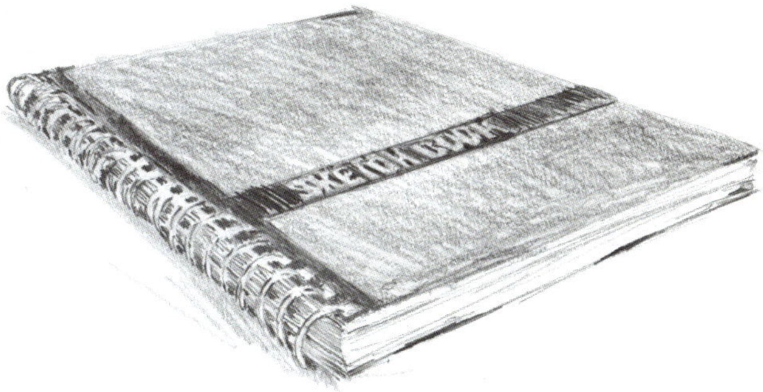

Sketchbooks

Price is a fair guideline for sketchbook quality. Cheap with lots of pages usually means it has inferior lightweight paper. Smooth paper does not hold pencil well, so choose something with a slightly abrasive surface texture or tooth. Archival quality is necessary if you want to preserve your work for generations to come, but most quality acid-free drawing paper will remain white for an average lifetime.

Keep a travel-size sketchbook with you at all times so you can sketch while waiting in airports, lobbies, parks, restaurants, etc.

2B Pencil on Rough 90-lb. (190gsm) Watercolor Paper

Some heavier papers have a decal edge. Different pressures fill more or less of the coarse texture.

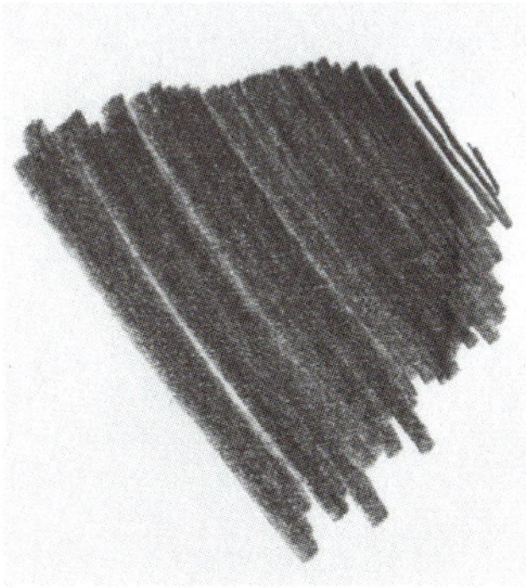

2B Pencil on Basic Sketchbook Paper

There is still enough tooth in the paper to show some surface interest.

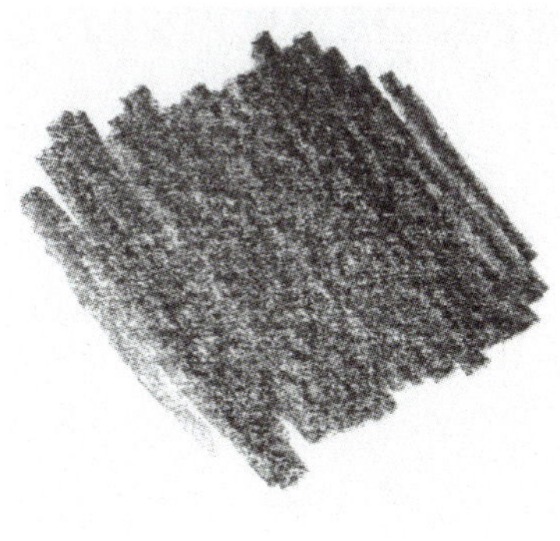

HB Pencil on Basic Sketchbook Paper

More pressure and harder lead flatten the tooth and fill in more.

CHAPTER 1

Graphite techniques

If you are new to drawing you will likely be concerned with proportion – getting shapes the right size, in the right place, and at the right angles and relationship to each other. Try to forget all that for now and just explore what you can do with a pencil. See what marks a simple pencil will make. The point leaves a certain type of line, the side a different mark. Different pressures and speeds have very different results. This type of experimenting might seem pointless at first, but you should be as familiar with the pencils you use as musicians are with their instruments. Doodling creates a connection with your eye, brain and hand that will be vital to your creation of successful drawings. This chapter will focus on helping you get command of the drawing tool and exploring graphite techniques that make the most out of the medium.

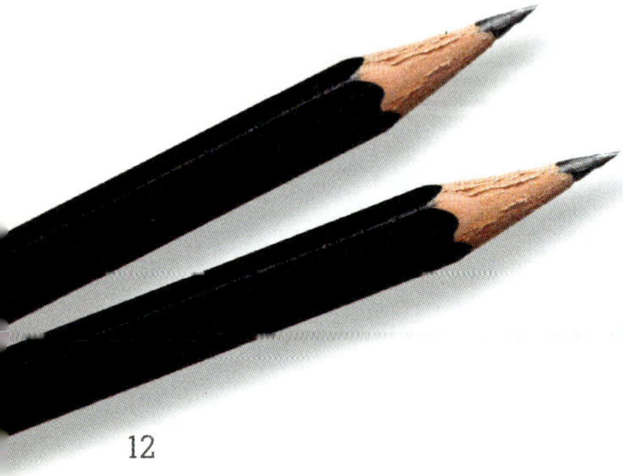

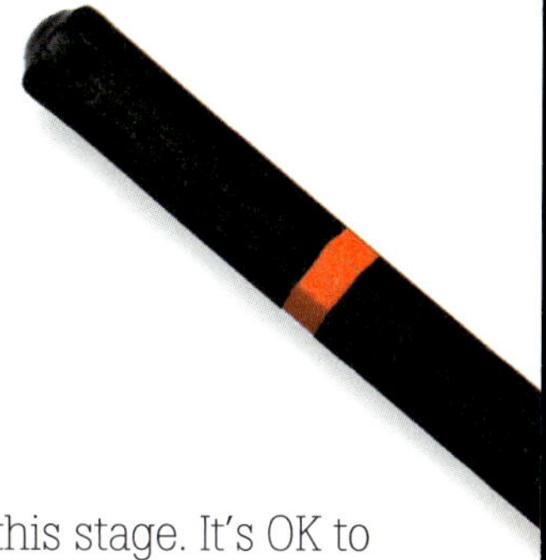

Line Quality

The line is the main ingredient in a drawing. Start with good quality ingredients.

Choose a simple household object to draw, like a coffee mug. Try to do the entire drawing without smudging. That means no blurring with the fingers to create light tones. Practice getting the different values (light and dark) just by changing pressure on the pencil.

Don't worry about erasing at this stage. It's OK to show several attempts to find the right place for a line. Go lightly at first, then apply more pressure as you learn where the contours are.

The lines should look as if the pencil was searching for the right place and then responded with enthusiasm when it was found.

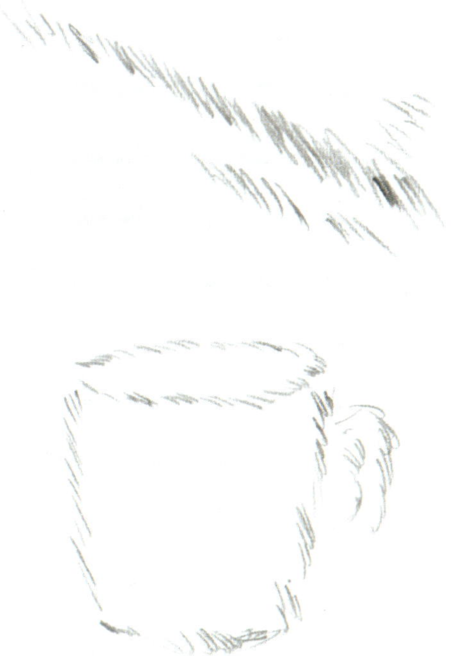

Too Sketchy

A common mistake when learning to draw. The lines reveal uncertainty and hesitation. Practice moving forward and keep the pencil on the paper rather than constantly lifting it. This requires boldness. You run the risk of losing proportion and shape, but you need to "feel" the paper through the pencil.

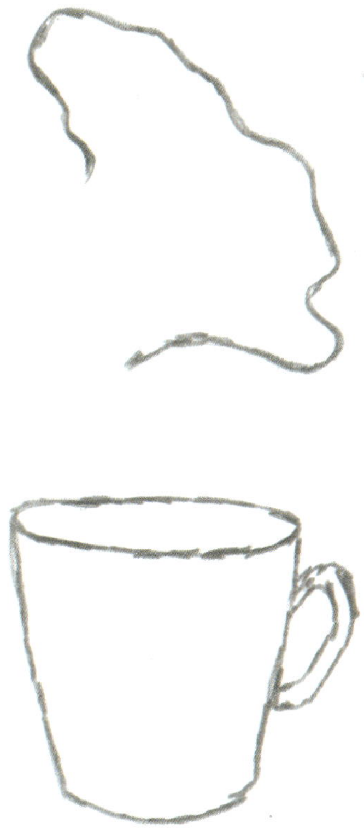

Too Boring

As you develop boldness and learn to keep the pencil on the paper, you will notice the lines getting monotonous. You are getting the idea, but the speed and pressure on the pencil is always the same.

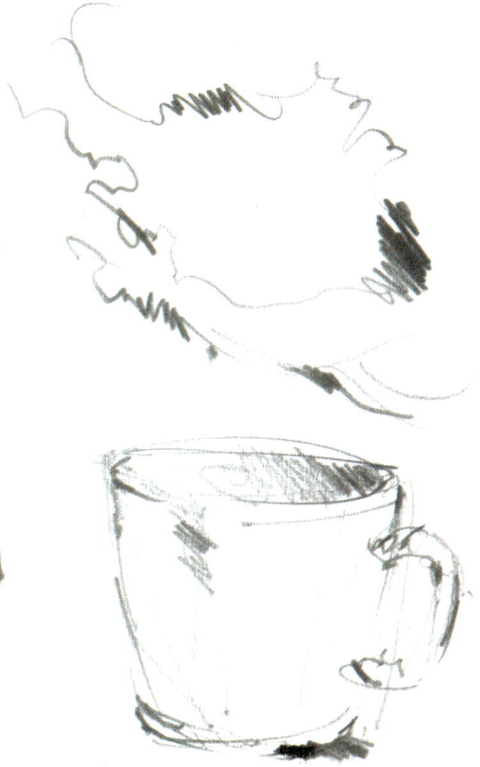

Good Variety

An example of the good line quality you want. Vary the speed and pressure. Use fast light lines, slower darker lines, wide and thin lines. You may lose the shape and accuracy at first, but the drawing will be exciting and lively. Line quality is more important than mathematical precision.

Blind Contour Drawing

This is an art-school exercise intended to improve hand-eye coordination. The idea is to stare at an object, find a starting point on the contour (outer edge) and begin to trace the shape onto a piece of paper. Oh yes – without looking at your hand, and without lifting the pencil off the paper!

It may seem silly but stick with it. Try to ignore the distorted line work on the paper. Don't think about the proportions right now. Just focus on the contour of the object. Notice whether it is smooth, rough, straight, curved, jagged, etc. Your drawing will probably look similar to the images on this page.

You might wonder if it is pointless to draw objects without paying attention to their proportions, but the goal of this exercise is to develop the quality of line. You will immediately notice a difference in your sensitivity and in the quality of your lines.

Once you have explored blind-contour drawing, use that same sensitivity you developed in the exercise to go back and draw normally. Study the contours of the subject, check your progress on the paper, and then study the subject again. You will begin to see more than you first realized, and that will soon show in your drawing.

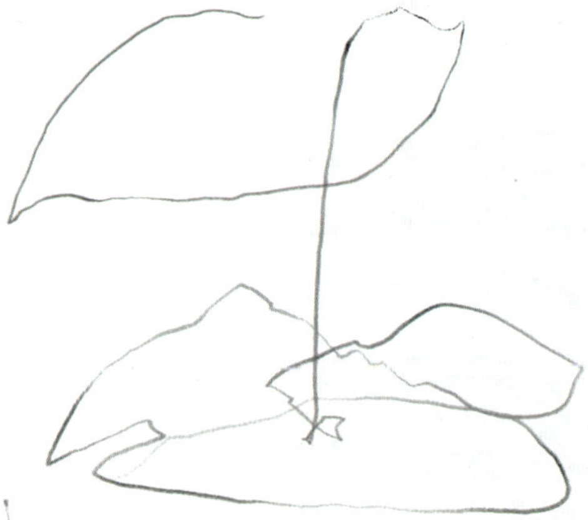

Plant

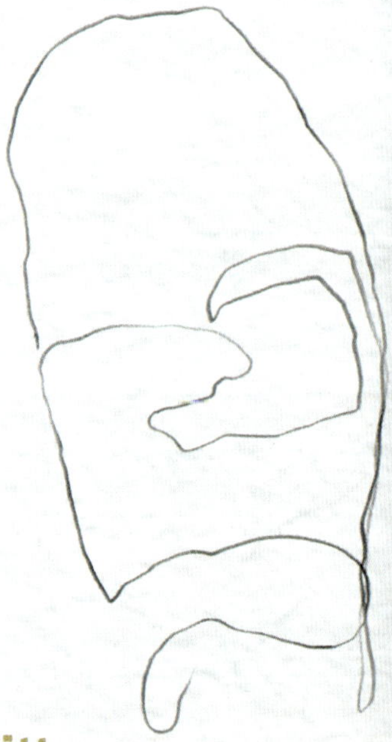

Mitten

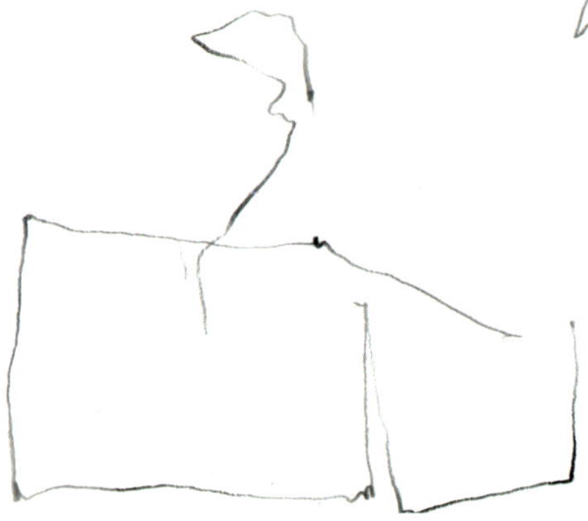

Box of Tissues

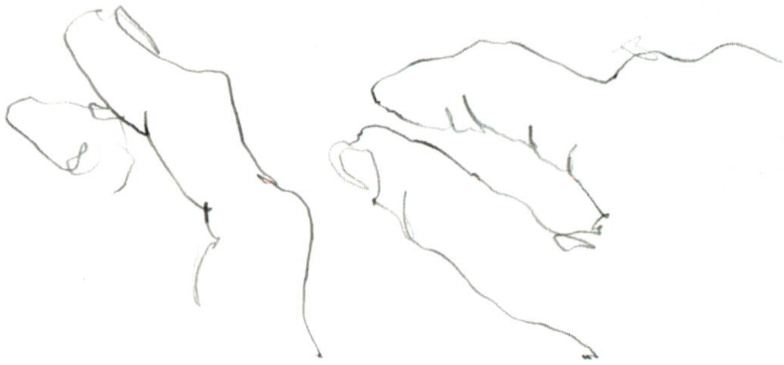

Fingers

PRACTICE WITH ORGANIC SHAPES

Organic shapes such as flowers are fun to practice, and they tend to be far more forgiving than structures or portraits.

Hardlines

Over the years I've observed that there seems to be a natural attraction between certain artists and certain types of subjects.

Many artists who draw or paint hard lines – structures such as buildings, boats and still life, will often struggle with soft-line subjects like figures, fabrics and floral treatments. Hard-line artists who have a talent for working with geometric shapes can be uncomfortable with subjects that do not have rigid, fixed edges.

On the other hand, soft-line artists have a natural flair for freehand work and do better with moving targets and subjects with flexible contours, but their drawings of rigid shapes may sometimes look tense and overworked.

Practice copying these drawings to get a feel for the different types of line work.

USE SHORT, REPETITIVE LINES AND VARY CONTRAST

In these examples, some of the lines were drawn with a straightedge. You can use a set square or ruler. Even though the lines are short and quite repetitive, there is still variation in pressure and speed. It is necessary to keep light and dark contrast, or the drawing gets mechanical and boring.

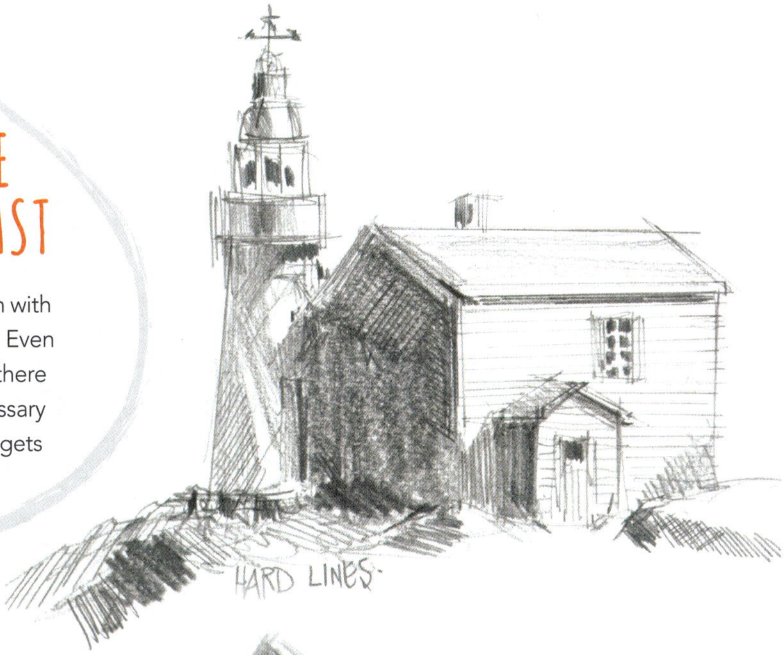

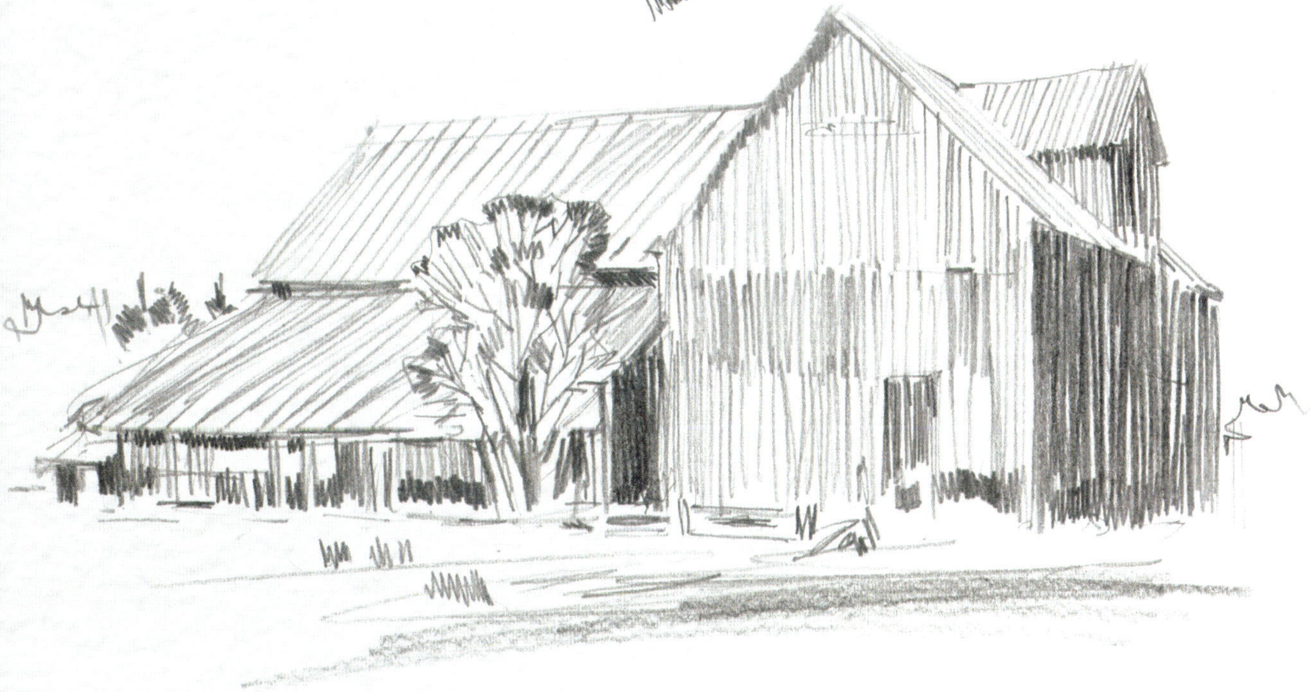

Rigid Lines Work Well for Certain Shapes

If the subject has an interesting shape, the short, rigid lines work quite well. It is important to preserve white areas in the drawing, along with dark, contrasting areas.

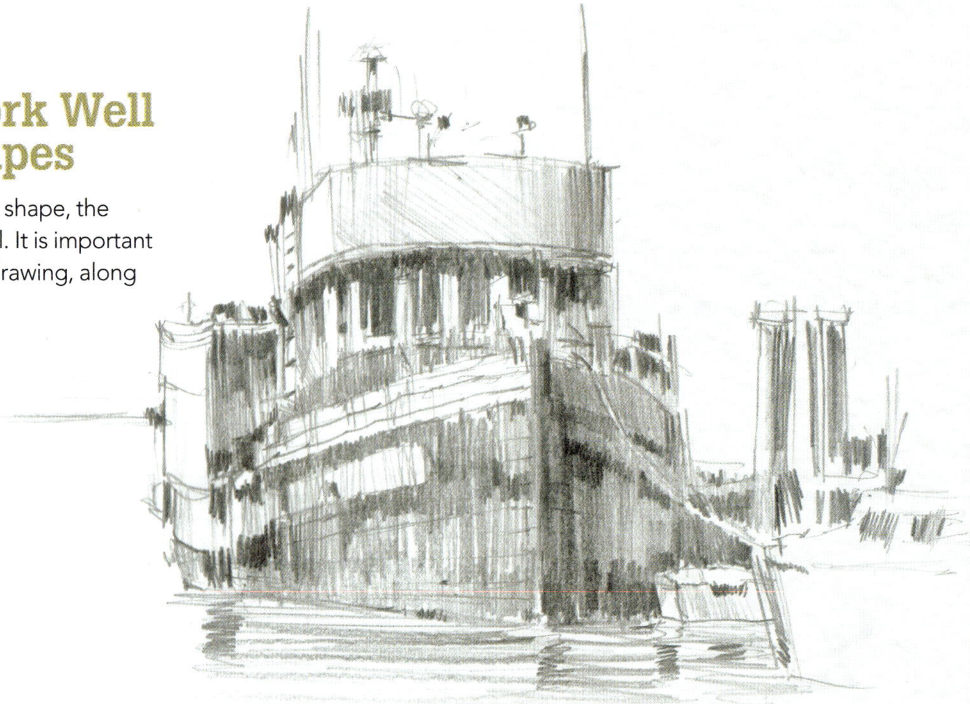

PRACTICE FREEHAND HARD-LINE SUBJECTS

Practice drawing straight lines without a straightedge. It's alright if the lines are not absolutely rigid as long as the structure is stable and not distorted.

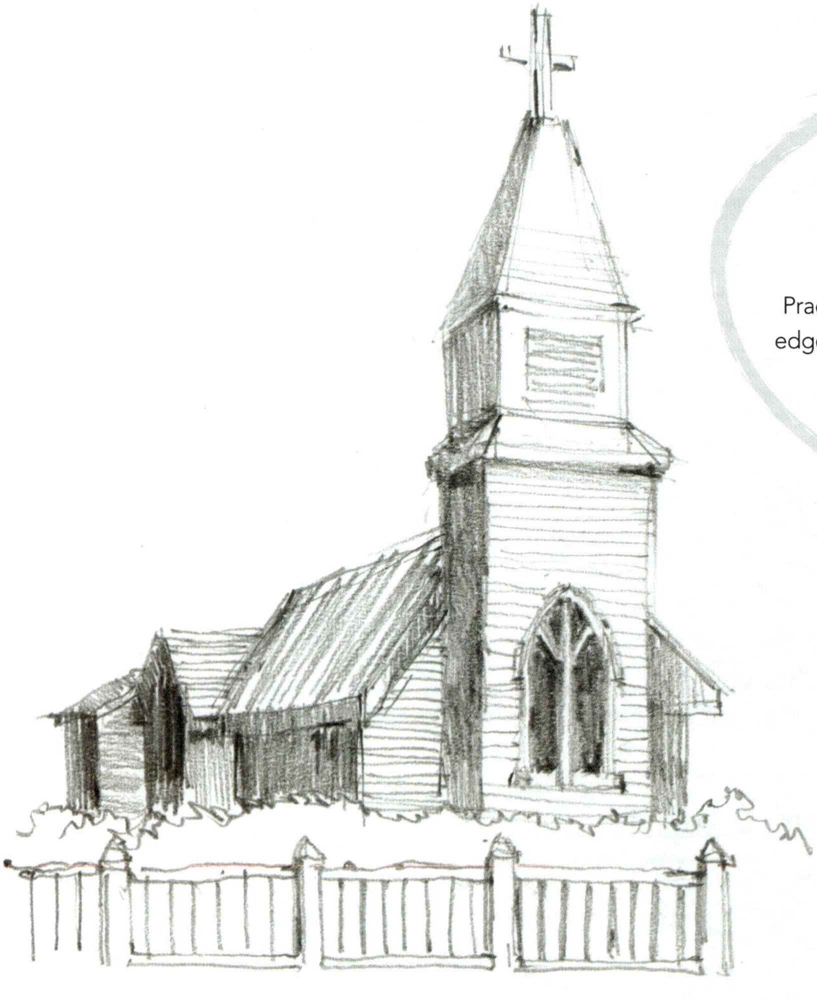

Freehand

This sketch is freehand, meaning it was drawn without a straightedge. The lines are a bit longer and wander more than previous examples. It is still a hard-line subject, but the line work is beginning to soften slightly.

Softlines

Here are some examples of soft-line subjects. Copy these onto some scrap paper. Try to work quickly, challenging yourself to draw the lines fast. You will find it easier to slow down later and focus on precision, but for now, give priority to speed rather than accuracy. Soon you'll be placing those speedy lines in the right place and feeling the thrill of accomplishment. You won't necessarily have the proportions right at this point, but there will be life and action in your work.

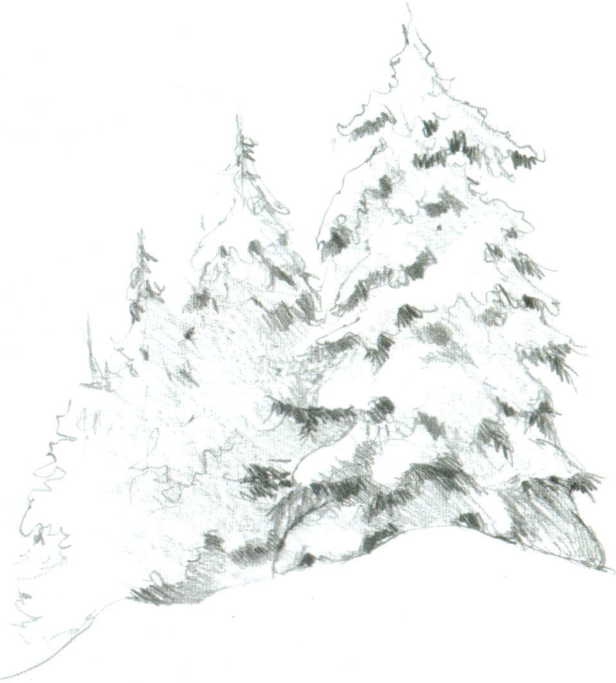

Vary Your Angle

Notice the different feel the pencil has when it is sharp compared to when blunt. It feels different when you increase pressure. Change the angle so that you vary between using the point and the side of the lead.

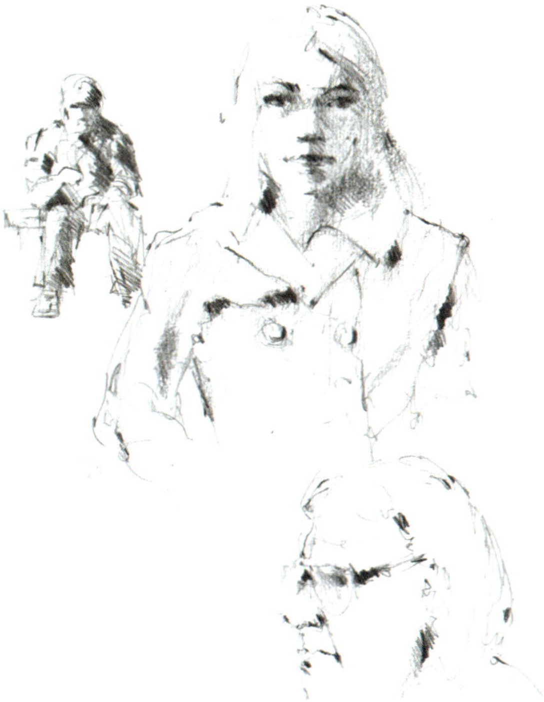

Traditional Approach

A more typical use of soft-line drawing. The line work is free and searching, even wandering in places. It makes use of variation in speed and pressure.

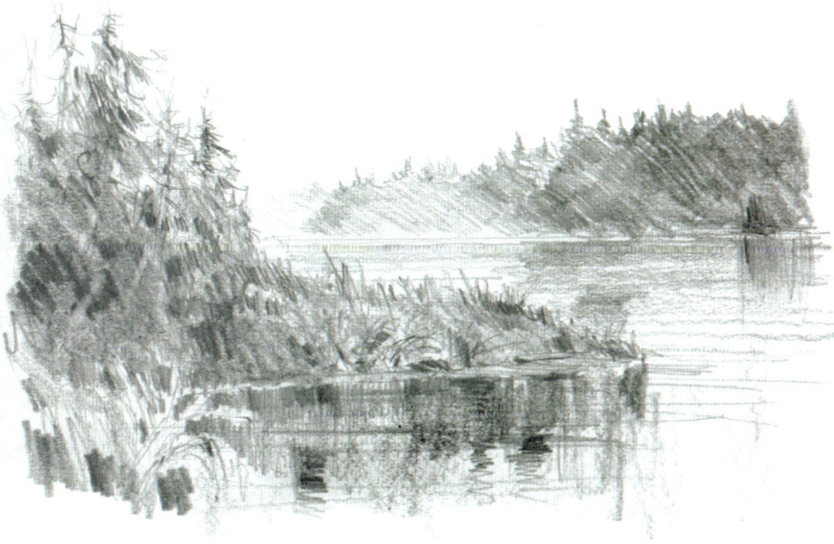

Tone Just As Important As Line

I consider this to be a soft-line work even though the drawing uses tone more than line. The shapes are not straight lines and they still need the lively "loose" treatment.

Learn to "See"

Have you ever noticed that although you are able to recognize countless objects at first glance, when you try to draw them from memory, you cannot recall enough information to make a good drawing? This is because your memory records key pieces of visual information about things as you look around, and your brain feeds back a "shorthand" version of your surroundings. This abbreviated method allows you to quickly identify all the objects around you, spot dangers, avoid collisions and find things.

After you draw an object, your memory has a vastly improved record of that object. After drawing it a few more times, you may find that you can draw it from memory. The down side, however, is that the quality deteriorates because you've taken your eyes out of the equation. No matter how good your memory is, it does not compare to what you see by looking at the real thing. Lighting, texture, subtle shapes and contours are all things that fade from memory very quickly.

As an artist, you must learn how to look at things as if you were seeing them for the first time.

Memory Fills in the Gaps

We can recognize objects from fragments of shapes and bits of information.

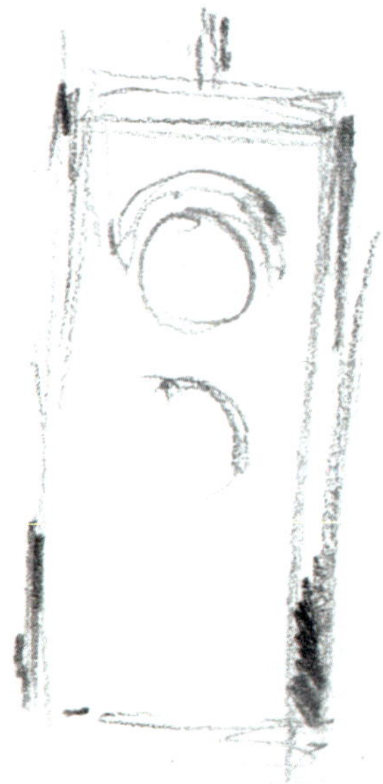

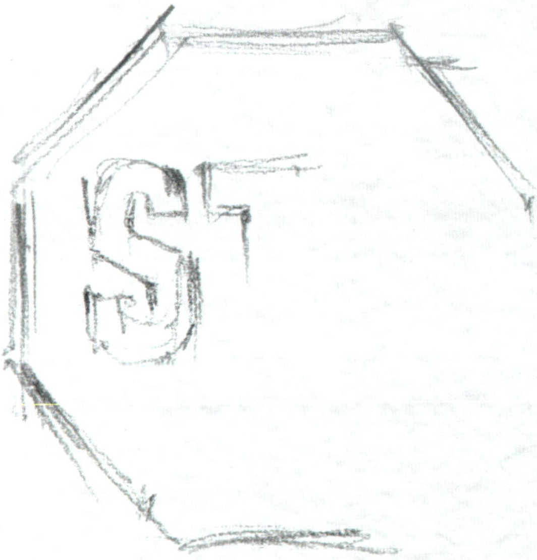

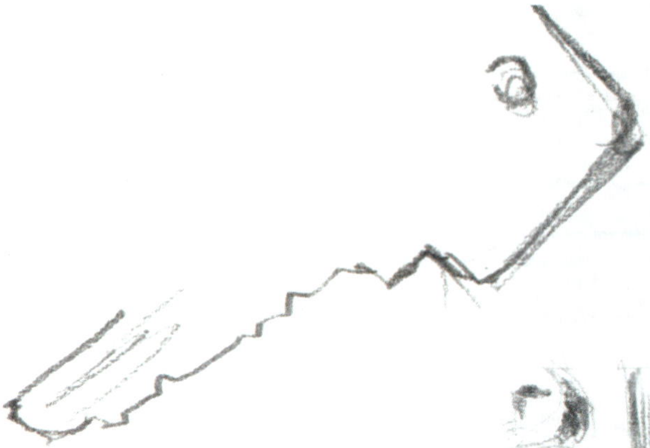

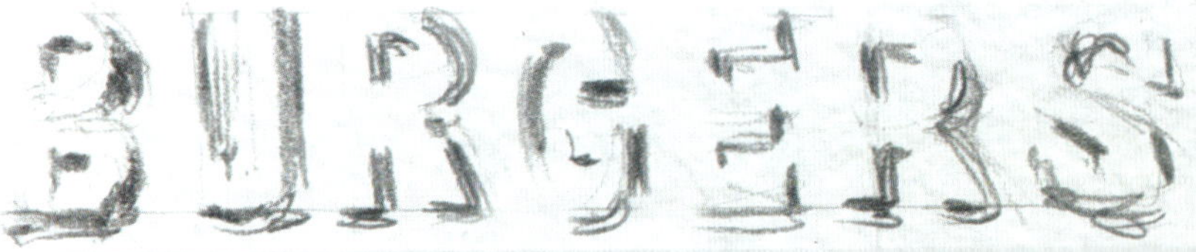

Upgrade Your Memory

Not only do we recognize fragments of objects, we also have a collection of highly simplified symbols in our memory. When we draw, we are competing with those symbols. It is important to concentrate on upgrading these images as we draw by committing new information to memory.

Draw a few household objects that are slightly uncommon. Don't select a table spoon or knife – they are so familiar that you will have symbols in your memory for those objects. However, tools like a can opener, kitchen whisk, egg beater or perhaps workshop tools, which are not likely embedded in your memory are better for this exercise. You'll need to study them as though you were seeing them for the first time.

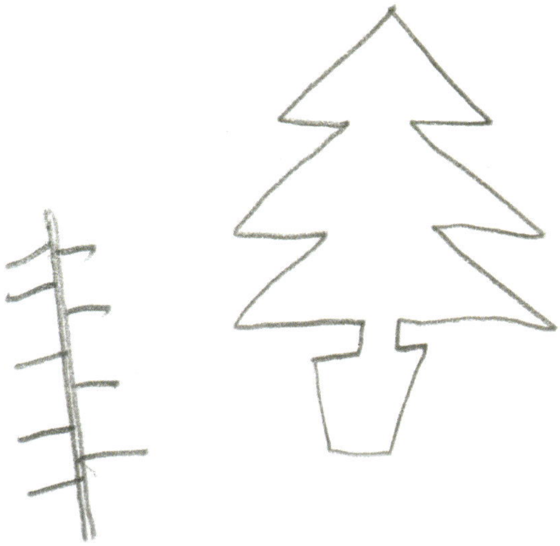

Memory Can Be a Roadblock

Because of the simplified symbols already present in our subconscious, when beginners are asked to draw something from memory the result is often similar to the images you see here. Upgrade your memory!

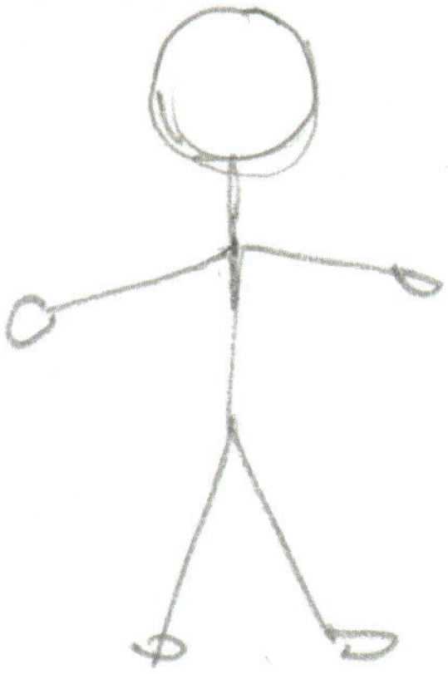

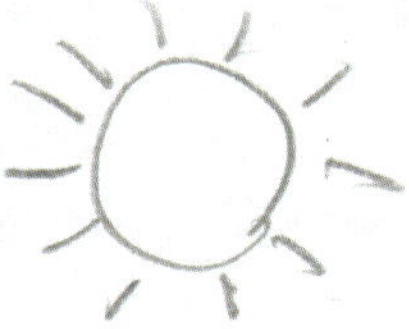

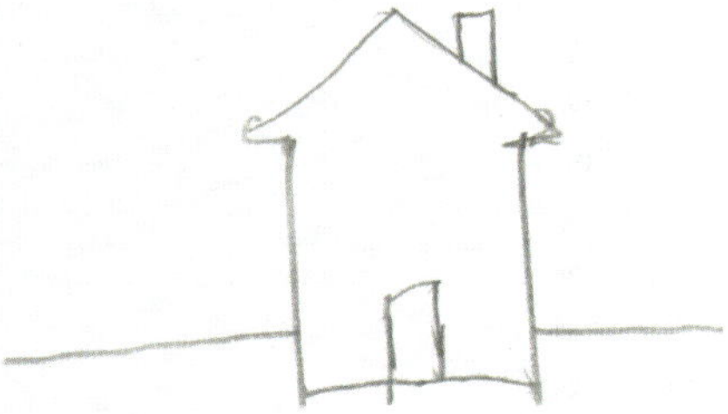

Draw Things in Order to Really See Them!

In the course of drawing unusually common objects, you will learn how things work – not scientifically, but how the parts connect and relate in size and shape. Drawing something as mundane as an electrical plug can be an adventure in seeing. You will begin to notice things that make you realize you have been looking but not really seeing.

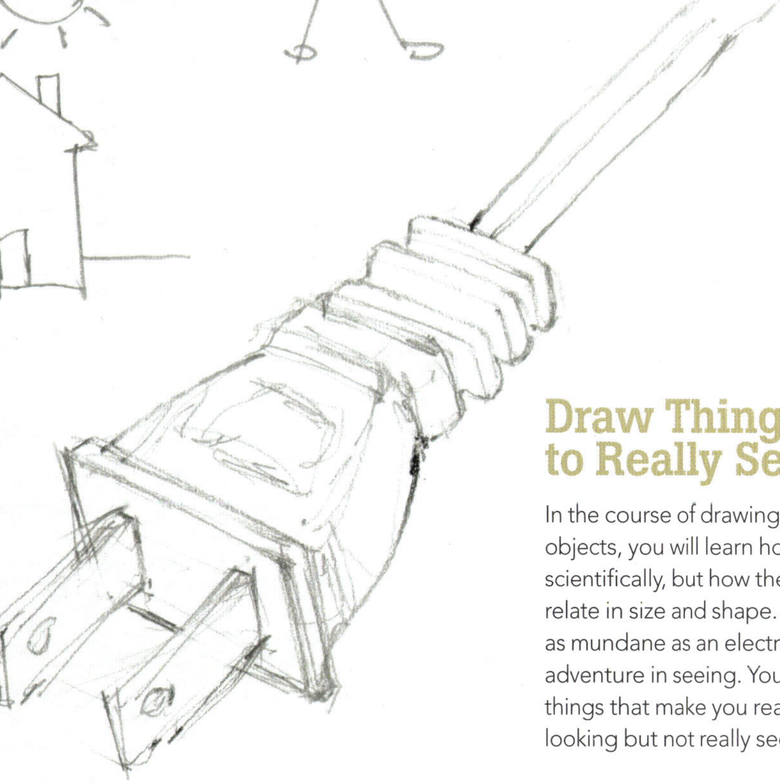

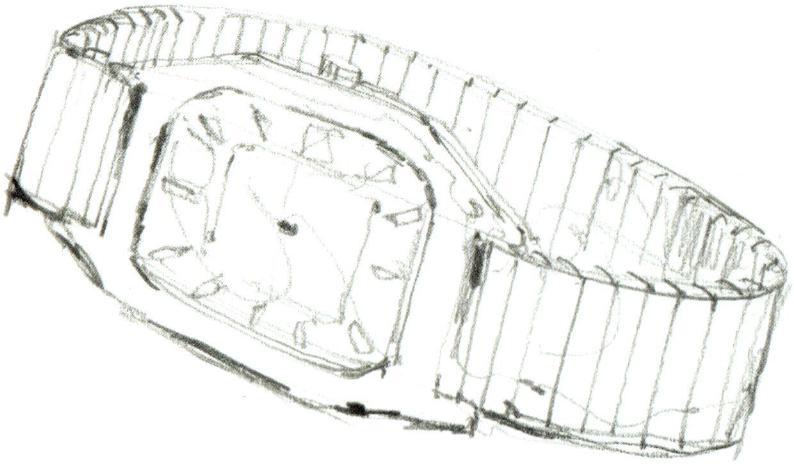

Draw What You See, Not What You Know

Even after only one drawing, you will notice so much more about your surroundings. It becomes a personal challenge to discover new information about things you have seen a thousand times.

Force Yourself to See

Many items that appear complex at first are really made up of simple geometric shapes. A camera is just a few ovals and rectangles, but seeing how they fit together makes the drawing process exciting. Force yourself to see. You know the camera lens is a circle, but from an angle the circle becomes an oval.

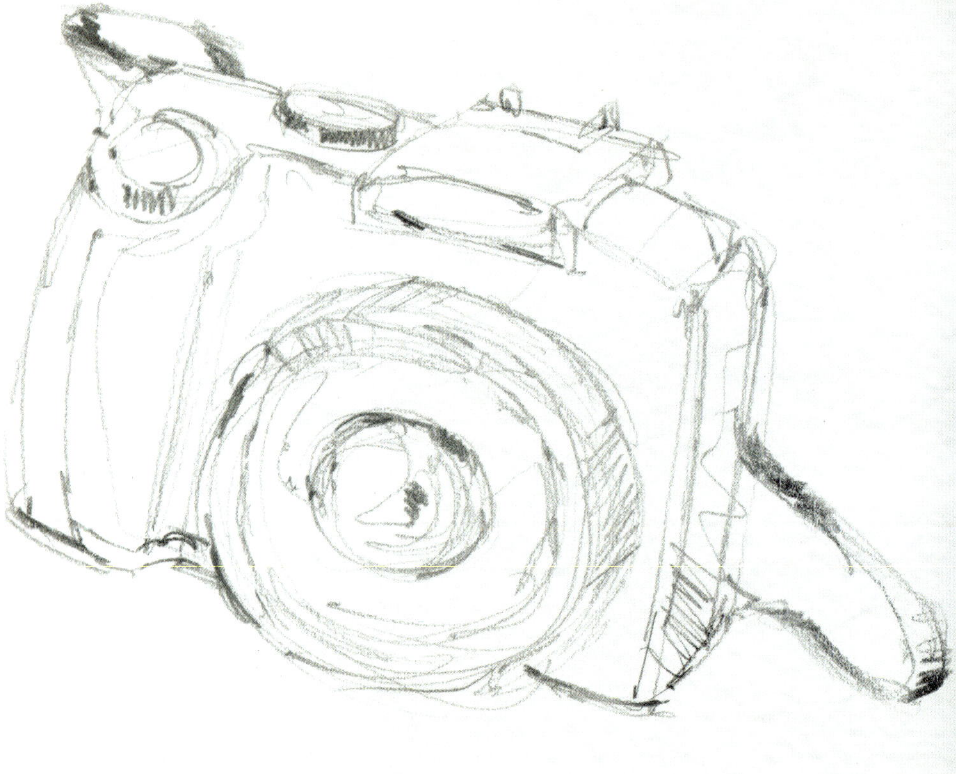

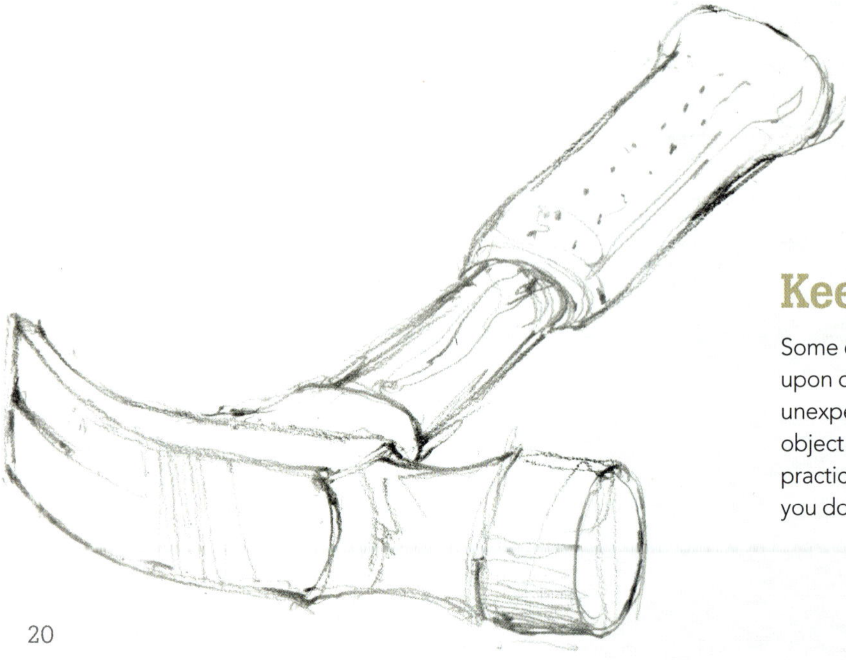

Keep Practicing!

Some objects look easy to draw, but upon closer examination, will present unexpected challenges. Making an object look convincingly real takes practice, so do not be discouraged if you don't get it right the first time.

More Practice

Look carefully at this drawing and then close the book. Draw as much as you can remember. Open the book to this page and compare. Modify your drawing but keep trying to hold as much in your memory as possible. You will be able to complete a drawing in fewer stages as your memory develops.

TRANSFER TECHNIQUES

Transfer a Drawing

Artists who draw or paint elaborate cityscapes and various architectural subjects will often use this method of transferring a drawing because it doesn't need to be redone from scratch if something goes wrong in the translation to paint or other media. This method also allows you to save your original so that it may be used again for another purpose.

In order for this to work properly, you will need to have drawn the original on a paper with a tough surface, such as illustration board or heavy cartridge paper. At the very least, choose a paper that can tolerate a lot of erasing. Even watercolor paper is good for this job.

MATERIALS

Surface
acid-free art paper
tracing paper

Graphite
HB or 2B graphite stick

Other
ballpoint pen
masking tape

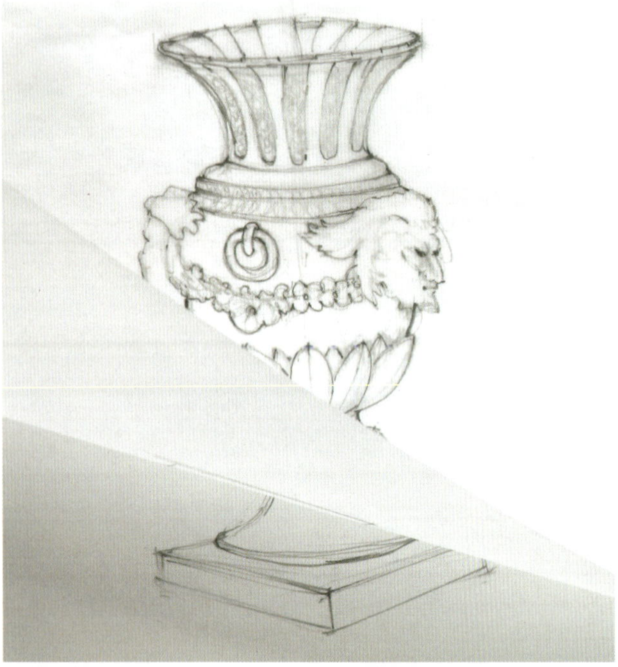

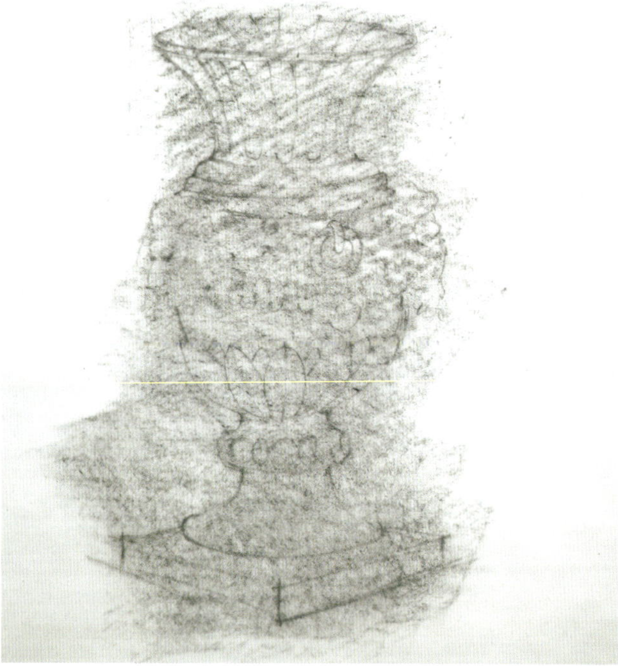

1 Trace the Drawing

Tape a piece of tracing paper over the original drawing and trace it. Tape only the top two corners so the tracing paper can be lifted to check any lines that may be too faint to see through the tracing paper. Low-tack masking tape is sold in hardware stores. It comes off easily without tearing the paper.

There is also special transfer paper commercially available at art supply stores that you may wish to purchase if you plan to use this method often.

2 Apply the Graphite

Flip the traced drawing over and rub an HB or 2B graphite stick over the back of it. (A soft pencil will also work but the side of a graphite stick is better.) It will need a good heavy coat of graphite so don't be shy about applying it.

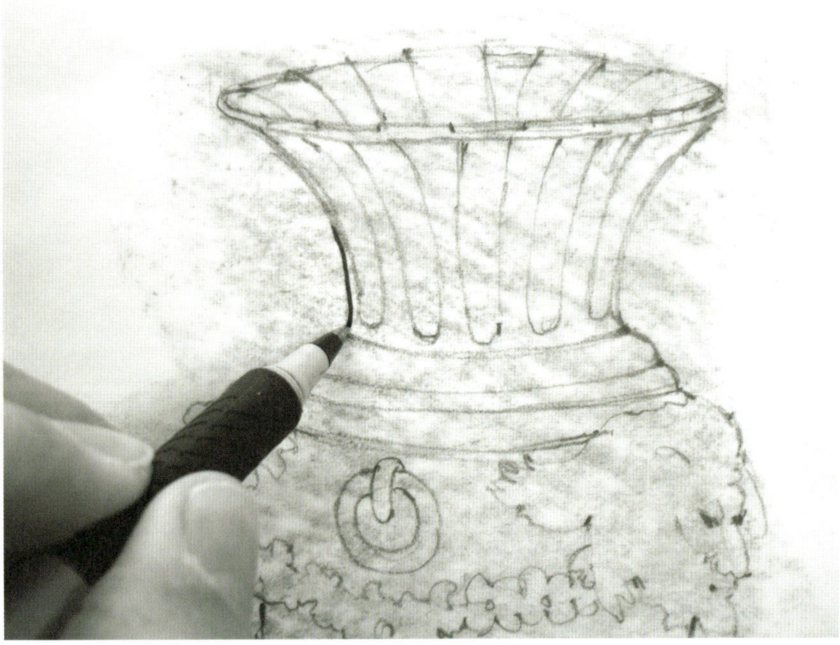

3 Transfer the drawing

Tape the tracing paper with the graphite side down to a new sheet of drawing paper. Once again, just tape the top two corners so it can be lifted to check your progress.

Transfer the image by drawing over the lines with a ballpoint pen. The pen will roll over the pencil lines without tearing the tracing paper and it will leave an ink line which is easy to distinguish.

Even though it is easy to see which lines have been transferred, it is still handy to lift the tracing paper and make sure the transfer is working properly.

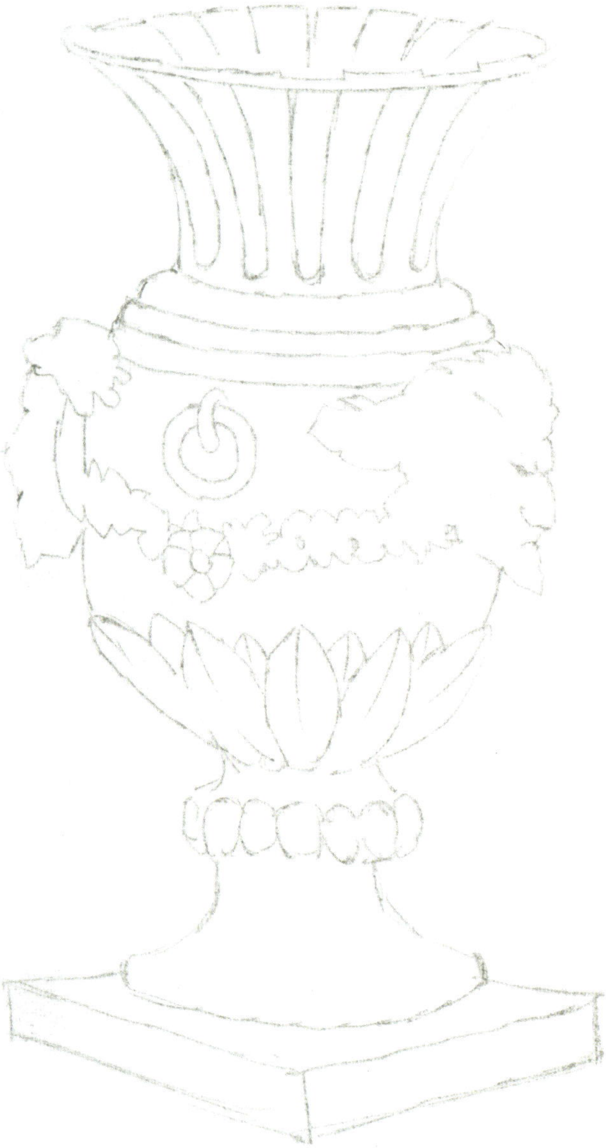

AVOID CARBON PAPER

Although you may see it available in many art supply stores, do not use carbon paper for transferring your images! It is extremely messy and can be difficult to erase the smudge marks after transferring to the final surface.

4 Clean It Up

Once the transferred drawing is on the final paper, it may require some touch-ups as well as a clean-up with an eraser. You will likely have some smudging from the tracing paper graphite, so use a kneaded eraser to work up to the lines and clean out any excess.

At this point, you would want to correct any problems with proportion and begin applying tone. The drawing could then be finished in paint, ink or colored pencils depending on the paper used.

CHAPTER

2

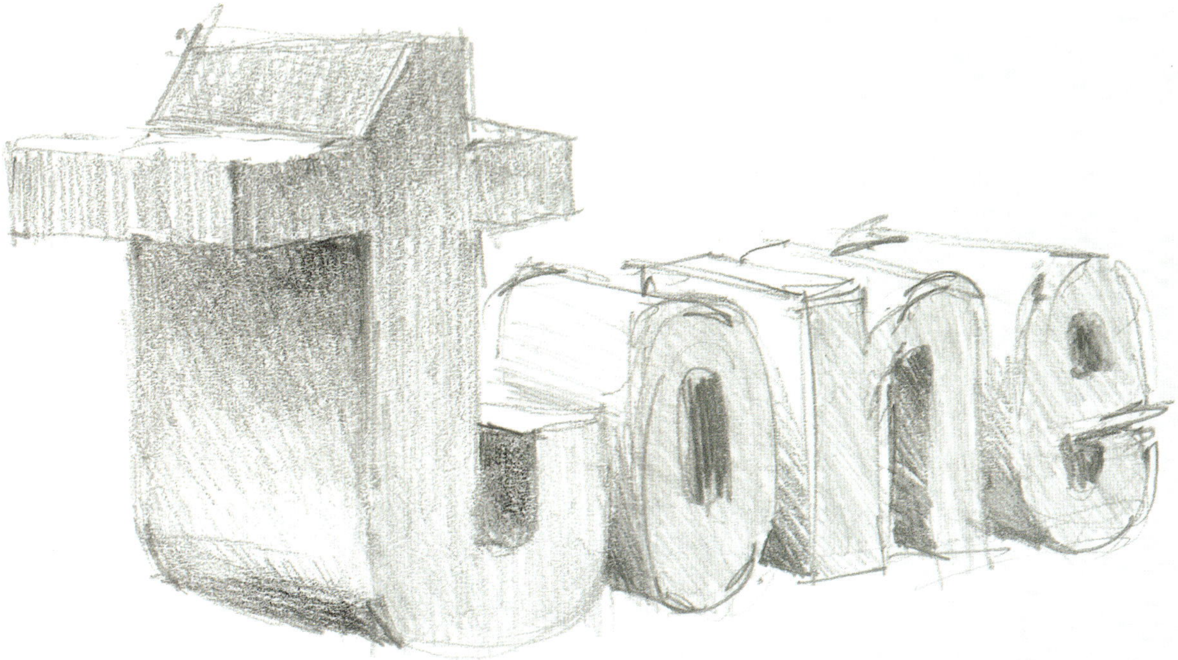

Tone is simply a more accurate term for shading and its various values. Some other media, such as ink, have only one value. But graphite gets darker the more vigorously it's applied. So the harder you press, the darker the value of the tone. In order to appreciate just how much tonal variation affects an image, study a simple black-and-white photograph. Try to duplicate the values. This increases your sensitivity to applying tone and also alerts you to how each object in the picture is defined by the value of the object next to it. There are no lines in the photo, just variations in the value of each shape.

As artists, we are entitled to convert contours of objects into lines in order to create our own interpretation, but if high realism is your goal, you need to become a master of applying tone.

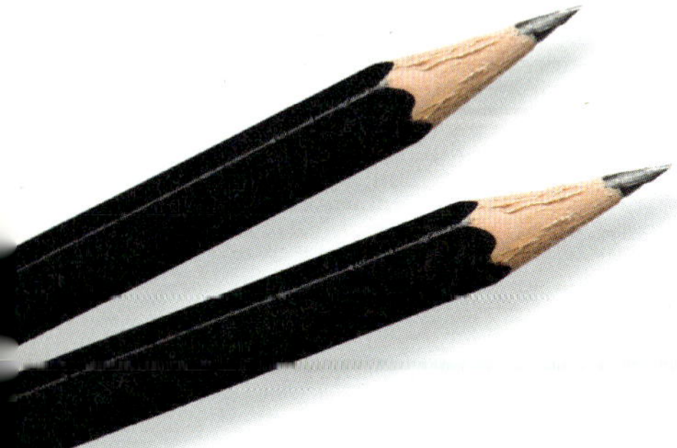

Faking 3-D

Making objects in a drawing look real means creating the illusion of a three-dimensional object on a two-dimensional surface. This requires an understanding of how light behaves when it illuminates various shapes. To study this, move an object around under the light, or place it in front of different windows. Sketch or photograph it in different light settings for future reference.

If you really look, you'll notice that everything is made up of cubes, spheres, cones and cylinders. Get used to breaking complex forms down into these basic geometric shapes, and you will have no trouble figuring out how to apply the tones and values that make them look three-dimensional.

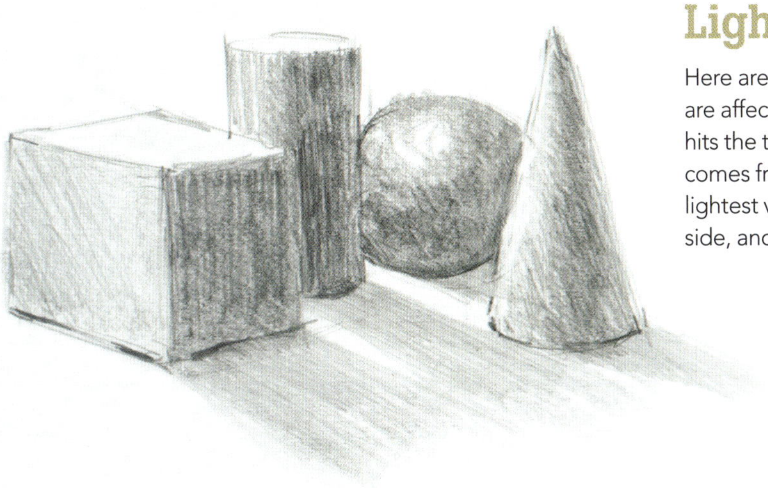

Light Angle Affects Value

Here are some basic shapes with a view of how they are affected when lit from one angle. Light normally hits the top of the object or near the top. If the light comes from the top left, the solid cube will have the lightest value on top, the mid-tone will be on the left side, and the darkest value will be on the back.

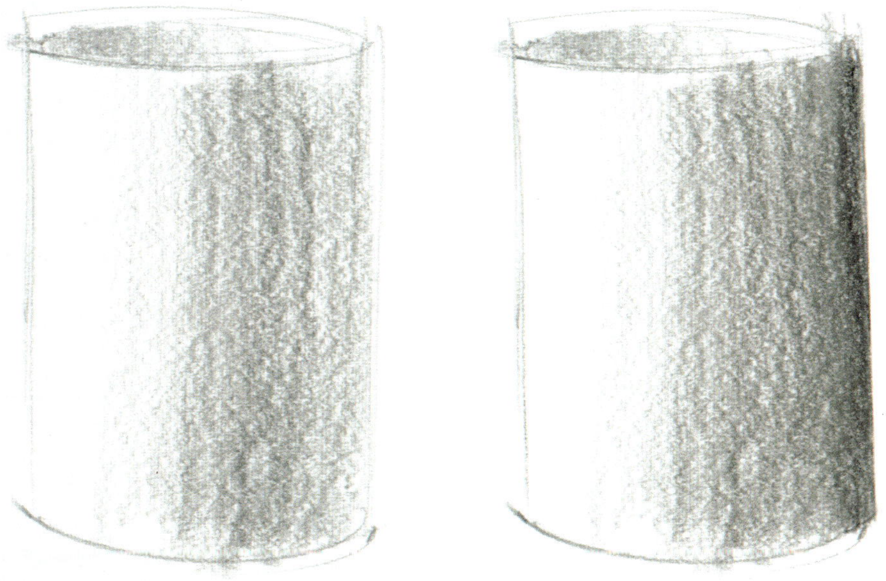

Value Affects Shape

The light in these examples comes from the left. In the left image, you see the darkest value as the surface turns away from the light. Then it gets slightly lighter on the right side to show the effect of reflected light. This makes the object appear round. In the right image, the value gets progressively darker towards the right edge, so it looks like a sharp corner rather than a round cylinder.

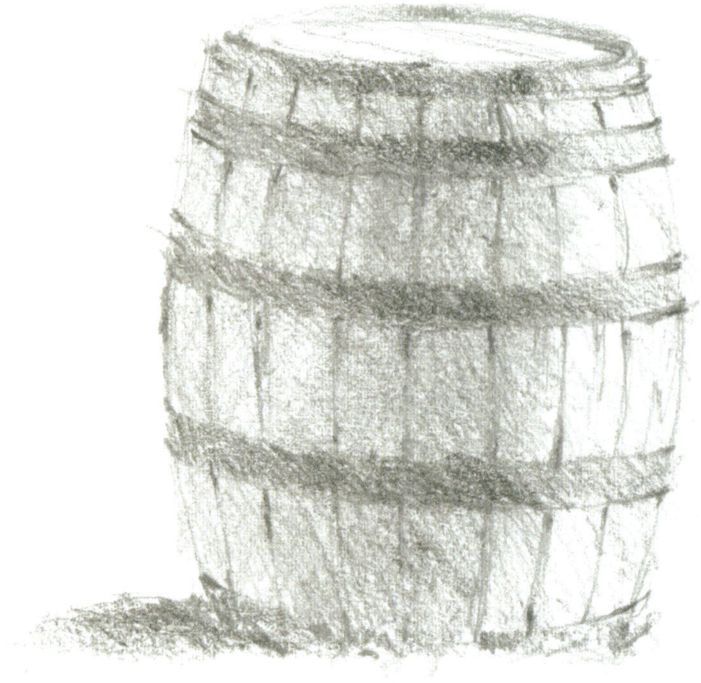

Large Objects Look Better When Showing Reflected Light

This barrel is a cylinder with a slight distortion in the center, giving it a convex shape. The direction of light is from the top right. The top of the barrel has the lightest value with a light tone on the right side. It then falls into shadow as it curves out of the light, and gets slightly lighter on the far left side due to reflected light.

Reflected light usually bounces off surrounding objects. But even if there are no other objects close by, the sky will provide reflected light.

Small Shadow Areas Don't Need to Show Reflected Light

This log is simply a cylinder on its side. Light from the top left hits each of the root cylinders the same way as the main log. As the root part turns upward, treat it like a vertical cylinder.

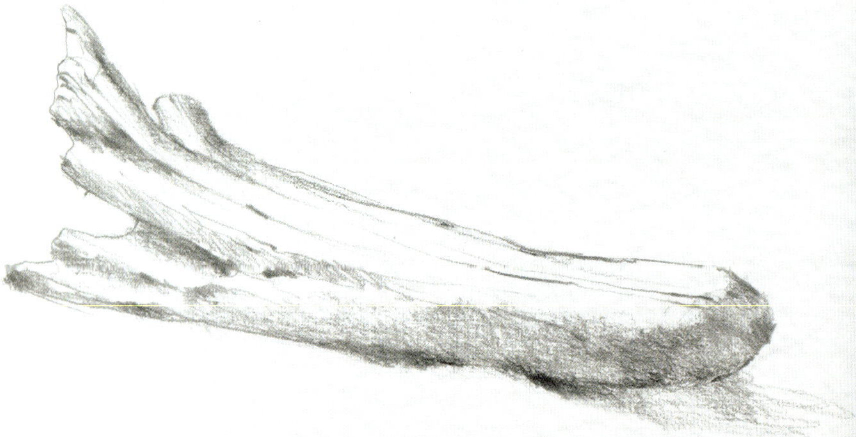

Same Theory, Different Shapes

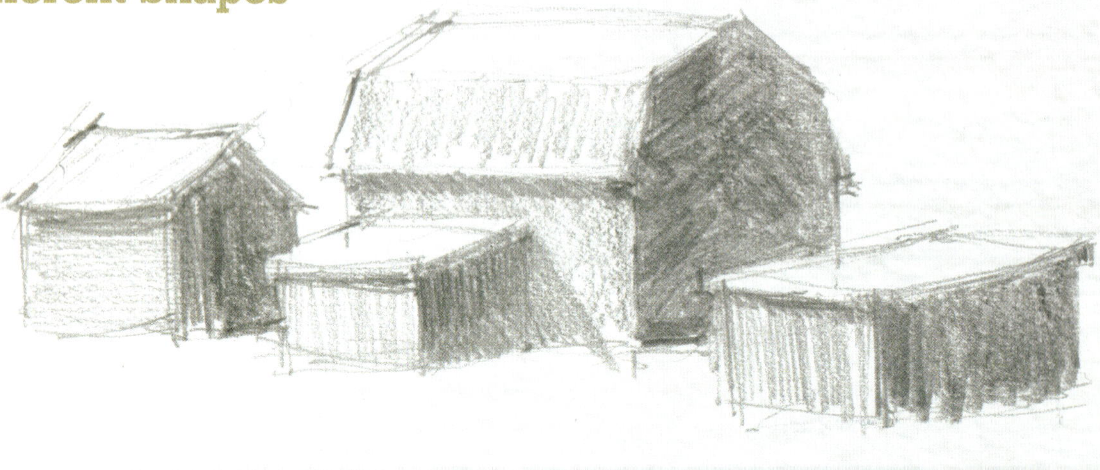

Break Complex Forms Into Basic Shapes

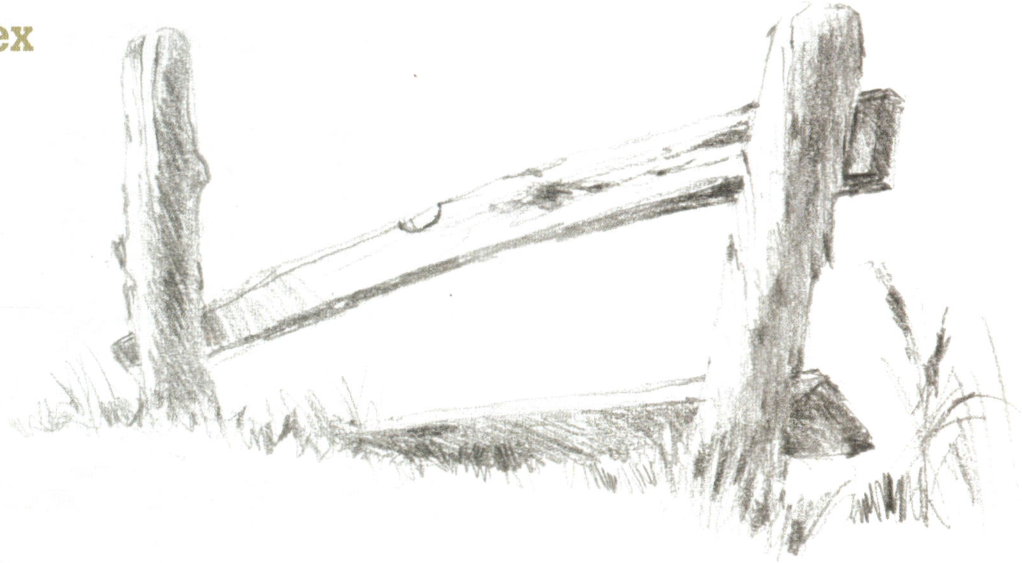

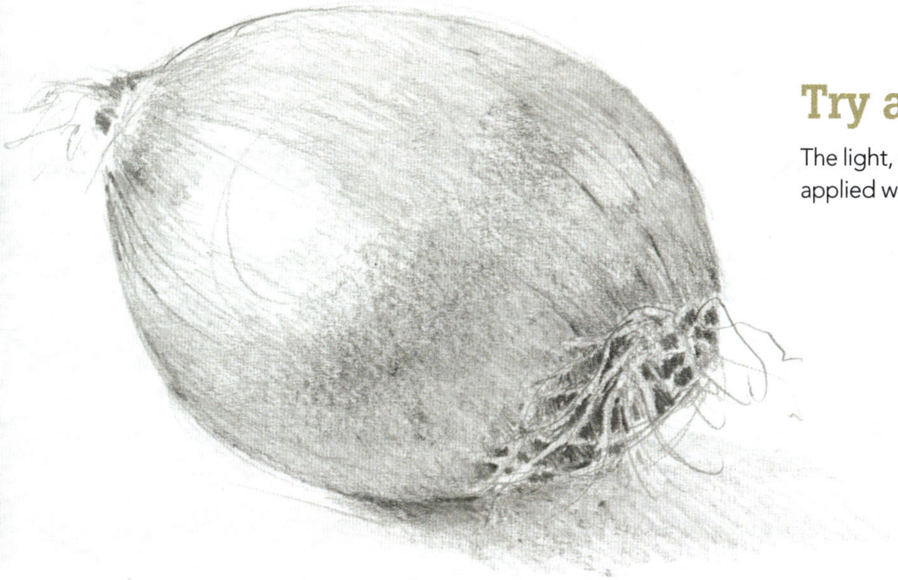

Try a Sphere

The light, subtle value on this onion was applied with a 2H pencil as the last step.

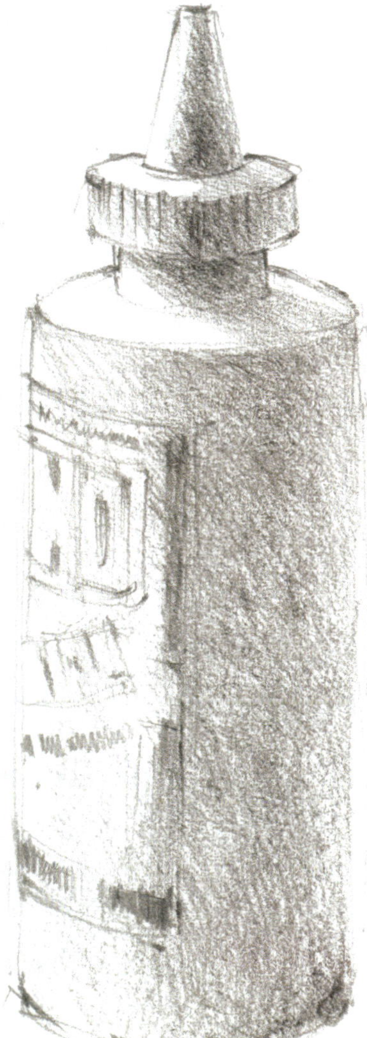

Treat Cones the Same as Cylinders

A cone shape is treated the same as a cylinder. Just keep in mind that it's a bit wider at the bottom, so the shadow will taper in proportion to the shape.

Applying and Blending Tone

When applying and blending tones, there are a handful of key objectives to keep in mind:

- Thinking in terms of only three values – light, medium and dark – will help to simplify even the most complicated subjects.
- Match the value of the tone with the original contours to avoid an outlined look.
- Don't get too dark too soon.
- Control pressure on the pencil for smooth transitions.
- Blend the different leads.
- Erase without leaving evidence.
- Prevent unintentional smudging by protecting the finished parts of the drawing from your hand. These important skills can all be developed with practice.

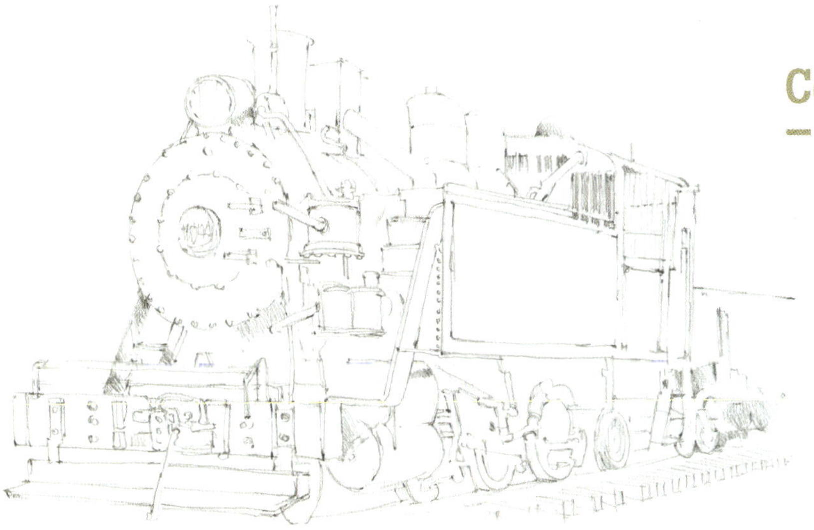

Contour Drawing – No Tone

Tone Applied

The tone was applied entirely with the point of B and HB pencils. No smudging was required because it is a hard-edge subject and suits the harsh linework.

A shape will have light, medium or dark value depending on how it faces the light. Even black machinery will be white where it is struck by the sunlight.

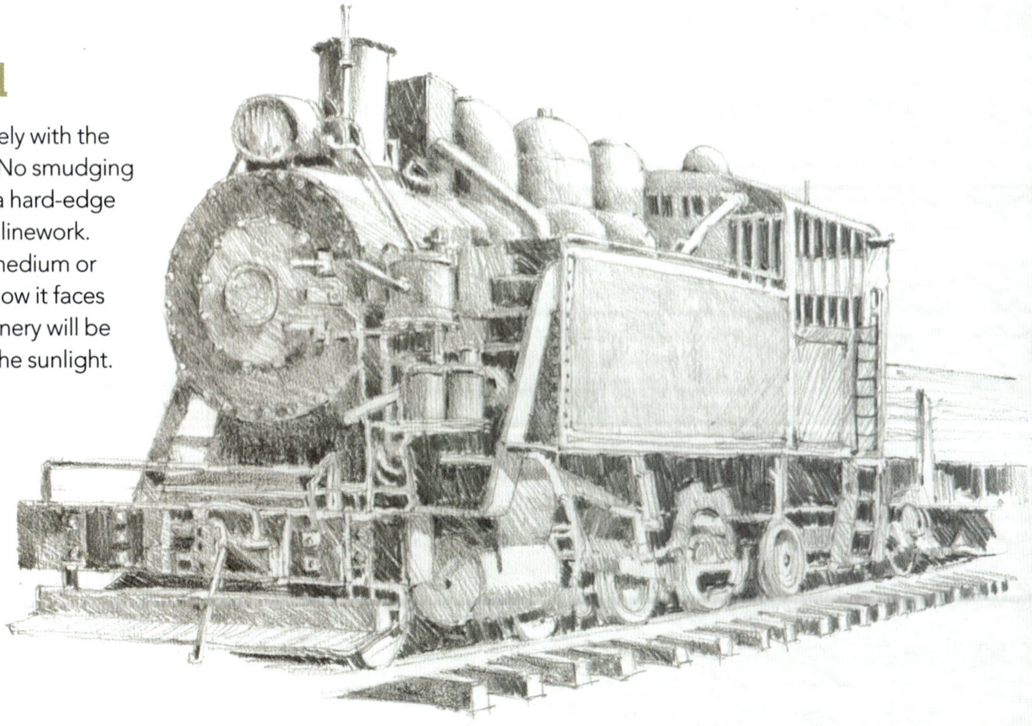

Smudging

If you desire a drawing with no texture from the pencil strokes or paper surface, you can blend the tones by smudging the graphite with a stump.

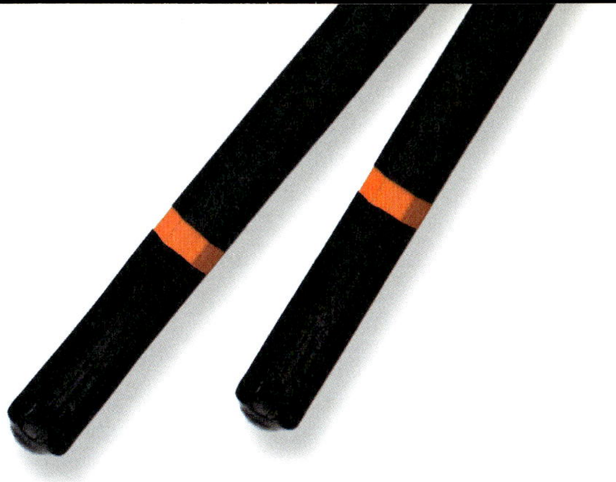

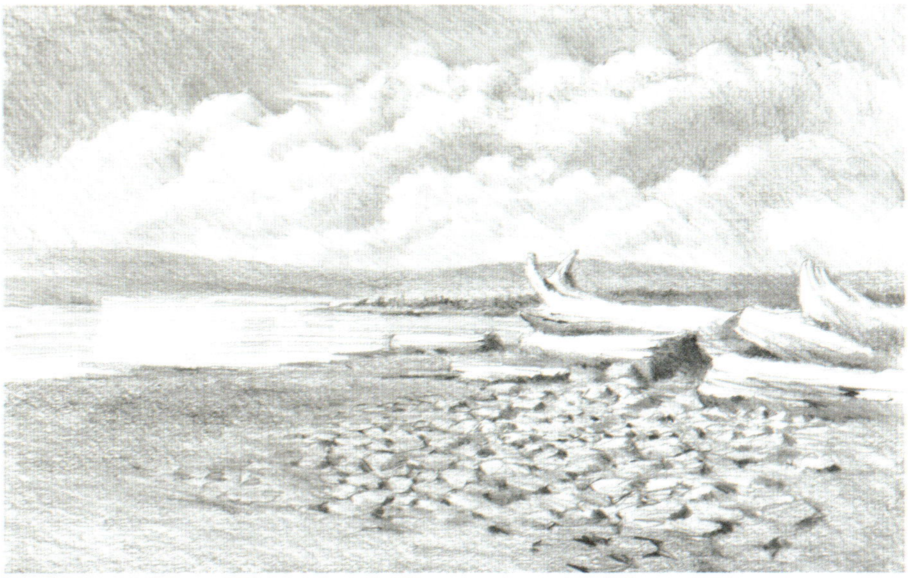

Tone Blended With Pencil

The tones in this drawing were applied with B and HB leads, and blended with a 2H wooden pencil. There was no smudging to blend the tones.

Tone Blended With Stump and Eraser

Here is the same drawing after a stump and eraser were used to blend and lift. This method works especially well for subjects that have soft edges, such as clouds and distant hills.

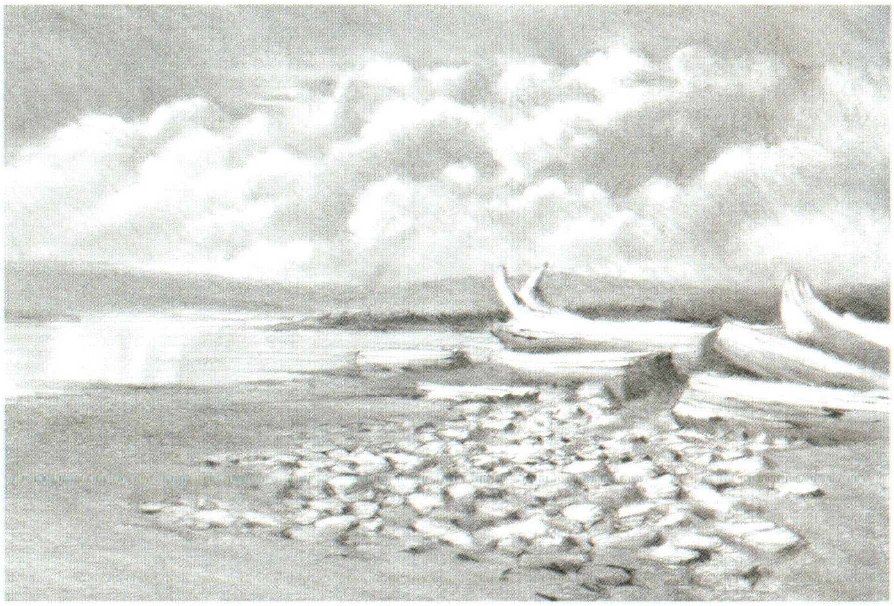

Create a 3-D Effect

Practice what you've learned about using value to achieve a 3-D effect. Plan on using just three values: light, mid-tone and dark. Imagine the direction of the light is coming from the top left.

MATERIALS

Surface
acid-free art paper

Graphite
HB wooden or mechanical pencil

Other
kneaded eraser

1 Sketch the Contour

If it is helpful, quickly sketch a cube first. Apply the three values to it – light on top, mid-tone on the side and dark on back. Now imagine that the rock is just a very eroded cube. Sketch the contour of the rock.

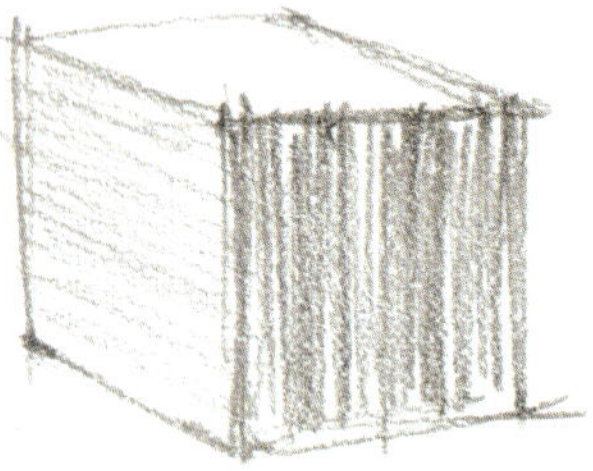

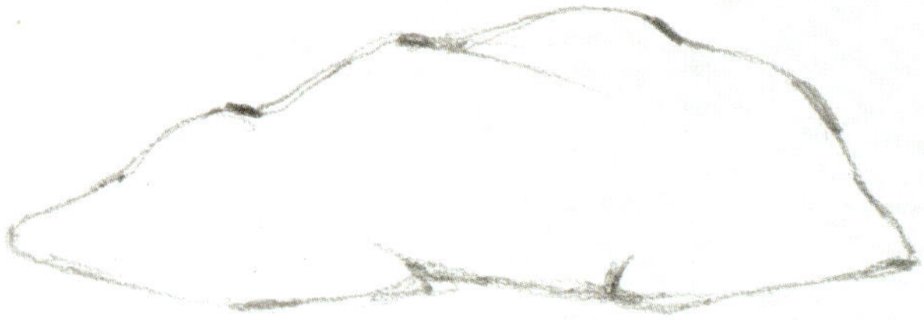

2 Apply Mid-Tones

Visualize the surfaces that face the light and add the mid-tone to the surfaces that angle away from the light.

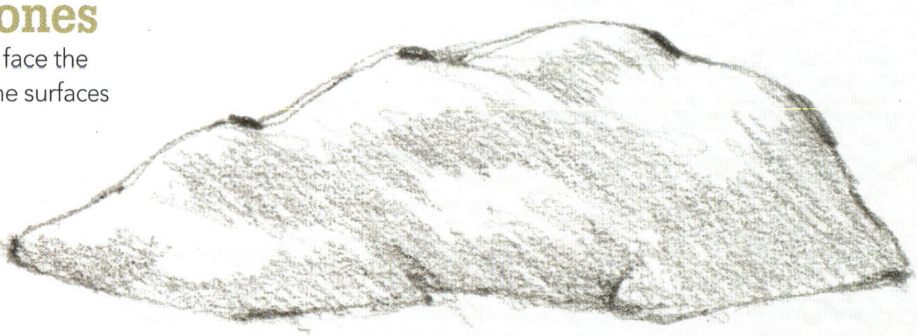

3 Add Dark Value

Apply the darkest value to the parts of the rock you want in shadow. Reflected light will not be significant on this small crusty surface.

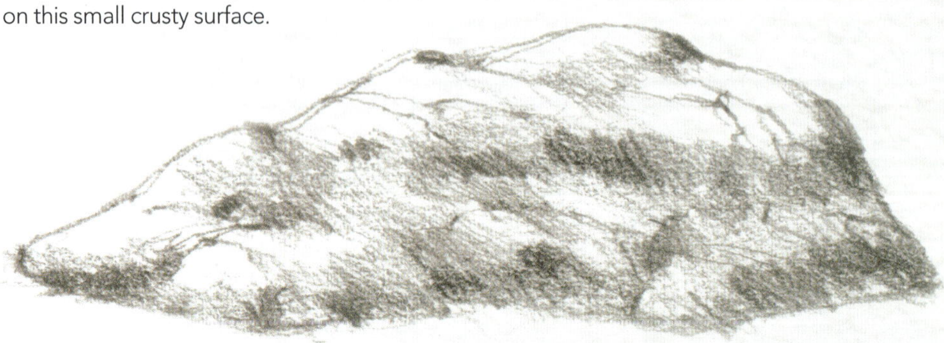

Blend Tones With a Stump

Practice smudging the graphite with a stump to blend the tones of your drawing. Use sandpaper to create a nice soft surface on the stump that will move the graphite, blend the pencil strokes and fill the paper texture.

MATERIALS

Surface
acid-free art paper

Graphite
2H, HB, B, 2B wooden pencils

Other
kneaded eraser, sandpaper, stump

1 Sketch the Candle

Sketch the contours of the candle with a wooden B pencil. As you start to build up graphite on the paper, begin blending it with a stump.

2 Blend the Light and Mid-Tones

Continue the drawing with the B pencil and alternate blending the light and mid-tones with a stump. You will notice that the stump tends to lift the darker values as the graphite builds up.

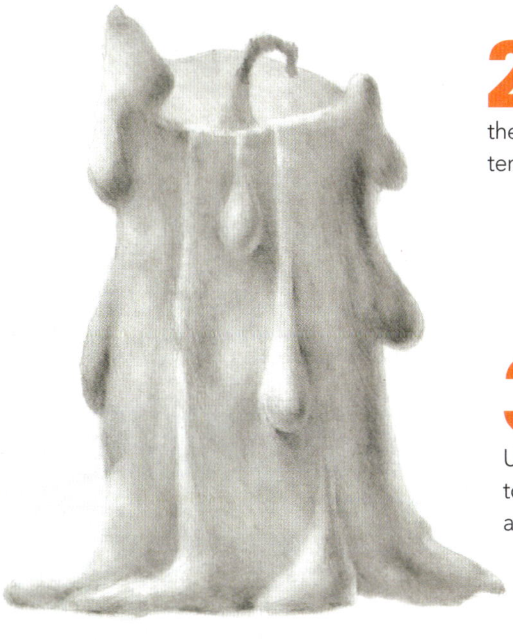

3 Add Dark Tones and Lift Highlights

Use 2H, HB and 2B pencils to work in the final dark tones without using the stump. Lift some light bits and highlights with a kneaded eraser.

TECHNIQUES

Apply Tone Without Smudging

This is a challenging exercise, but it will take your drawing skills to a new level. It's so tempting to smear graphite in order to get a lighter value and save the time it takes to meticulously apply the subtle variations in tone. But if you discipline yourself to use only the pencil and avoid smudging techniques for now, you'll gain much more control of the graphite and discover ways to avoid accidental smudging.

MATERIALS

Surface
acid-free art paper

Graphite
HB graphite stick
B mechanical pencil
2H, HB wooden pencils

Other
kneaded eraser
paper towels

1 Sketch the Drawing and Apply Light Tones

Sketch the drawing with a mechanical pencil using a B lead. When you are happy with the contours and proportions (see Chapter 3 on proportion), use a 2H wooden pencil to begin, applying the tone very lightly.

2 Apply the Mid- and Dark Tones

Use a softer pencil such as the HB wooden or the B mechanical to apply the mid- and dark tones on the bird.

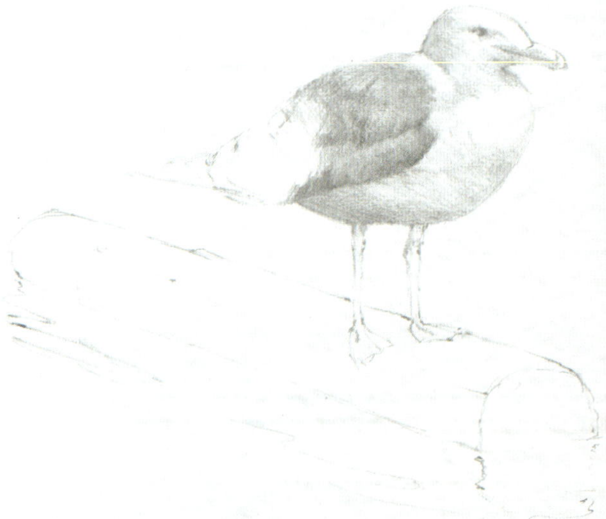

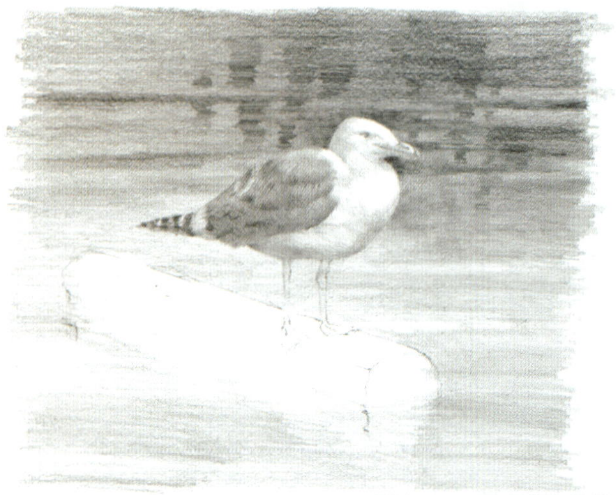

3 Add the Background

For the background, use an HB graphite stick. The side of the stick is good for broad areas, and the end works well for darker patterns in the water. To avoid accidental smudging, lace a paper towel under the hand you're holding the paper with.

TECHNIQUES

Blend Tones With a Stump

Practice smudging the graphite with a stump to blend the tones of your drawing. Use sandpaper to create a nice soft surface on the stump that will move the graphite, blend the pencil strokes and fill the paper texture.

MATERIALS

Surface
acid-free art paper

Graphite
2H, HB, B, 2B wooden pencils

Other
kneaded eraser, sandpaper, stump

1 Sketch the Candle

Sketch the contours of the candle with a wooden B pencil. As you start to build up graphite on the paper, begin blending it with a stump.

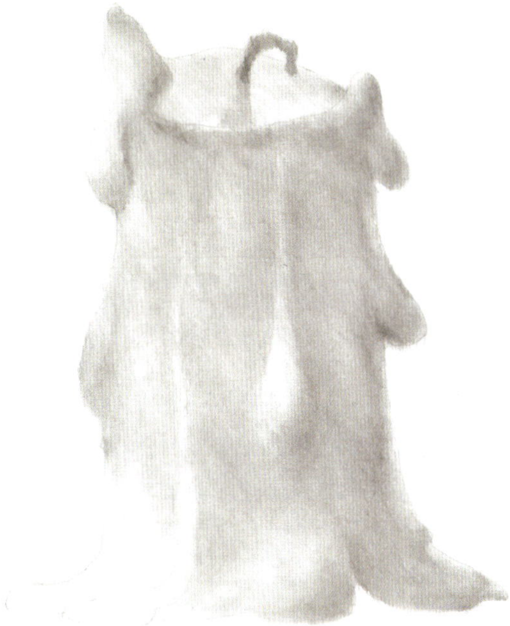

2 Blend the Light and Mid-Tones

Continue the drawing with the B pencil and alternate blending the light and mid-tones with a stump. You will notice that the stump tends to lift the darker values as the graphite builds up.

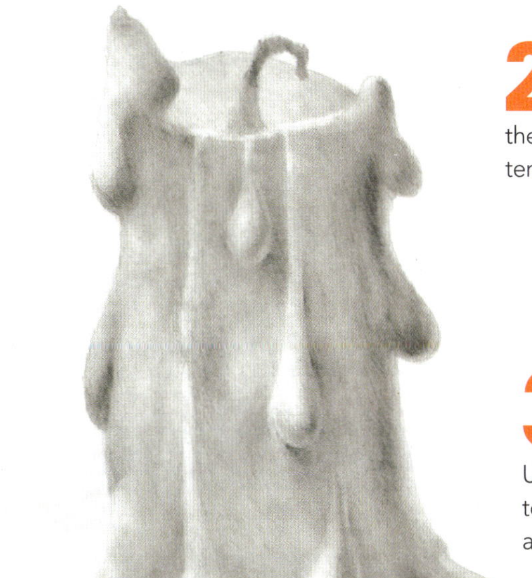

3 Add Dark Tones and Lift Highlights

Use 2H, HB and 2B pencils to work in the final dark tones without using the stump. Lift some light bits and highlights with a kneaded eraser.

TECHNIQUES

Apply Tone Without Smudging

This is a challenging exercise, but it will take your drawing skills to a new level. It's so tempting to smear graphite in order to get a lighter value and save the time it takes to meticulously apply the subtle variations in tone. But if you discipline yourself to use only the pencil and avoid smudging techniques for now, you'll gain much more control of the graphite and discover ways to avoid accidental smudging.

MATERIALS

Surface
acid-free art paper

Graphite
HB graphite stick
B mechanical pencil
2H, HB wooden pencils

Other
kneaded eraser
paper towels

1 Sketch the Drawing and Apply Light Tones

Sketch the drawing with a mechanical pencil using a B lead. When you are happy with the contours and proportions (see Chapter 3 on proportion), use a 2H wooden pencil to begin, applying the tone very lightly.

2 Apply the Mid- and Dark Tones

Use a softer pencil such as the HB wooden or the B mechanical to apply the mid- and dark tones on the bird.

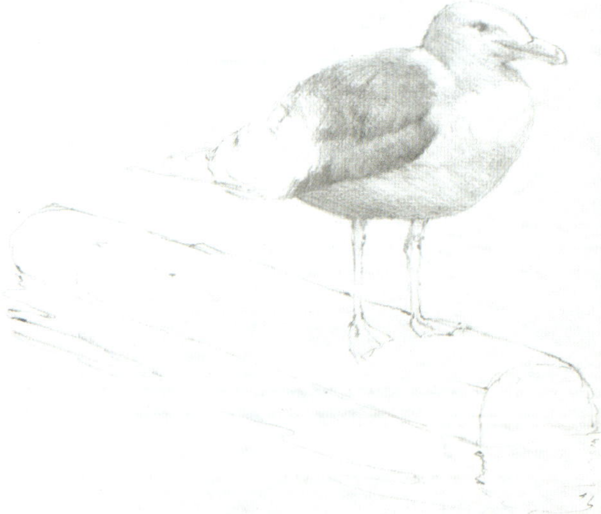

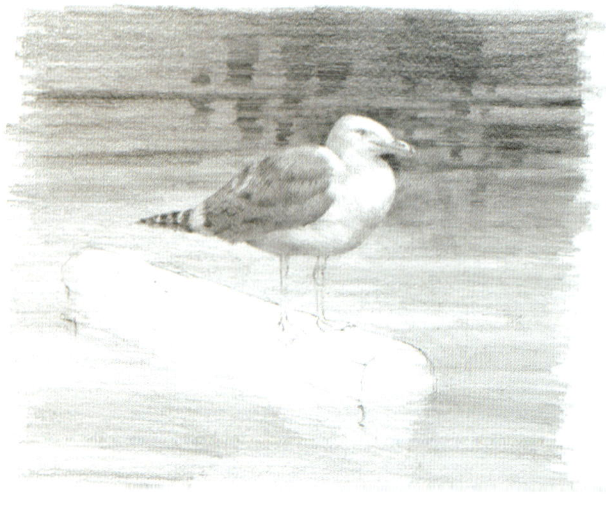

3 Add the Background

For the background, use an HB graphite stick. The side of the stick is good for broad areas, and the end works well for darker patterns in the water. To avoid accidental smudging, lace a paper towel under the hand you're holding the paper with.

Smudging

If you desire a drawing with no texture from the pencil strokes or paper surface, you can blend the tones by smudging the graphite with a stump.

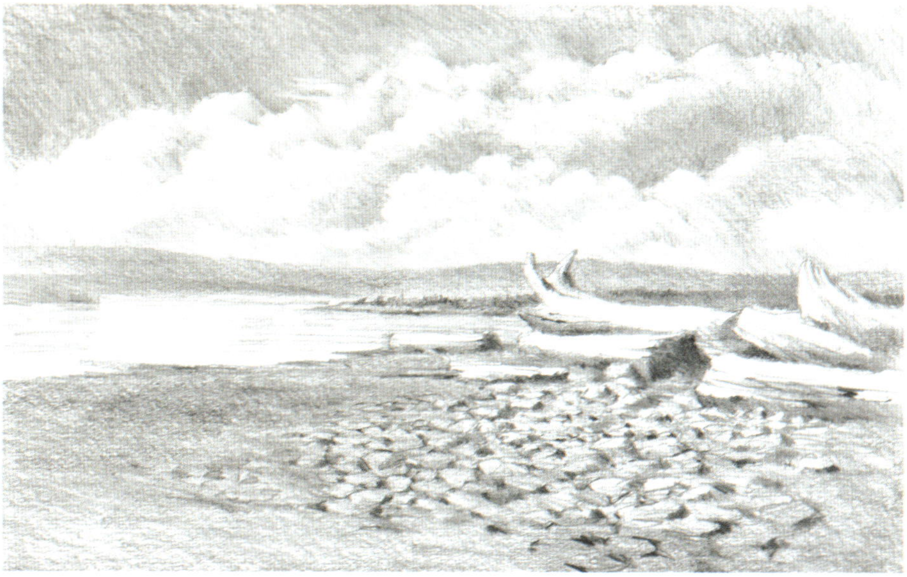

Tone Blended With Pencil

The tones in this drawing were applied with B and HB leads, and blended with a 2H wooden pencil. There was no smudging to blend the tones.

Tone Blended With Stump and Eraser

Here is the same drawing after a stump and eraser were used to blend and lift. This method works especially well for subjects that have soft edges, such as clouds and distant hills.

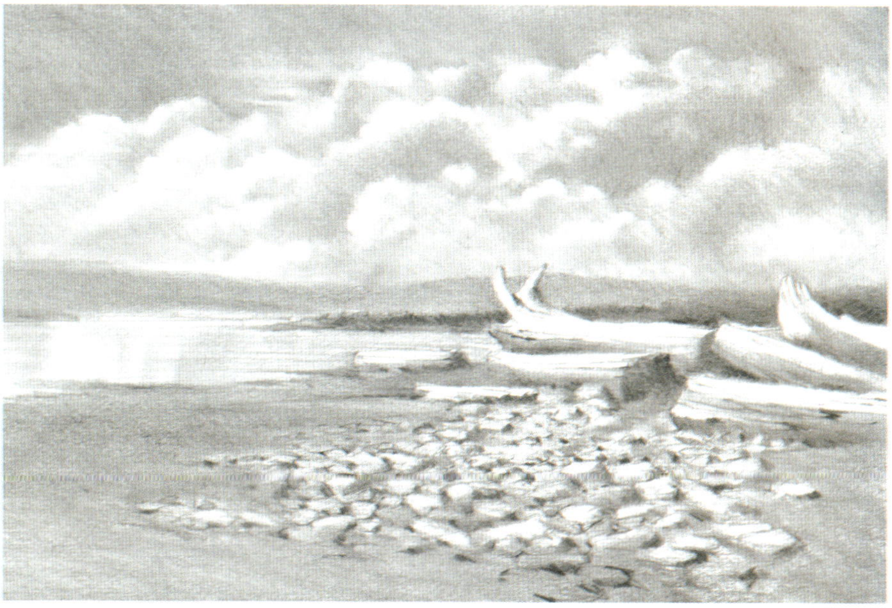

TECHNIQUES

Create a 3-D Effect

Practice what you've learned about using value to achieve a 3-D effect. Plan on using just three values: light, mid-tone and dark. Imagine the direction of the light is coming from the top left.

MATERIALS

Surface
acid-free art paper

Graphite
HB wooden or mechanical pencil

Other
kneaded eraser

1 Sketch the Contour

If it is helpful, quickly sketch a cube first. Apply the three values to it – light on top, mid-tone on the side and dark on back. Now imagine that the rock is just a very eroded cube. Sketch the contour of the rock.

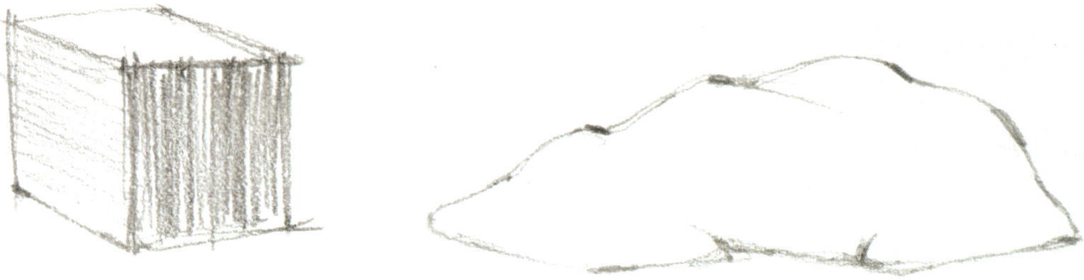

2 Apply Mid-Tones

Visualize the surfaces that face the light and add the mid-tone to the surfaces that angle away from the light.

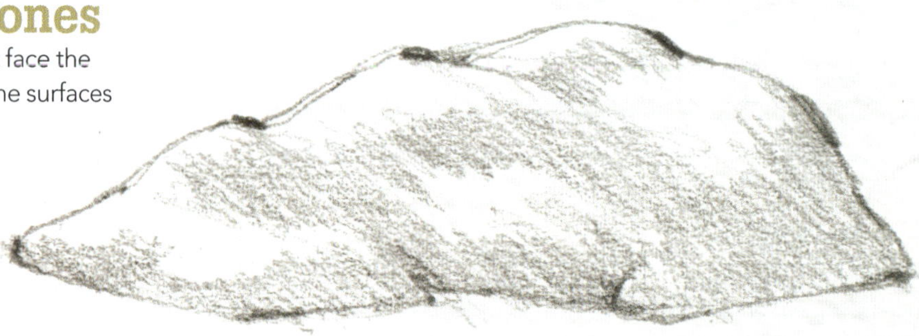

3 Add Dark Value

Apply the darkest value to the parts of the rock you want in shadow. Reflected light will not be significant on this small crusty surface.

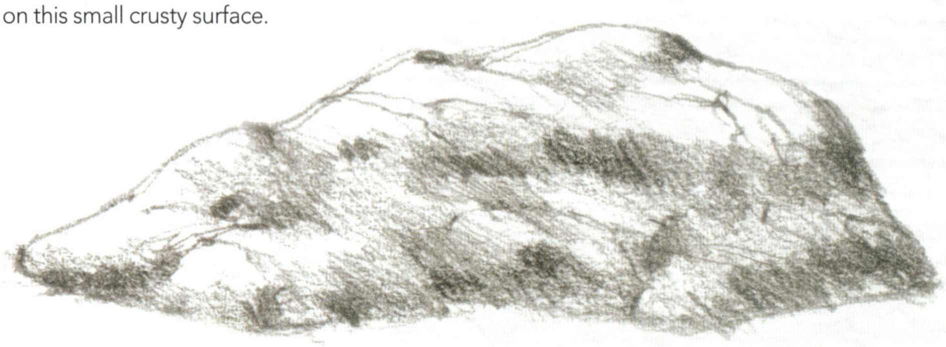

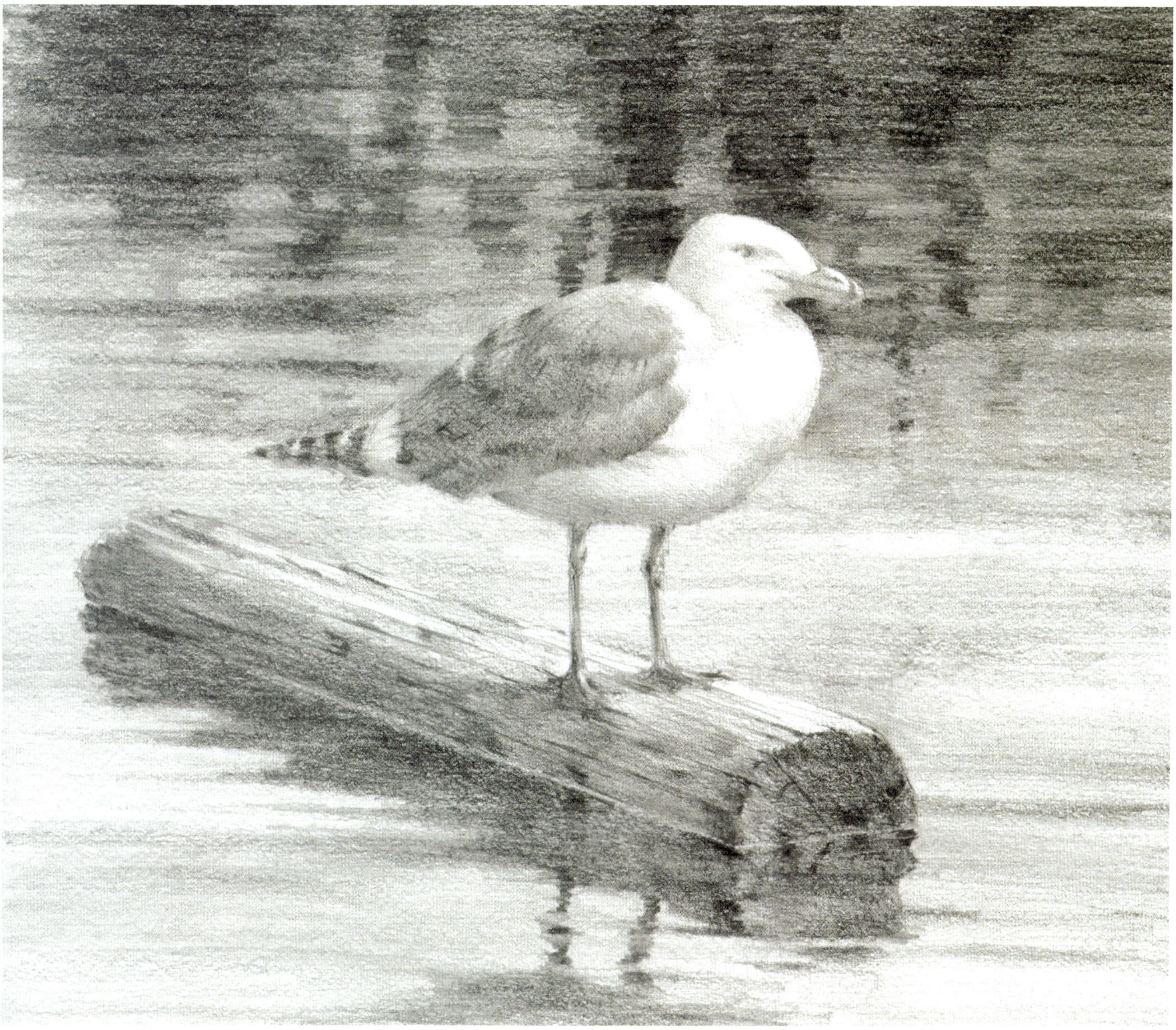

4 Add Finishing Touches

Use a sharp HB wooden pencil to cut in around the bird. Remember to keep the paper texture prominent. Do not attempt to smudge or fill it in. (It is possible at this stage to begin working with a stump to smooth out the graphite and get a more photographic look to the drawing.)

TRANSFER TECHNIQUES

Blend Tone With a Pencil

Practice using a pencil to blend tones in a drawing. The temptation to smudge here will be overwhelming, but this exercise is intended to develop your control over blending tone with a pencil. There will be plenty of opportunity for smudging later.

MATERIALS

Surface
acid-free art paper

Graphite
HB graphite stick
2H, HB, B wooden pencils

Other
kneaded eraser

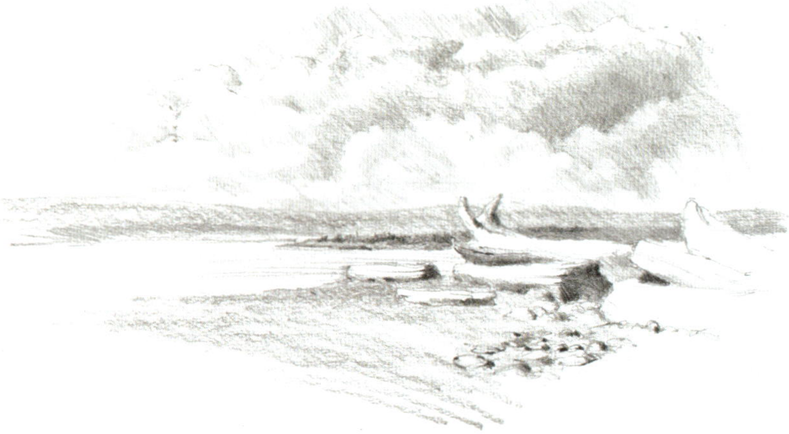

1 Sketch the Contour Drawing

Sketch your contour drawing with the B pencil, making it light enough so that the lines will blend and virtually disappear when you add tone. You do not want to have outlines showing in the final product.

2 Focus on the Sky

With an HB pencil, carefully bring the sky value up to the edges of the clouds. Either make it as dark as the contours of the clouds, or lightly erase the cloud contours to lighten and blend them with the value of the sky.

Retain a convex shape on the clouds to avoid cutting into them. The clouds should look puffed up like they are expanding, but when you are working around them in the background (negative drawing), cut into them leaving concave areas in their contour.

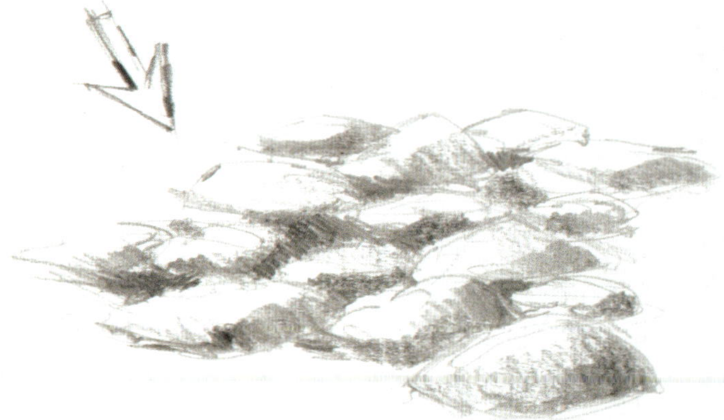

3 Focus on the Stones

Vary the size and shape of the stones on the beach and give them a consistent light source. For example, if the light comes from the top left, apply tone to the right side. Be sure to apply dark tones in between the stones as well.

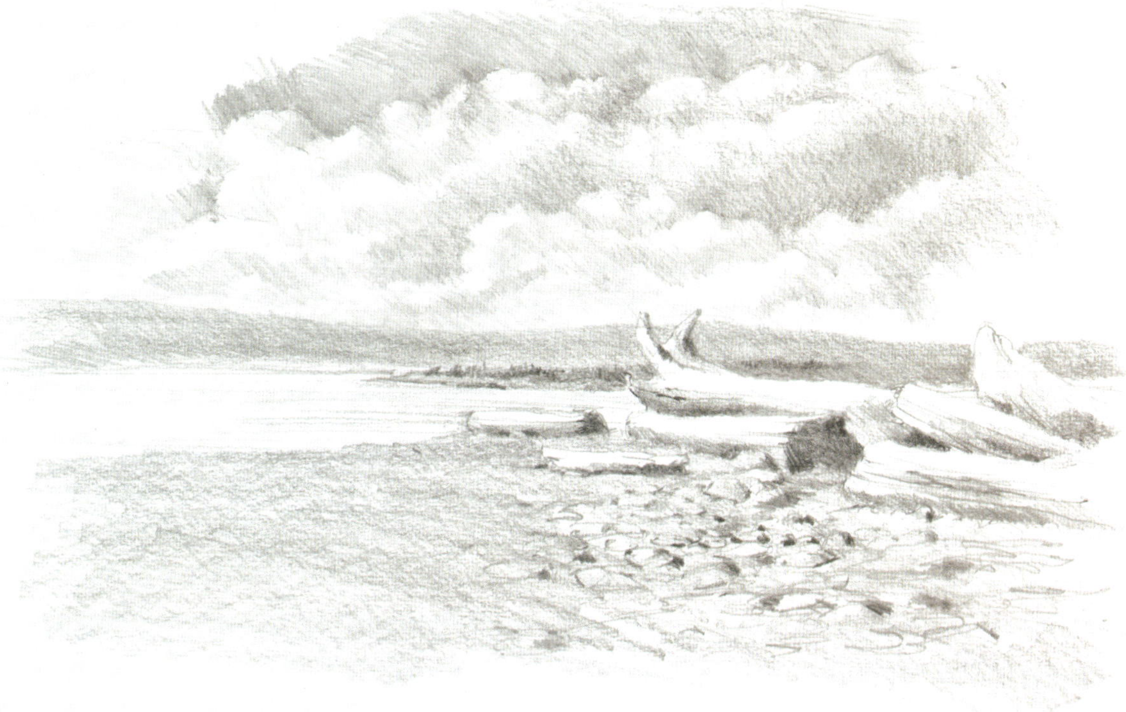

4 Fill In the Sand and Darken the Hills

Fill in the sand with an HB graphite stick. Apply darker tones to the distant hills. Be careful not to make them too dark, or they won't look distant.

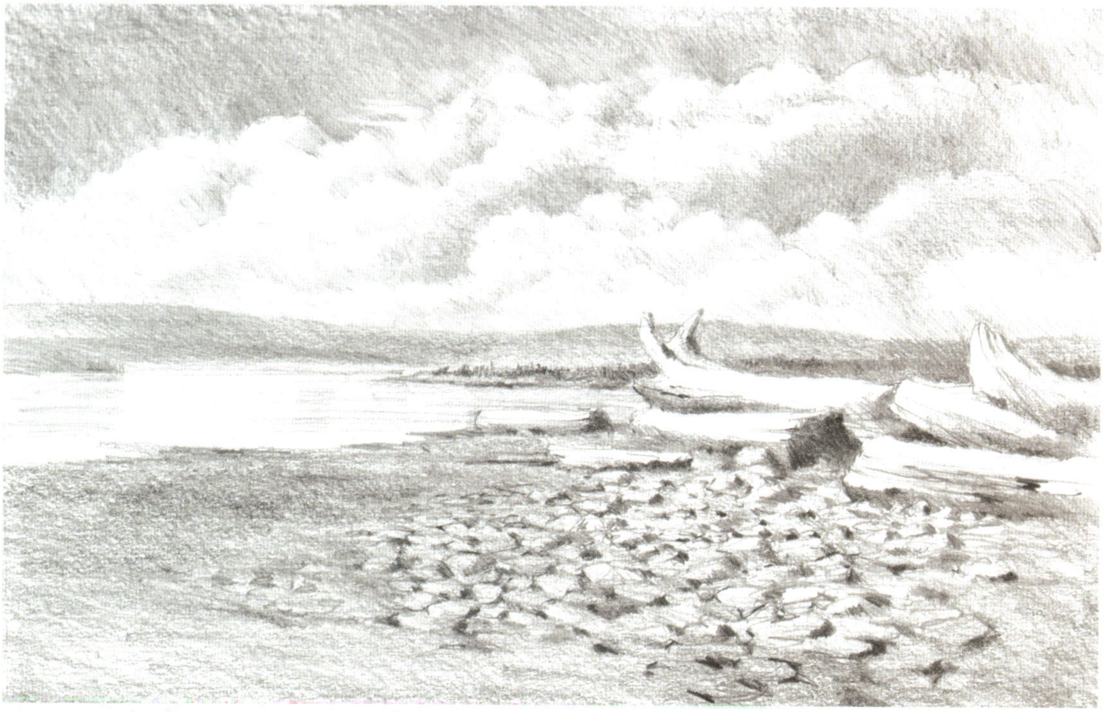

5 Blend the Tones to Finish

Use a 2H pencil to blend the various tones. It won't smudge the existing tone, and it will add its own stroke while slightly moving the graphite on the surface.

CHAPTER

3

PROPORTION

Learning to get proportions right in a drawing can be a challenging task. It requires that you adjust your way of seeing from simply identifying objects, to comparing their height and width, their parts in relation to each other.

It's possible to practice this even when you're not actually drawing. Keep those relationships in mind as you look at objects around a room or watch people passing by. How long are people's legs compared to their torsos? How tall is the back of a chair compared to its legs, or compared to its width? Angles are also important to capturing a pose or more complex objects that don't have many horizontal and vertical contours. Start to measure things in your mind using not only vertical and horizontal imaginary guidelines, but diagonals as well.

You will be amazed at how much more you notice when you start thinking this way. You'll soon be calculating the size and position of countless objects and their components. This reflects in your drawing and makes getting correct proportions a much easier process.

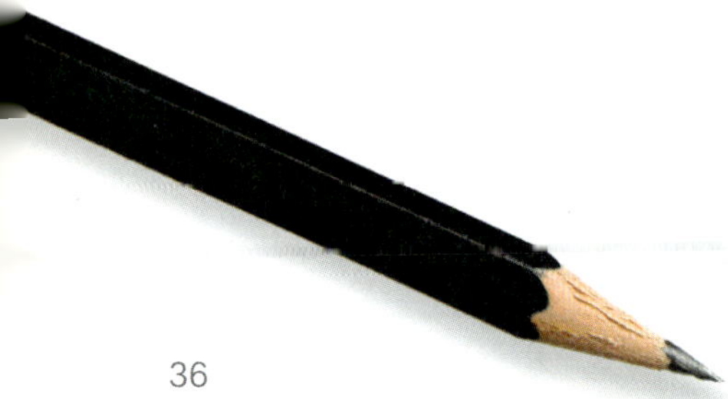

Plotting Proportion

The movie version of an artist at work often has a figure in a beret and smock holding a pencil at arm's length and squinting seriously. This not only looks great, there is also an actual function being performed. The artist is using the pencil as a ruler, usually comparing height and width.

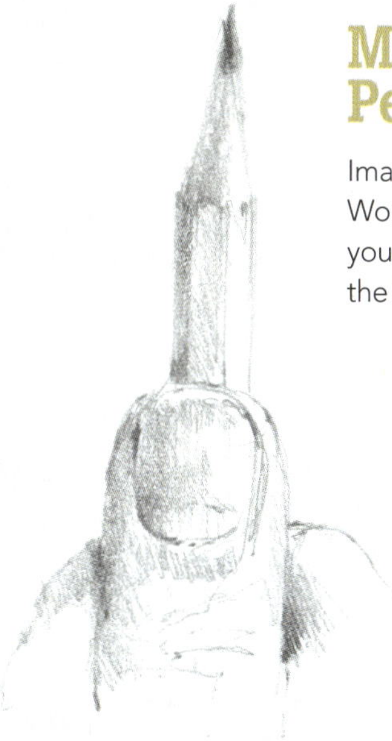

Make Your Pencil a Ruler!

Imagine you are working on site. Working at arm's length, use your pencil as a ruler to measure the building you want to draw.

Measure Height

It looks like the building is 2 and a bit pencil lengths high. On your drawing paper, use that "2 and a bit" to establish the height. You now have a fair proportion for the building.

If you are doing a high-realism rendering, you will need to plan the drawing with greater precision, possibly working from photos. This is plenty accurate enough for our purpose, though.

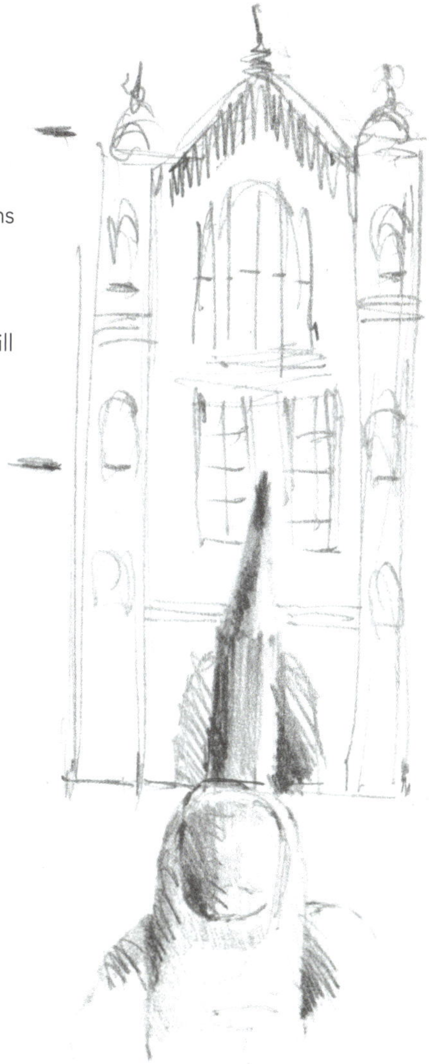

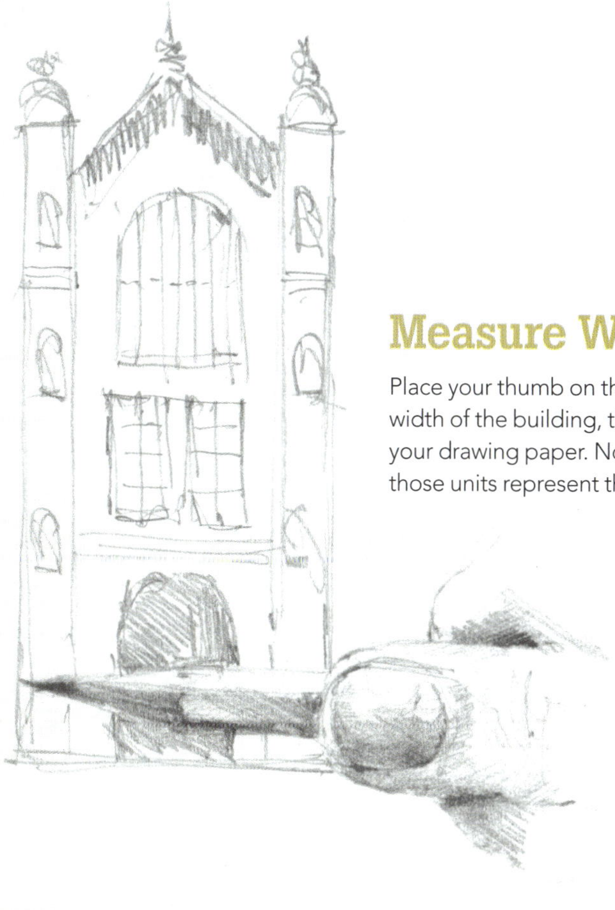

Measure Width

Place your thumb on the pencil to mark the width of the building, then mark that width on your drawing paper. Now, see how many of those units represent the height of the building.

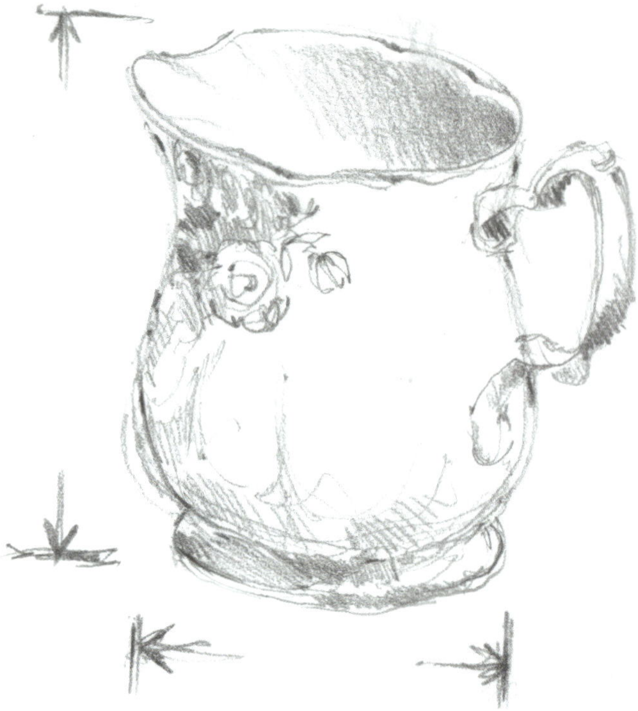

Estimate Scale With Guidelines

This piece of china is about 1¼ times as tall as it is wide. You could use a ruler to measure when scaling it up to a larger size, but you could also just estimate with light guidelines before you begin to draw.

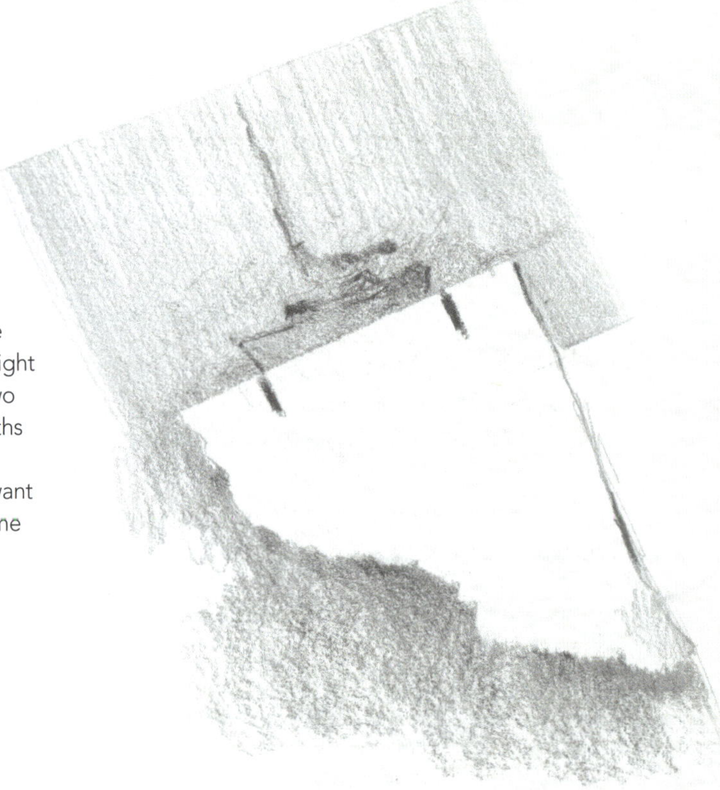

Use Scrap Paper as a Ruler

This example shows how to work from a photo and make your own ruler with a scrap of paper. Using the clean straight side of the paper, I marked the length of the boat with two pencil lines. Now it is easy to figure how many boat lengths equals the height of the mast.

When you scale your drawing, decide how long you want to make the boat and then make the mast height the same relationship. Here, my mast was about 1 boat length tall.

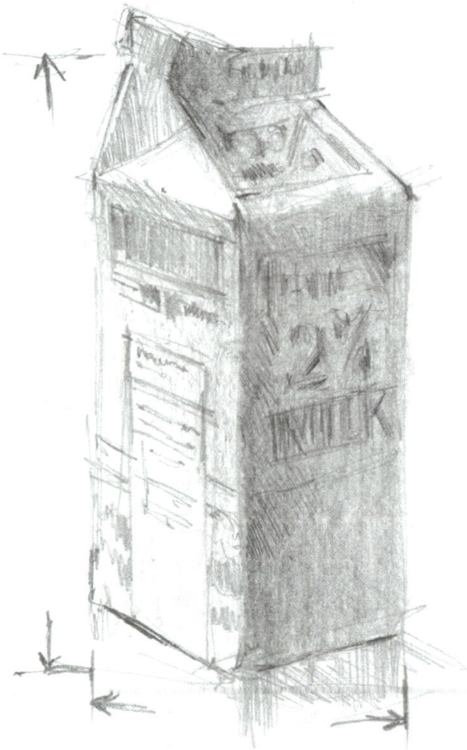

Now Practice...

Try the thumb and pencil trick on a real milk carton and then try the scrap of paper method on this drawing from the book.

Foreshortening

Proportions change dramatically when we view objects from different angles. To establish a sense of space and increase the illusion of 3-D, we need to study these distortions. Artists refer to this as foreshortening.

Foreshortening Helps 3-D Effect

This drawing of a pencil is shorter in width than it would be if drawn face on. However, the pointed end is much larger than the eraser end, giving it the illusion of 3-D.

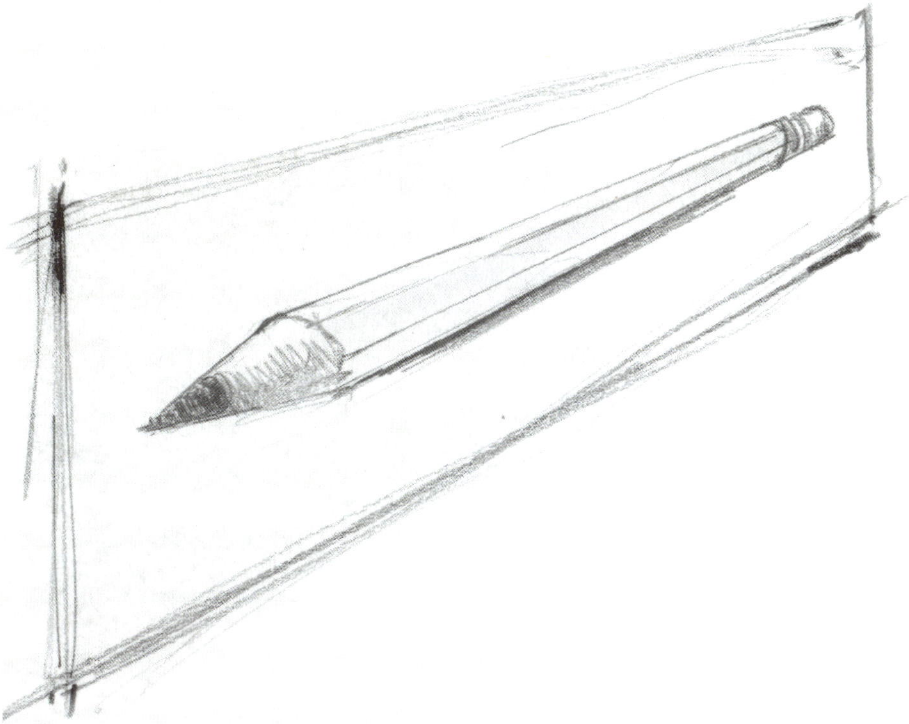

Reversed Proportions

In reality, the handle of this spaghetti claw is longer than it is wide. But from this angle, those proportions are reversed. Line A (handle length) is shorter than line B (width of the claw). You may need to verify that with a ruler because it contradicts what is already in our memory.

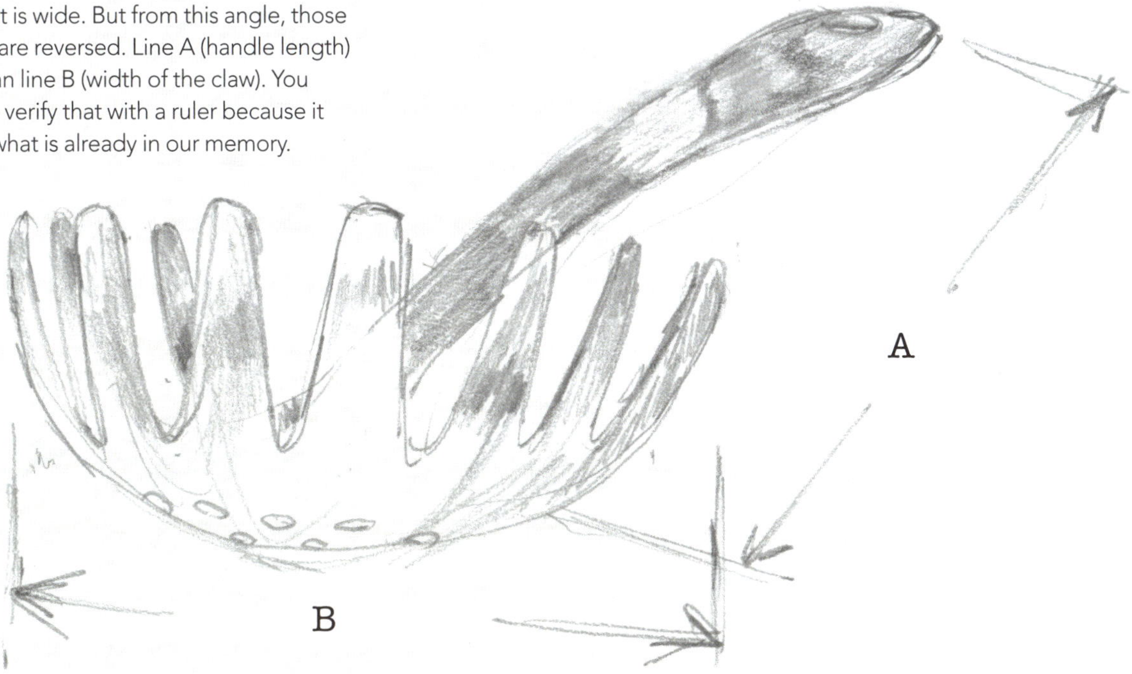

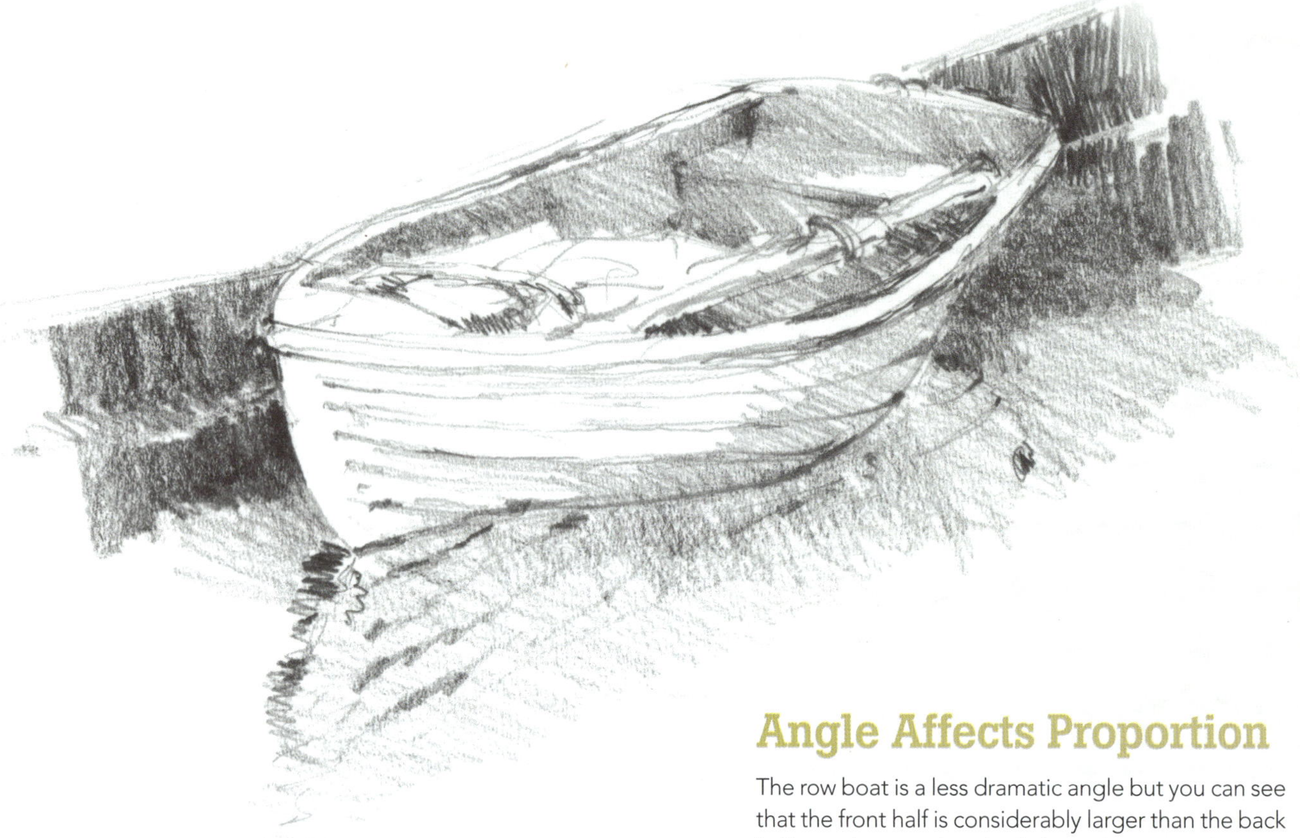

Angle Affects Proportion

The row boat is a less dramatic angle but you can see that the front half is considerably larger than the back half in order to make it look three-dimensional.

Direction Affects Foreshortening

One of the more difficult shapes to foreshorten is a branch that tapers toward you. The thickness still needs to diminish but at a slower rate than it would if the branch were tapering away from you.

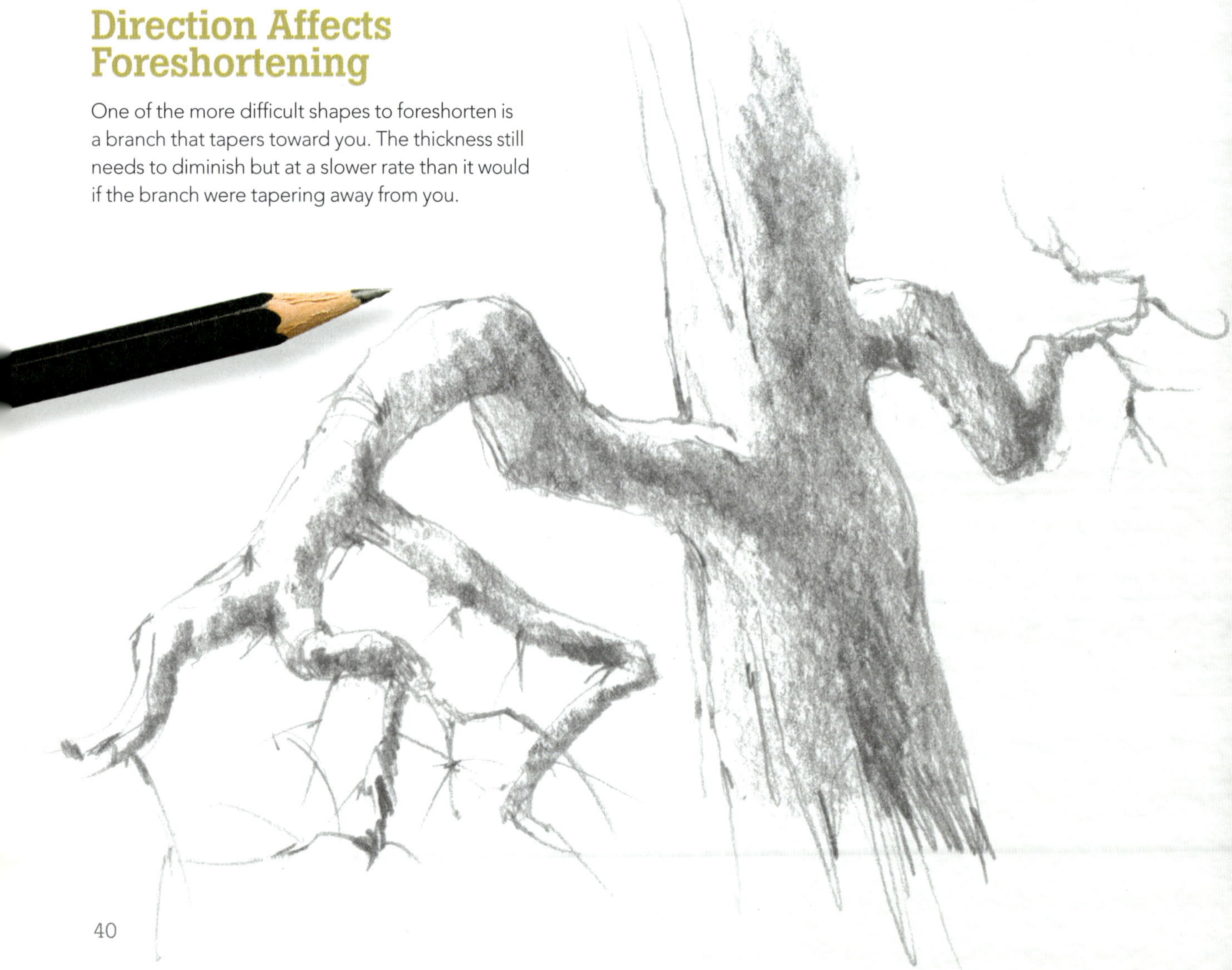

Contours Aid Direction

Notice how the contours explain much about the direction of the subject.

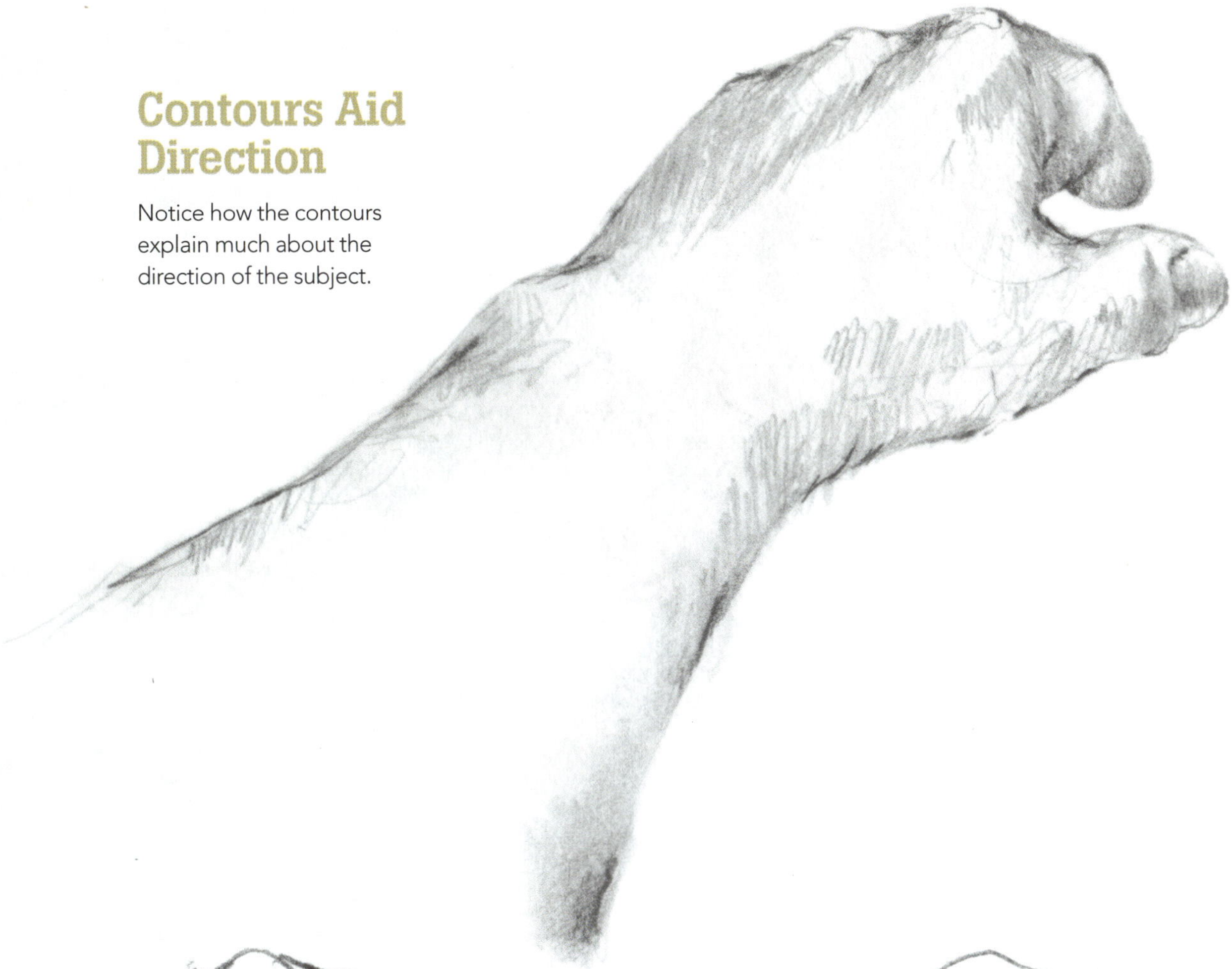

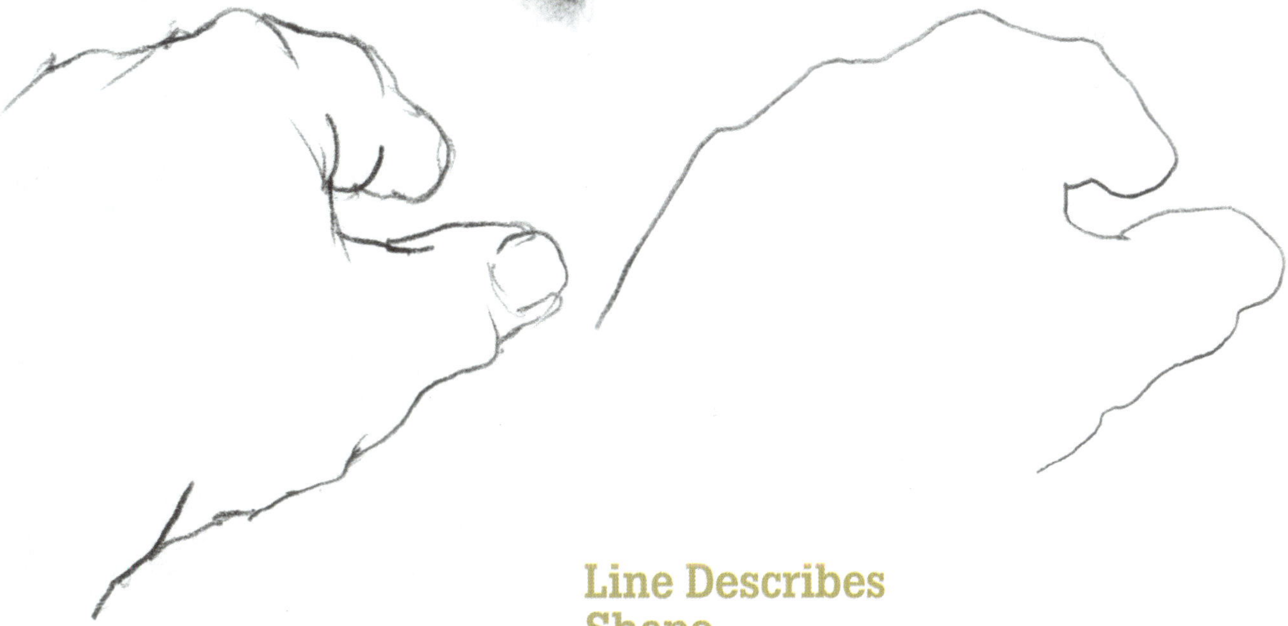

Line Describes Shape

The line must describe a series of overlapping shapes, not just a plain outline.

3

TECHNIQUES

Draw a Cat in Proportion

Spend some time practicing how to plot proportions. It is best to find a good reference photo of your own, but for this exercise you could also use the finished drawing as a reference.

MATERIALS

Surface
acid-free art paper

Graphite
HB graphite stick
2H, HB, B wooden pencils

Other
kneaded eraser

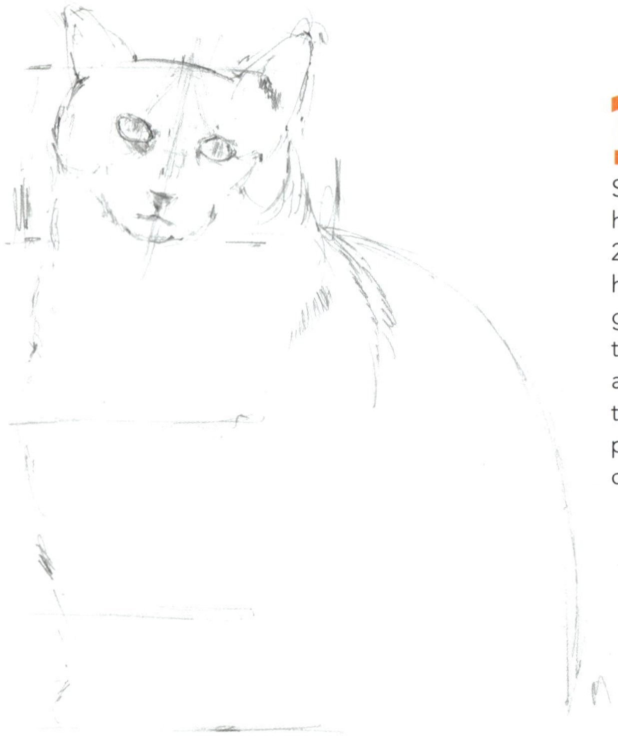

1 Sketch the Shape and Plot Proportions

Start with an HB pencil and make the width of the cat's head about 1¼ times the height of the head (or about 25 percent wider). Set the height of the cat's body at 3½ heads. Make the body 2 heads wide. Draw a diagonal guideline in the center of the head to establish the tilt. (Animals and figures look better when the head is angled slightly.) Set other guidelines at 90 degrees to the center line to ensure you get the eyes and mouth properly aligned. Block in the facial features and take care making the eyes the same size and shape.

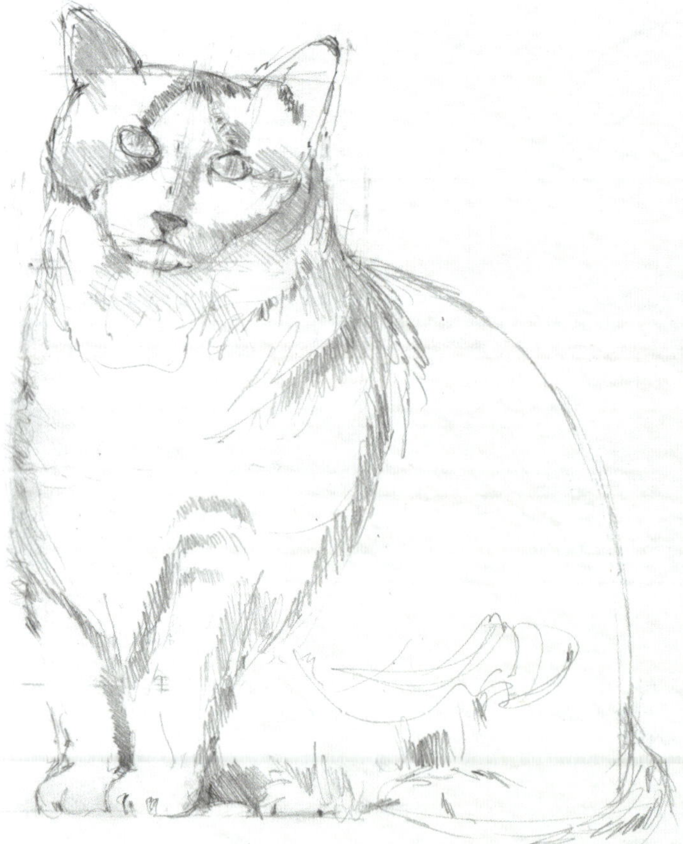

2 Define Fur Patterns and Add Texture

Once the shape has been established, use a B pencil to define the fur pattern where the darkest value meets the lightest value. Use a 2H pencil to suggest the texture of fur in the light areas.

Erase the guidelines when you no longer need them. Clean any smudges with a kneaded eraser as you go. They may get more difficult to remove as the drawing becomes more elaborate.

3 Fill In the Dark Areas

Use the side of the B pencil to fill in the dark areas. Because these areas are so large, you may want to use an HB graphite stick for the broad strokes.

Draw back into any of the darks that need to be reinforced. Use an HB pencil for any of the fine dark work because the lead is soft enough to deposit more graphite, but hard enough to press the paper texture flat and fill in the white bits.

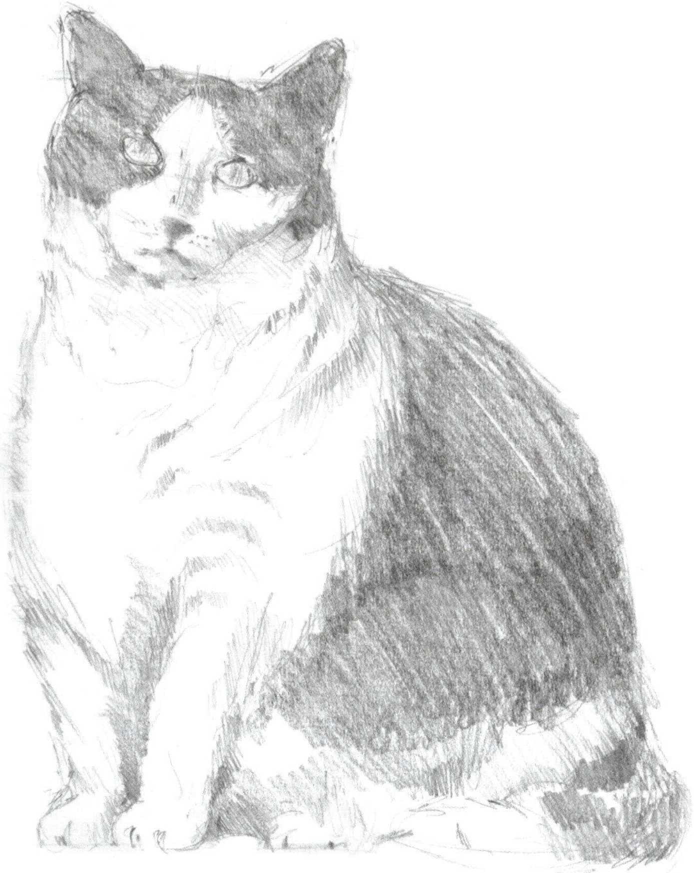

4 Continue Filling In and Refine the Details to Finish

Always think in terms of three values: light, medium and dark. Other subtle shades will find their way into the drawing as you refine the shapes. Don't attempt to get photorealistic at this stage. Focus on getting the size relationship of the various parts working together. The proportions and values are more important than fine detail such as rendering fur. In fact, the suggestion of fur may be all you want here.

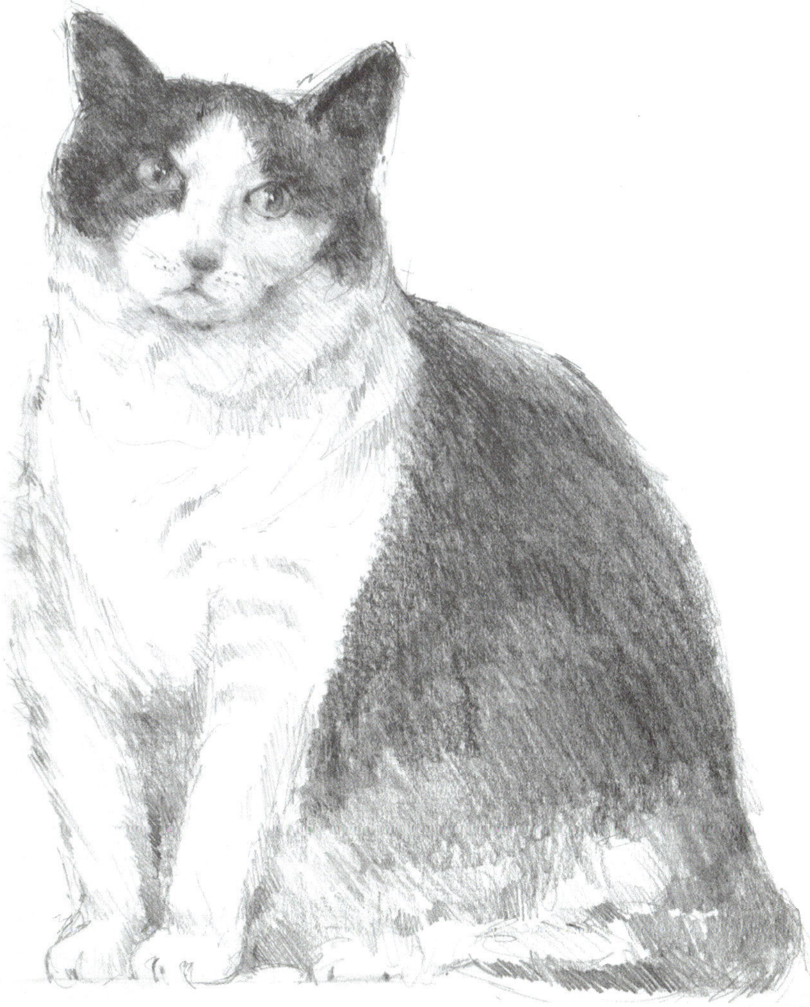

LEAD SHAPING

Use a scrap of paper or very fine sandpaper to shape the lead as needed.

TECHNIQUES

Draw a Coffeepot in Proportion

Draw your coffee pot, tea pot, kettle or some other household object. Start by establishing the proportions. With this particular coffeepot, the proportions were fairly easy to establish because it is simply twice as tall as it is wide.

This is just another way of working with pencils and creating a slightly different end appearance.

MATERIALS

Surface
acid-free art paper

Graphite
HB graphite stick
2H, HB, B wooden pencils

Other
kneaded eraser
paper towels

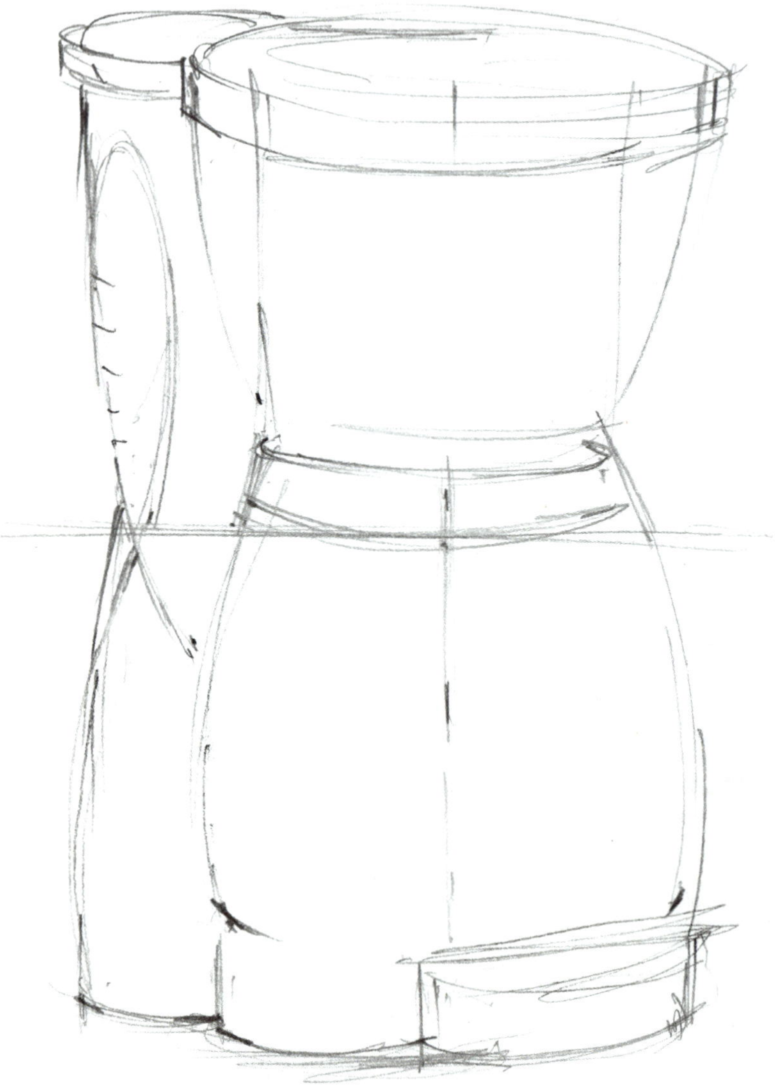

1 Sketch the Shape and Establish Proportions

With an HB wooden pencil, draw a horizontal guideline for the center, dividing the top half and bottom half. Then draw a vertical guideline, in this case you want the center of the carafe portion. That vertical center line is vital to getting the bowl shapes symmetrical. It is so much easier to compare the two halves of the pot by using a center guideline.

The next challenge will be getting the ovals right. Keep your eraser handy because this will involve a lot of trial and error.

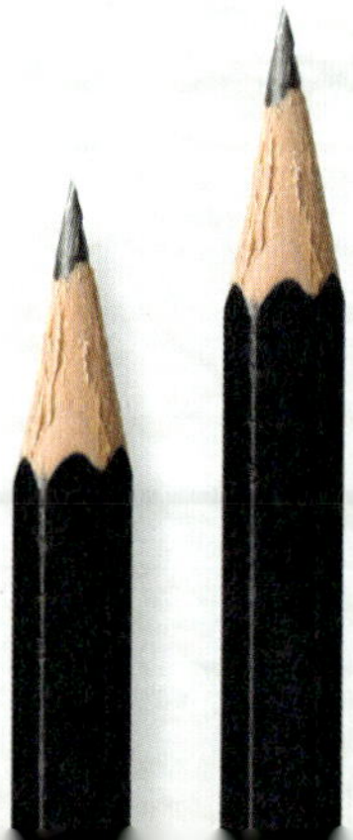

2 Complete the Contour Drawing

Once you have the basic shapes established, erase the guidelines and some of the extraneous marks. Adjust any distortions and add the extra parts of the coffeepot. (In this case I completed the handle and fixed the switch panel on the bottom front.)

It will help the bulk of the pot if you draw some coffee in it, because the oval contributes to the three-dimensional illusion. It will also provide a dark value for contrast.

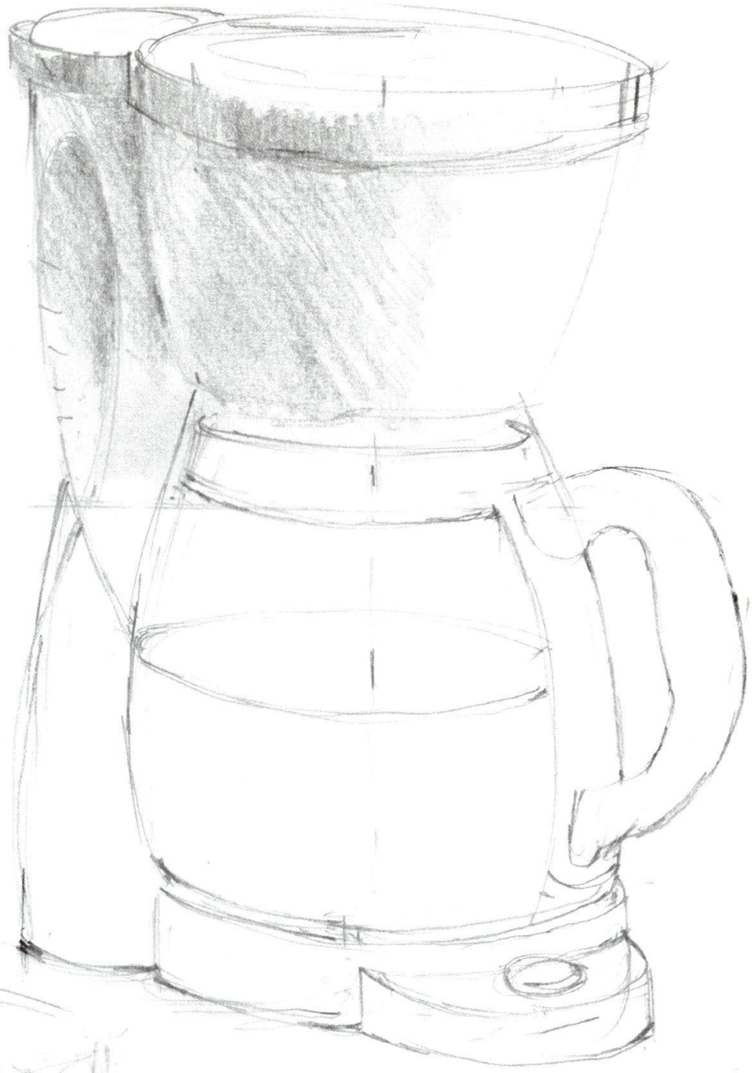

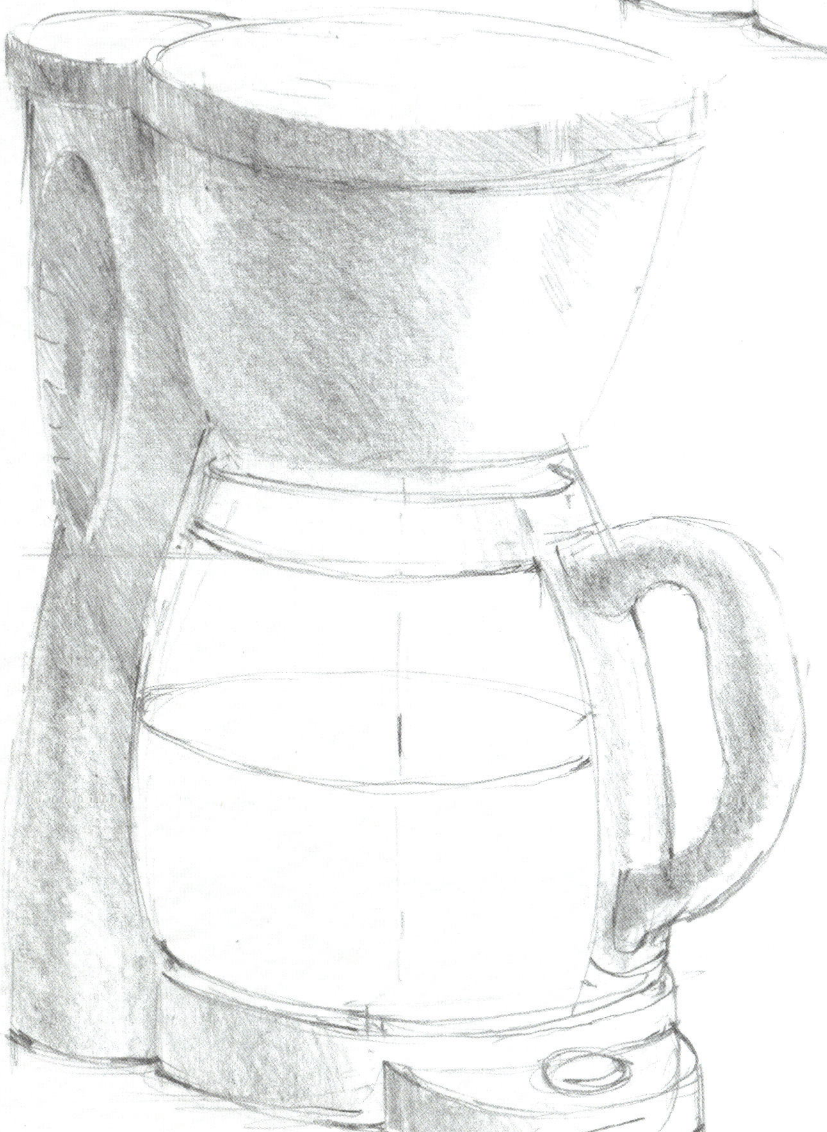

3 Apply Value and Tone

Make the light come from the top right side. Your lightest surface will be the top. (Because the local color of the basket holder on this particular coffeepot is white, I left the right side white as well.)

Apply the tone with the side of an HB graphite stick. Then gently go over that with the side of a 2H wooden pencil to help blend the graphite and hide some of the pencil strokes.

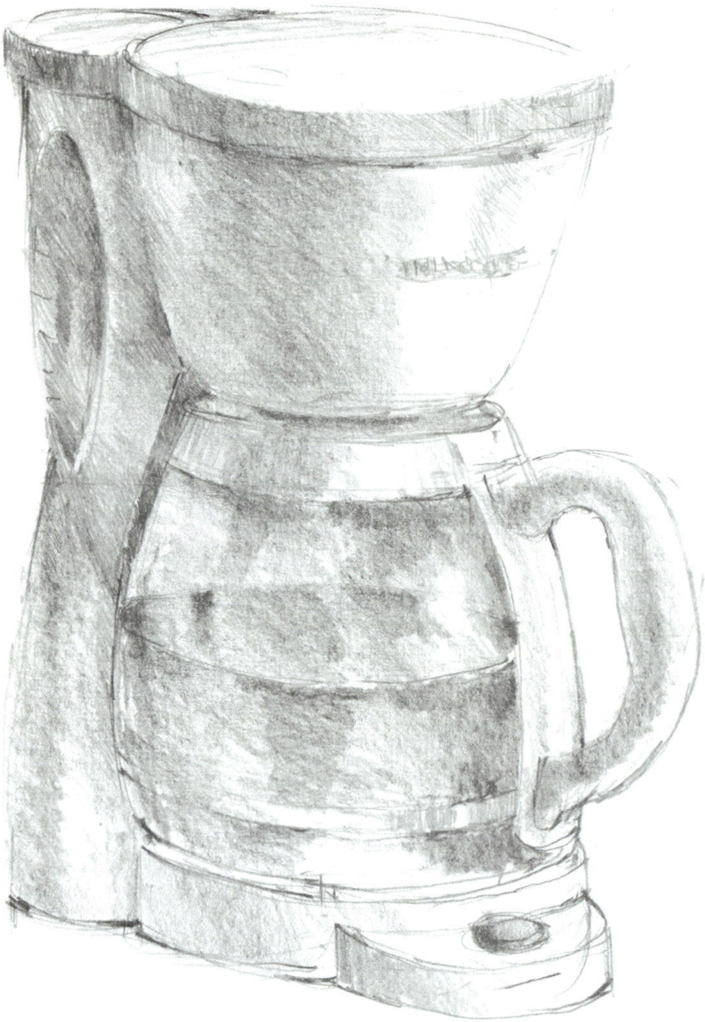

4 Continue Adding Light and Mid-Tones

Start with the lightest values first and go through the whole drawing, placing those values in their appropriate places.

Still using the 2H pencil, add the medium values by increasing the pressure. When you are satisfied with those mid-tones, proceed to adding the darks.

5 Apply the Dark Tones

Use B and HB pencils to apply the darker tones. Place a paper towel under your drawing hand to avoid smudging the work. By this time, there is a lot of graphite on the paper and it will be easily moved.

Note the darkest areas could still be made much darker. This is evident by the amount of white paper fiber showing through in the coffee.

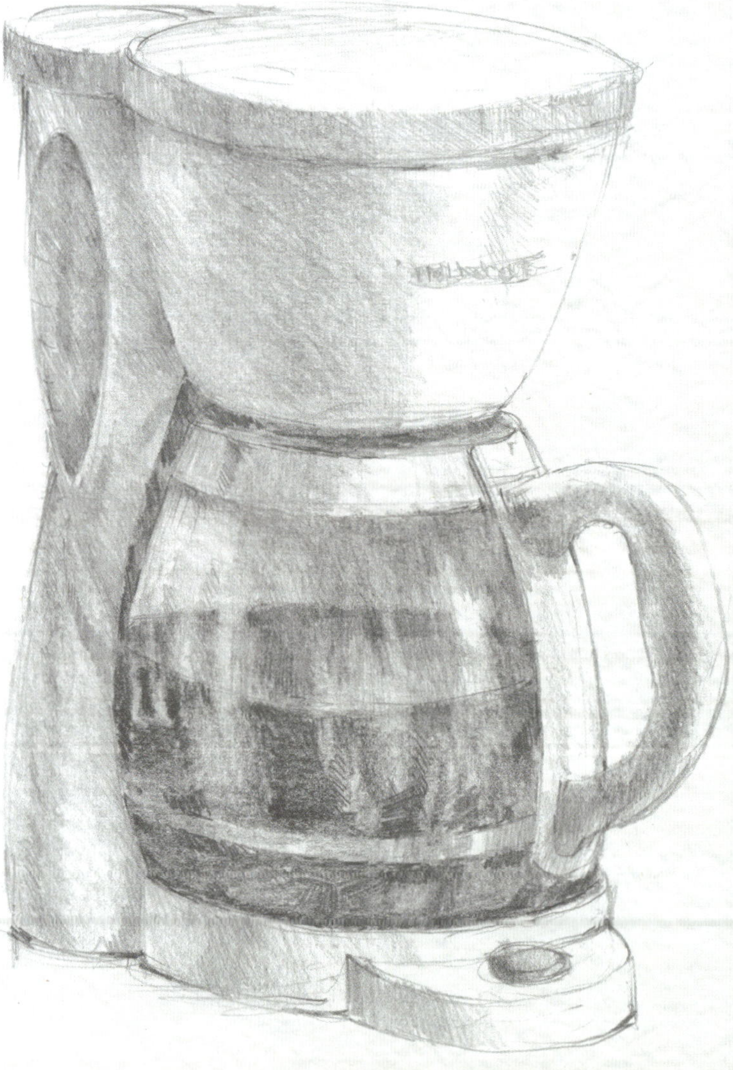

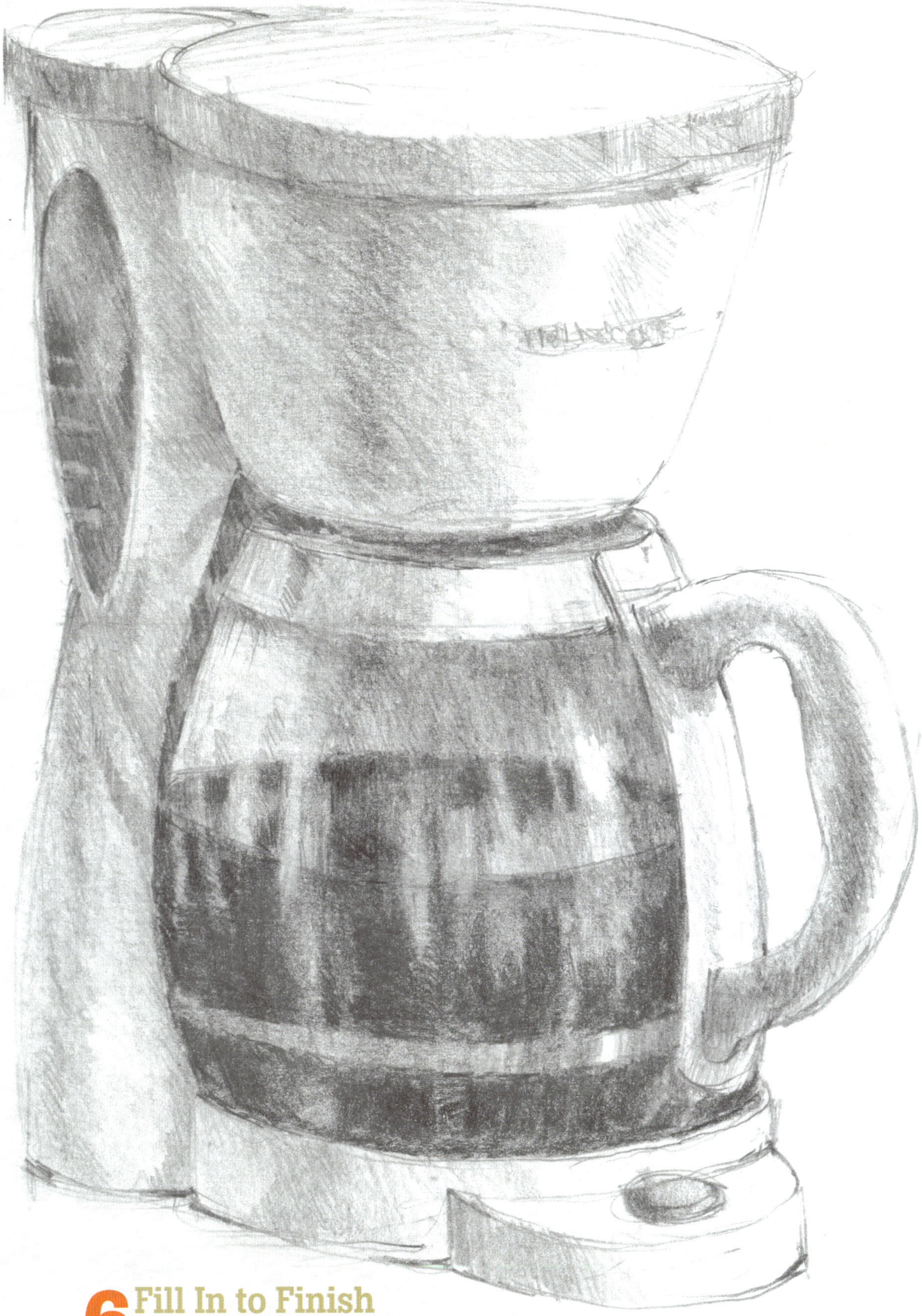

6 Fill In to Finish

Fill in a bit more of the paper fiber by pressing hard with an HB or even a B pencil. This will give the blacks that little extra contrast.

TECHNIQUES

Scale a Drawing With a Grid

Occasionally you may need to enlarge a subject that is a bit too complicated to work freehand. This manual grid method will enable you to get accurate proportions without the aid of a computer or photo enlarger.

MATERIALS

Surface
acid-free art paper

Graphite
HB wooden or mechanical pencil

Other
kneaded eraser
set square (or T-square)
straightedge
transparent sleeve

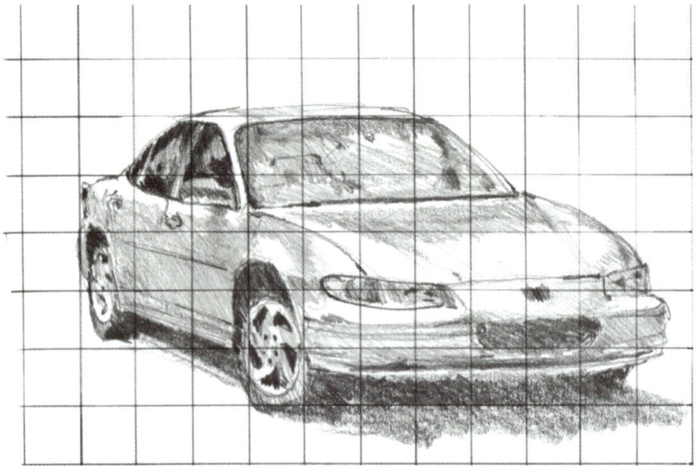

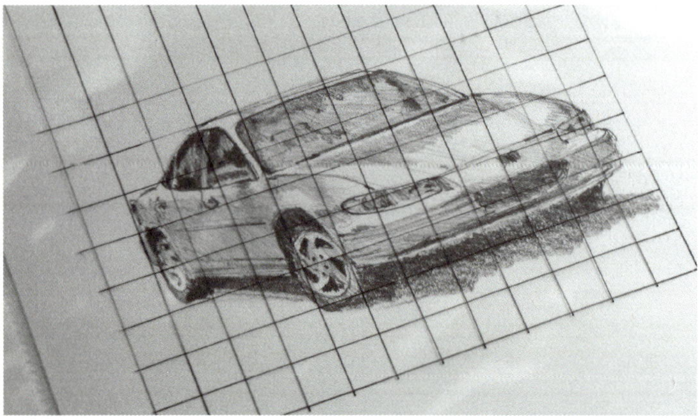

1 Draw a Half-Inch Grid

Imagine you want to double the size of an original drawing. Place your original drawing in a transparent sleeve and draw half-inch (1.3cm) squares on the outside of the film.

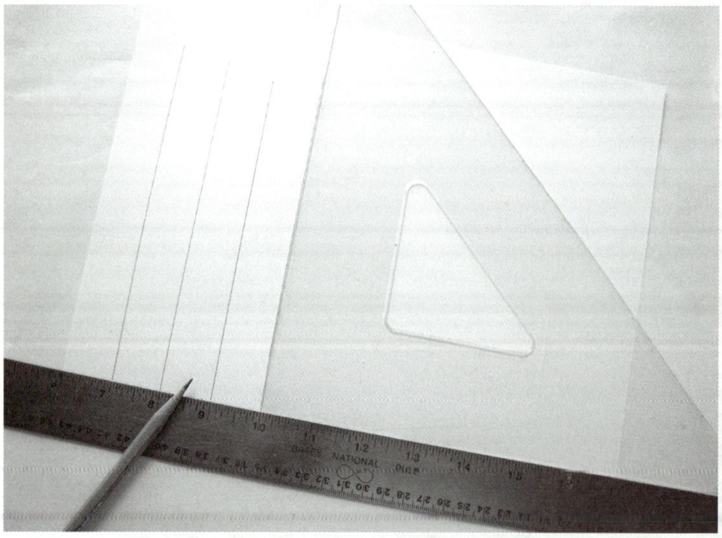

2 Draw a One-Inch Grid

Lightly draw the same number of squares on your new drawing paper but make them one-inch (2.5cm) squares. Hold the straightedge still and slide the set square along in order to get the lines parallel. It is important to keep your grid lines very light, as the squares will be erased once the contours are drawn. (I have shown them much darker here for the purpose of this demonstration.)

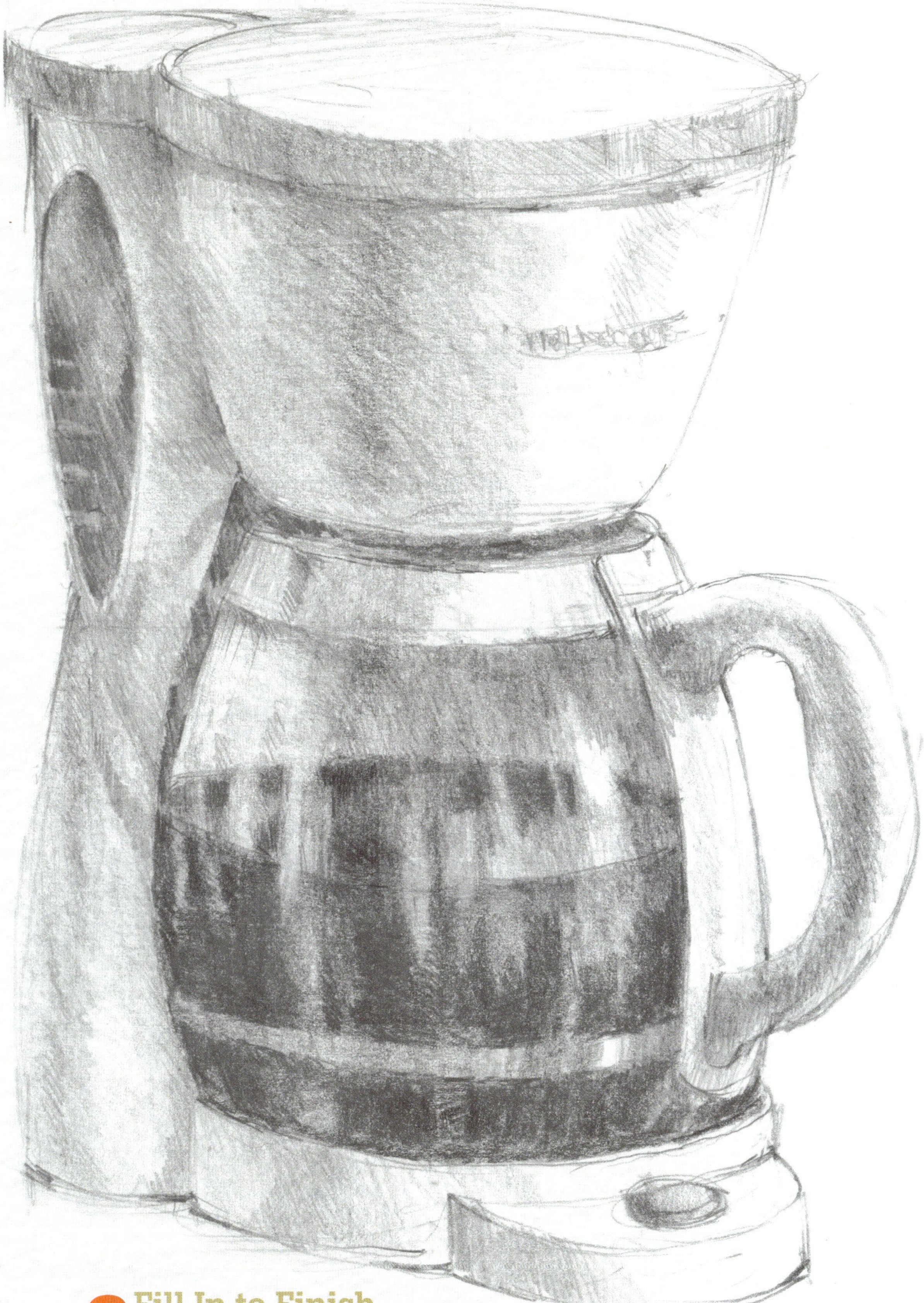

6 Fill In to Finish

Fill in a bit more of the paper fiber by pressing hard with an HB or even a B pencil. This will give the blacks that little extra contrast.

TECHNIQUES

Scale a Drawing With a Grid

Occasionally you may need to enlarge a subject that is a bit too complicated to work freehand. This manual grid method will enable you to get accurate proportions without the aid of a computer or photo enlarger.

MATERIALS

Surface
acid-free art paper

Graphite
HB wooden or mechanical pencil

Other
kneaded eraser
set square (or T-square)
straightedge
transparent sleeve

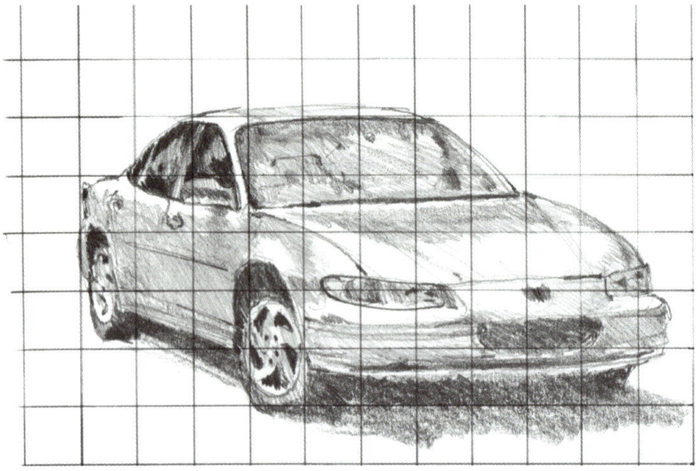

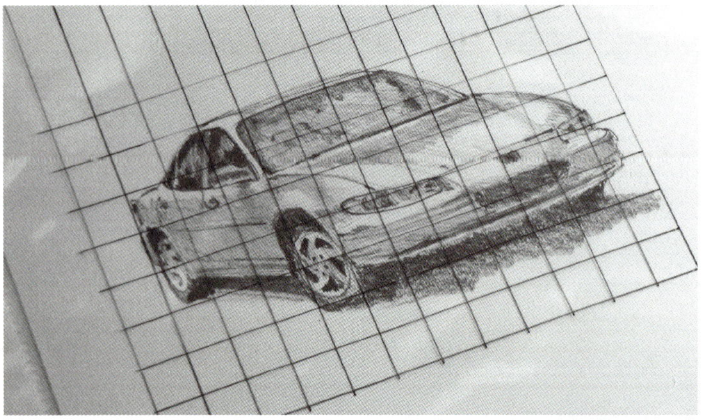

1 Draw a Half-Inch Grid

Imagine you want to double the size of an original drawing. Place your original drawing in a transparent sleeve and draw half-inch (1.3cm) squares on the outside of the film.

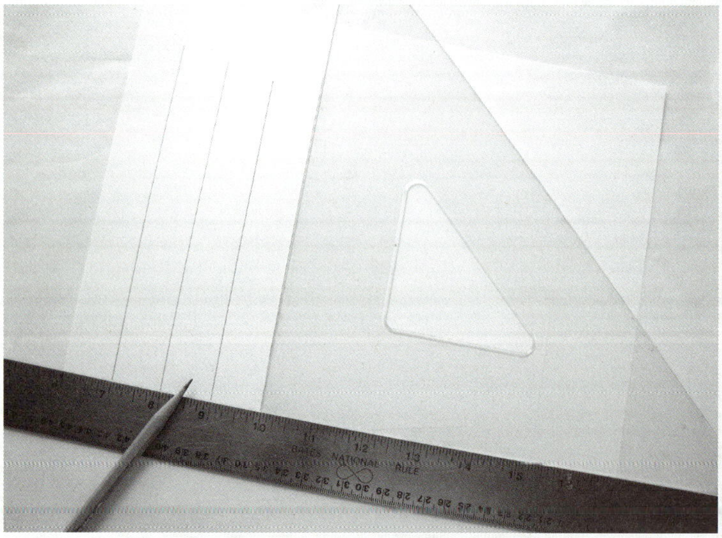

2 Draw a One-Inch Grid

Lightly draw the same number of squares on your new drawing paper but make them one-inch (2.5cm) squares. Hold the straightedge still and slide the set square along in order to get the lines parallel. It is important to keep your grid lines very light, as the squares will be erased once the contours are drawn. (I have shown them much darker here for the purpose of this demonstration.)

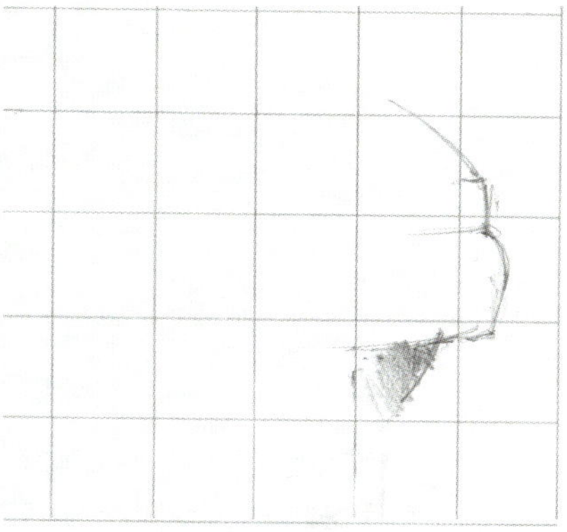

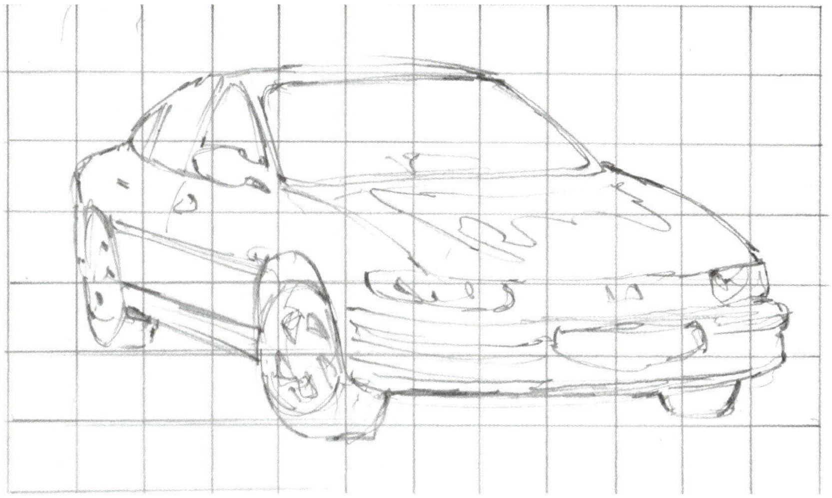

3 Draw the Subject on the New Paper

Draw the subject of the original drawing onto the new paper, one square at a time. Refer back to the original and continue comparing it to your new drawing as you go. It is so much easier to compare and draw these small pieces bit by bit, than attempting to draw the whole object at once.

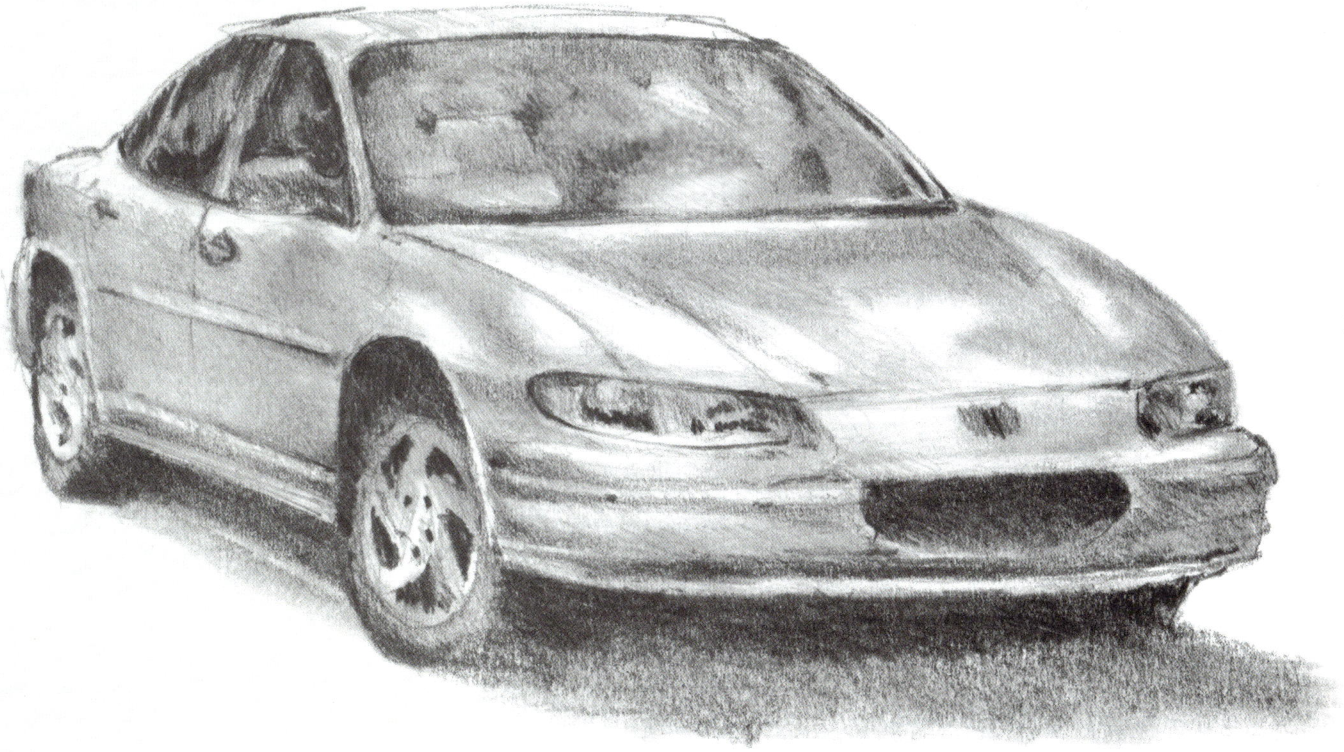

4 Erase the Grid Lines and Add Details to Finish

Continue drawing the contours of the subject. When you are happy with the completed contour drawing, go ahead and erase the grid lines. Be careful not to smudge your drawing. Apply tone and add whatever finishing details you like.

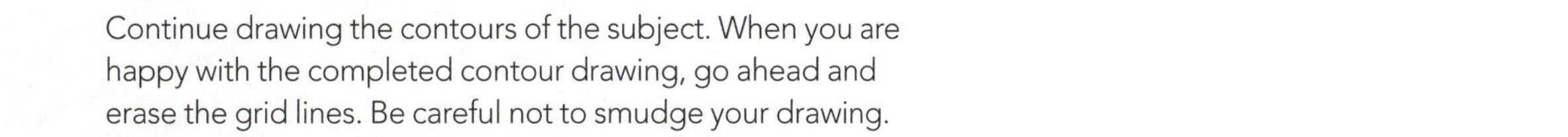

CHAPTER 4

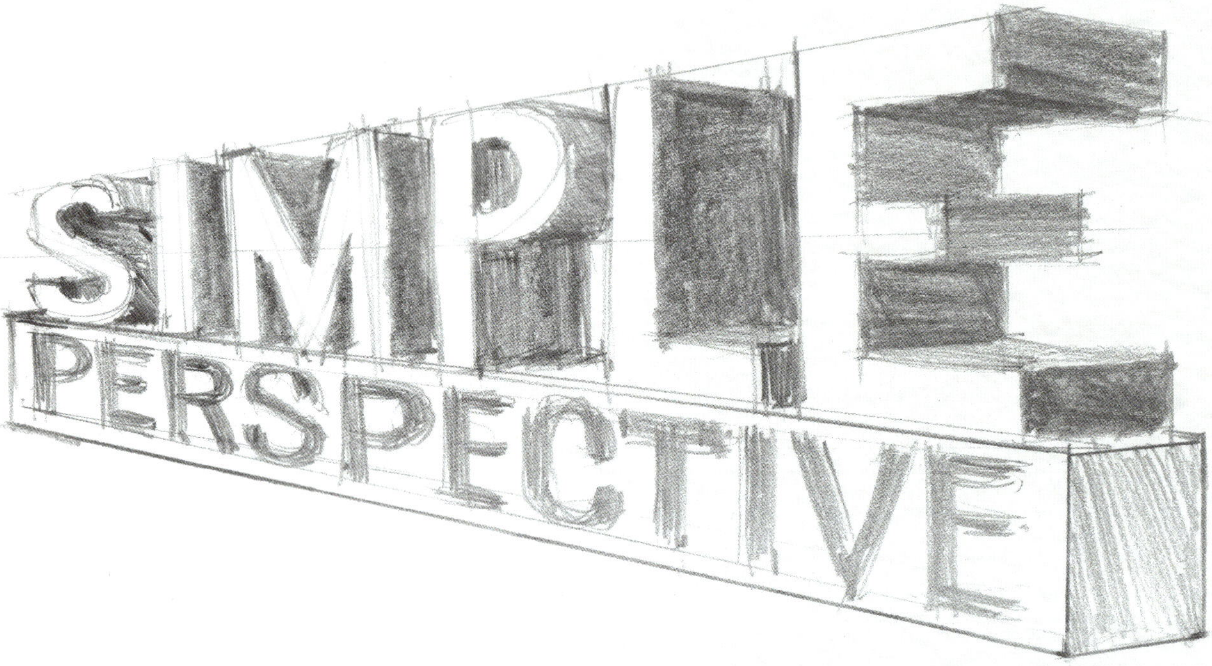

Unlike architects and engineers, artists simply want to make the structures we draw look good. Although we don't need to build the real thing from our drawings, it is important to create convincing perspective in order to get a realistic end result.

Achieving the illusion of three dimensions on a two-dimensional surface requires an understanding of how to use the horizon line and vanishing points to establish guidelines that insure the angles are correct. You will need to trust your own judgement when it comes to things such as how far apart to space the vanishing points when working with two point perspective. With a bit of practice, you'll get a feel for it, and eventually you'll become quite comfortable with establishing perspective in your drawings.

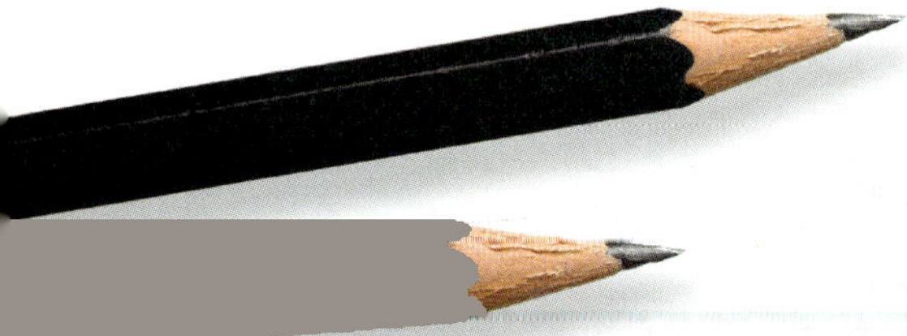

One- and Two-Point Perspective

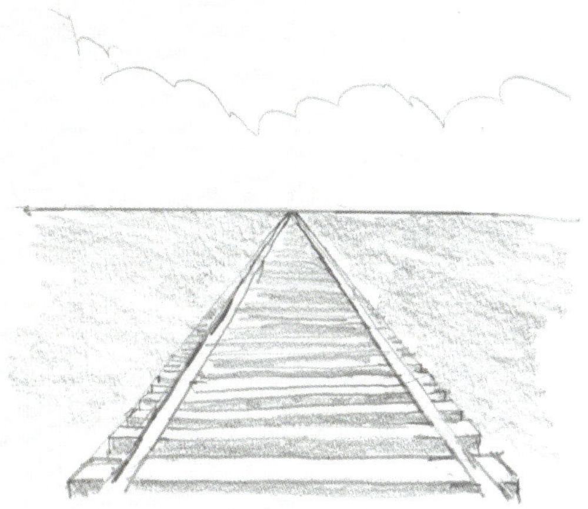

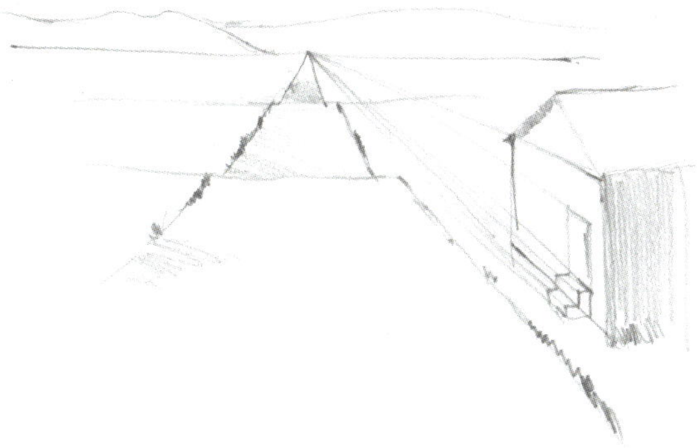

One-Point Perspective, Single Vanishing Point

In this view from the direct center of a railroad track, the track appears progressively smaller as it goes farther away until it finally disappears on the horizon. The place where the track meets the horizon is called the vanishing point. Because this composition is positioned directly in the center, there is only one vanishing point.

Different Drawing, Same Concept

The same is true in this composition. Although you may begin to see minor distortions, it is safe to draw the building beside the road to the same vanishing point as the road. You can assume that the building is parallel to the road. Any other structures that are also parallel to the road would use the same vanishing point.

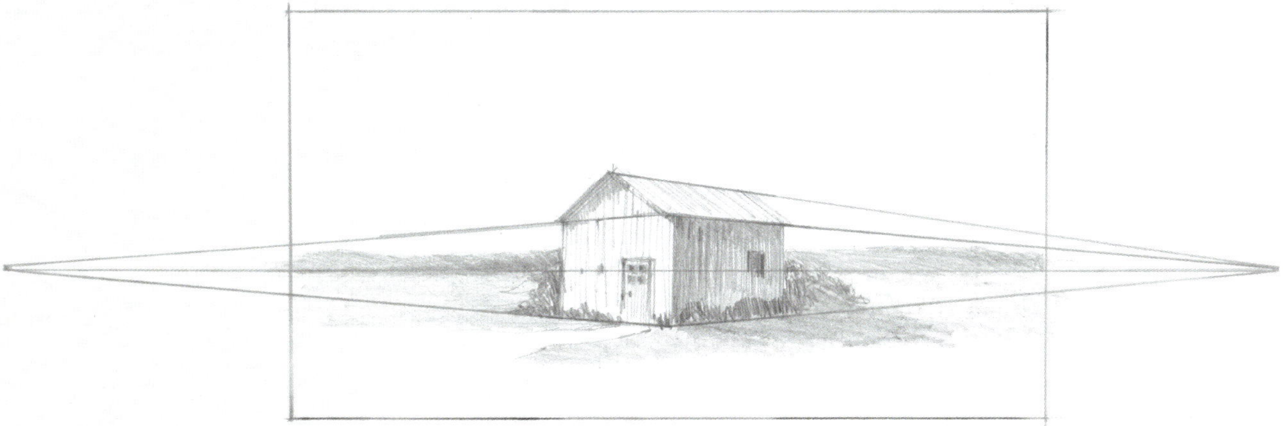

Two-Point Perspective – Two Vanishing Points

Note the relationship between the angles of the roof and walls with the horizon. The sides are vertical but the top and bottom of the walls are angled toward a point on the horizon. The top and bottom of the right-side wall (and roof because the roof is on the right side of the building) can be extended to the vanishing point on the right. The top and bottom of the left wall are projected to the left vanishing point.

FIND THE HORIZON

The horizon will always be at your own eye level. If you can't see the horizon from a particular place, you can always establish it on your drawing by looking straight ahead and noticing how it relates to your subject. Normally, the vanishing points are on the horizon. The only exception would be floating forms or extreme viewpoints.

Cast Shadows in Perspective

It is important not to confuse shadows and reflections. Shadows are cast across a surface. Unlike reflections, they are not mirror images.

Shadows can be plotted using the light source, similar to the way a vanishing point is used.

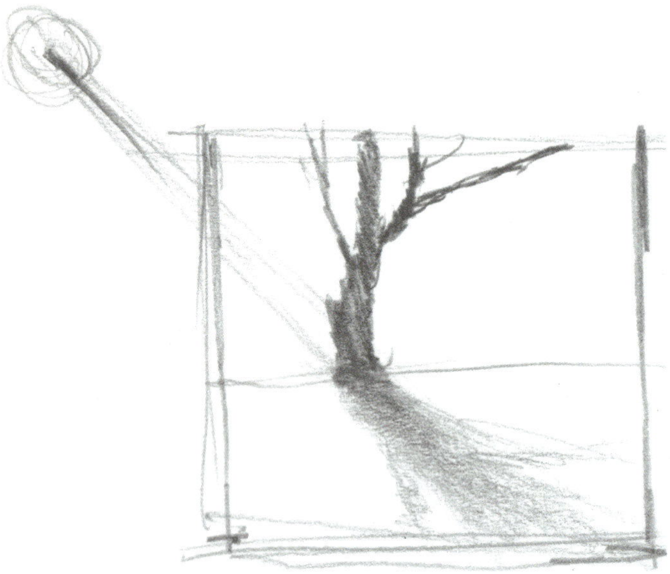

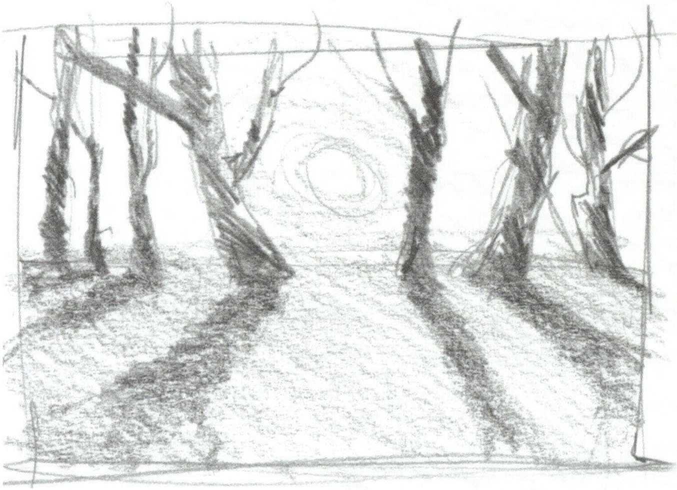

Back Lighting

When the object is backlit, the shadow is cast forward and appears to get larger as it gets closer.

Center Lighting

If the sun is directly in the center, the result is much like the one-point perspective. Draw angles from the center of the light source as though it were a vanishing point.

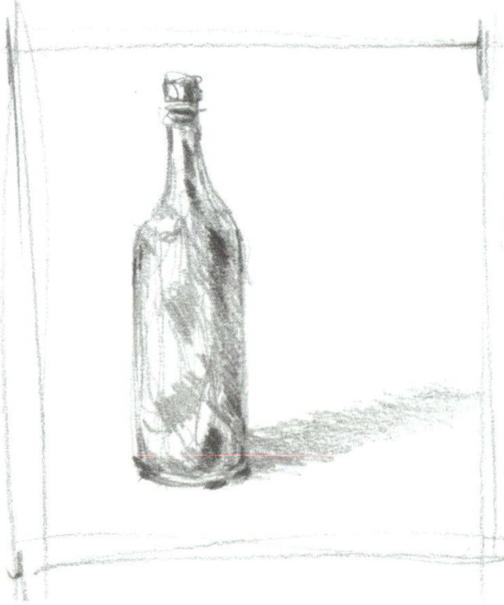

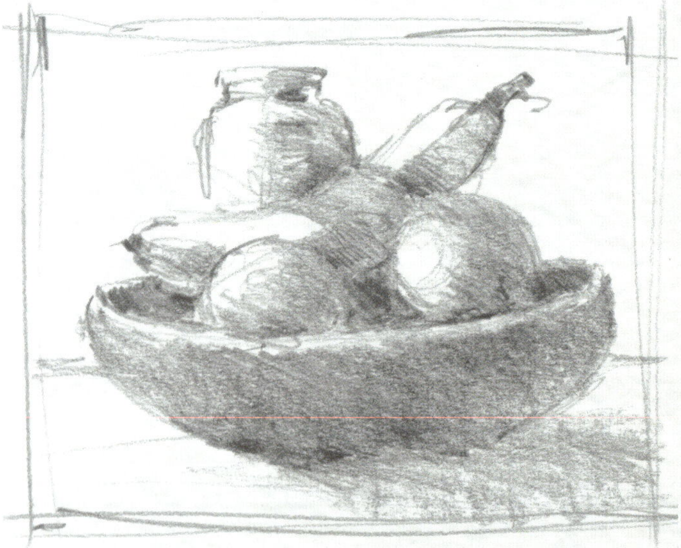

Front Angled Lighting

With an object that is lit from the front at a slight angle, the shadow is cast running away. Obviously the shadow is cast directly opposite to the light source. In this case, the shadow will appear to get smaller in perspective, but there is also the flare effect causing the shadow to fade, with softer edges toward the end.

Irregular Surfaces

When shadows are cast on additional objects or very irregular surfaces, any relation to perspective is obscured. This example is strictly a study in lighting and not perspective.

Perspective and Shapes

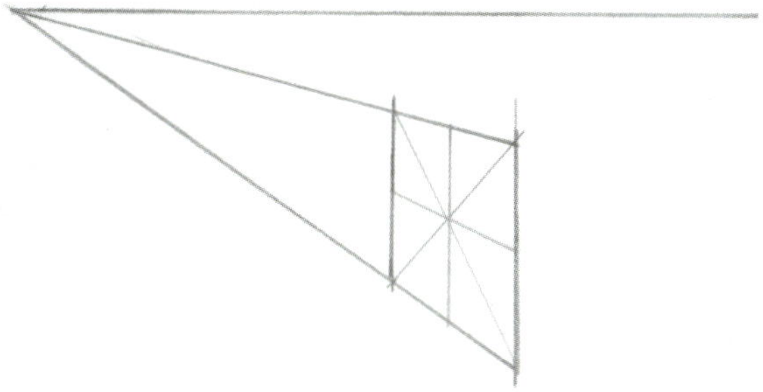

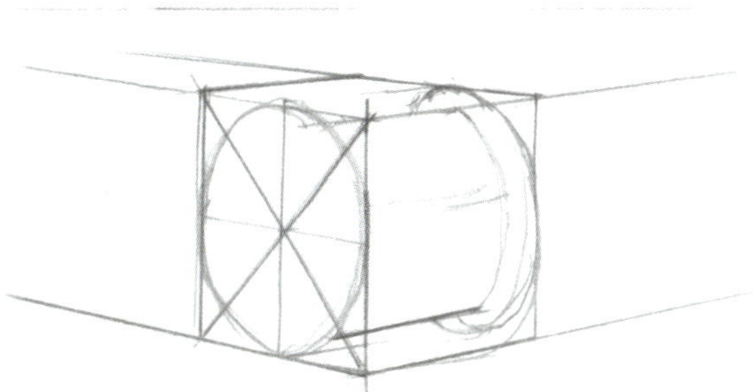

Flat Plane in Perspective

Draw a flat plane in perspective. Divide it with diagonal lines and a vertical line through the center. Add another line extending from the vanishing point through the center. You now have a segmented guide to aid in drawing an oval in perspective.

You'll need to guess the proportion of height versus width when deciding where to place the second vertical. Avoid lengthy math problems but make sure the plane looks square in perspective.

Cube in Perspective

Drawing a cube in perspective will provide you with a guide for developing other shapes such as a cylinder, which was the foundation of the paddle wheel in the drawing below. This method can be used for boats or cars and other objects that need foreshortening but do not have straight edges.

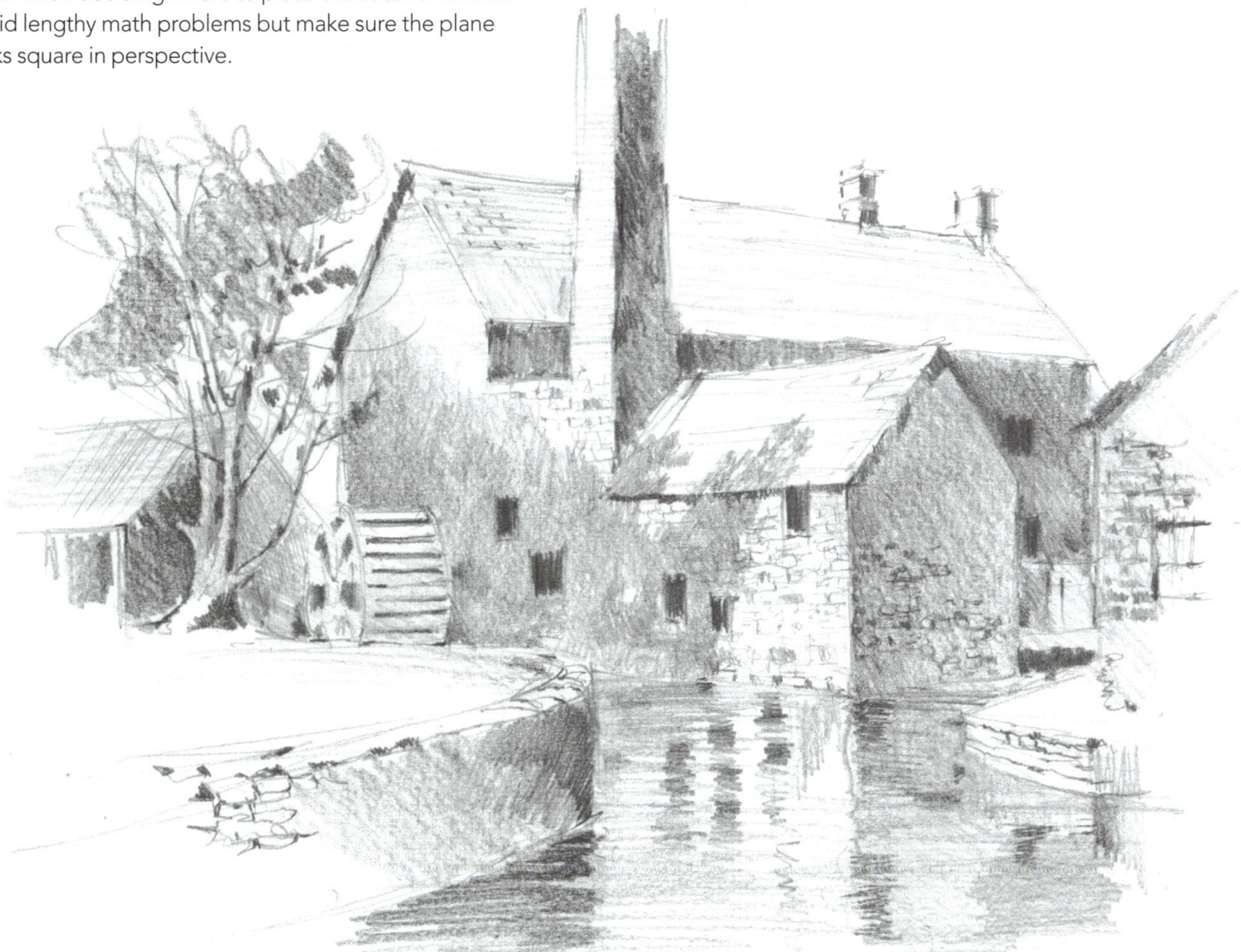

Bringing It All Together

Visualize where the horizon and vanishing points are in this drawing. Note the direction of the light source. Study the cast shadows as well as the reflections.

PLAYING WITH PERSPECTIVE

Practice Two-Point Perspective

Much of this method of drawing perspective requires guesswork and trial and error. With practice, you will begin to see immediately where the vanishing points should be and will be able to draw accurate structures without any horizon or guidelines on the paper.

MATERIALS

Surface
acid-free art paper

Graphite
wooden or mechanical pencil

Other
kneaded eraser

1 Draw the Horizon Line

Draw the horizon line and choose a place to position the front corner of the building. Decide how tall you want to make it.

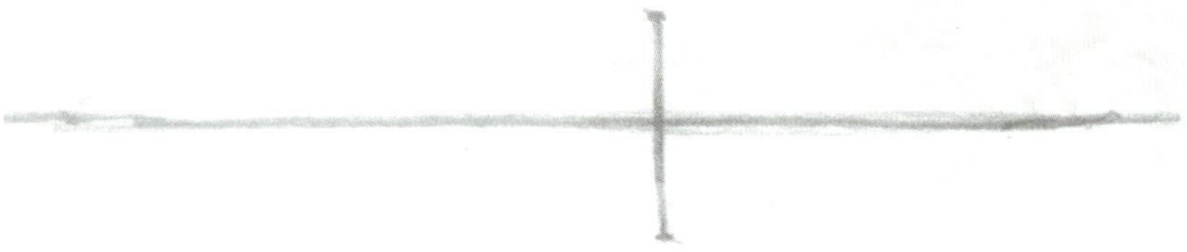

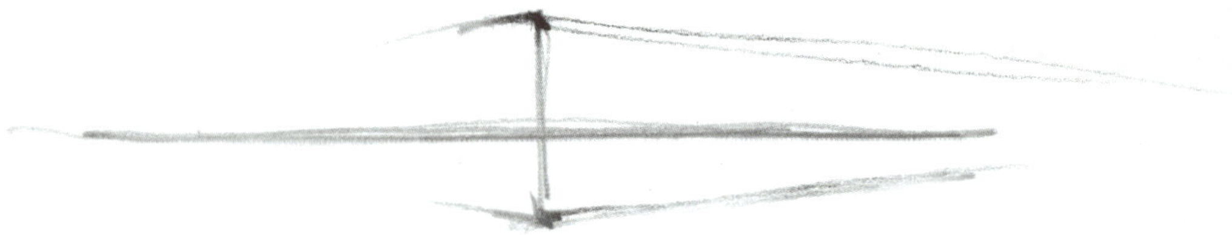

2 Sketch the Wall Angles

Sketch the approximate angles of the left and right walls. Find a good reference photo if you have difficulty visualizing these angles.

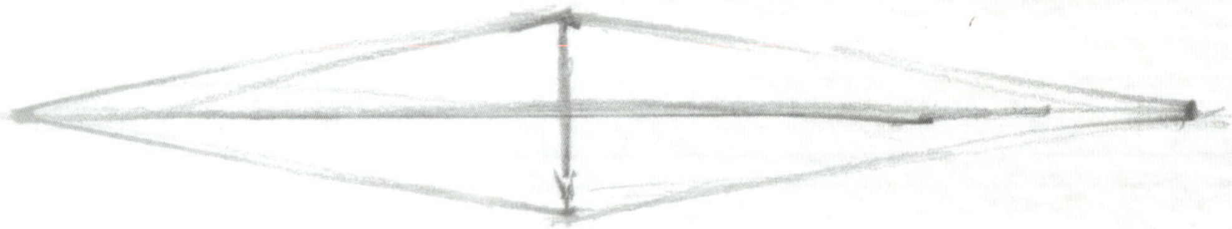

3 Establish Vanishing Points

Decide how far apart the vanishing points should be. If they are too close together, the drawing will be distorted. It is safe to make them right off the page. With a straightedge, extend the walls to the horizon. This will establish the left and right vanishing points.

4 Add Vertical Lines

Draw the vertical lines that will determine the length of each wall. This is basically a judgment call on your part. Make the building as long or as wide as you like.

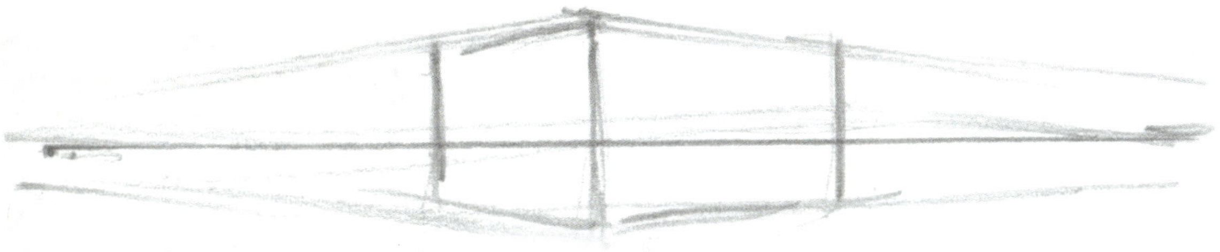

5 Establish the Roof Peak

Diagonals will intersect at the "optical" center. Draw an X on the end wall and a vertical line through the center of the X to establish the peak for the roof.

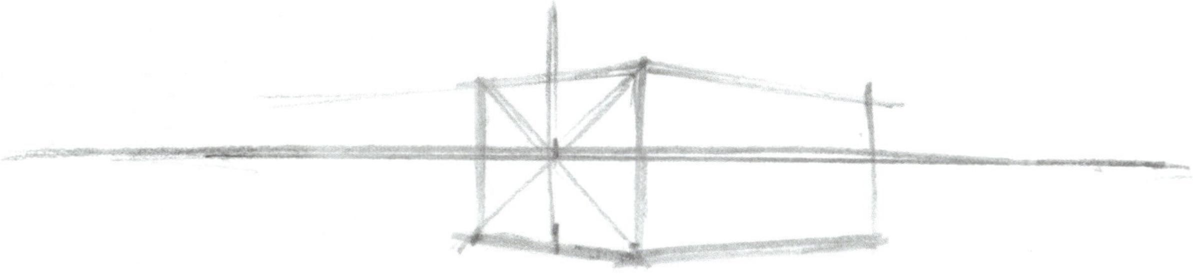

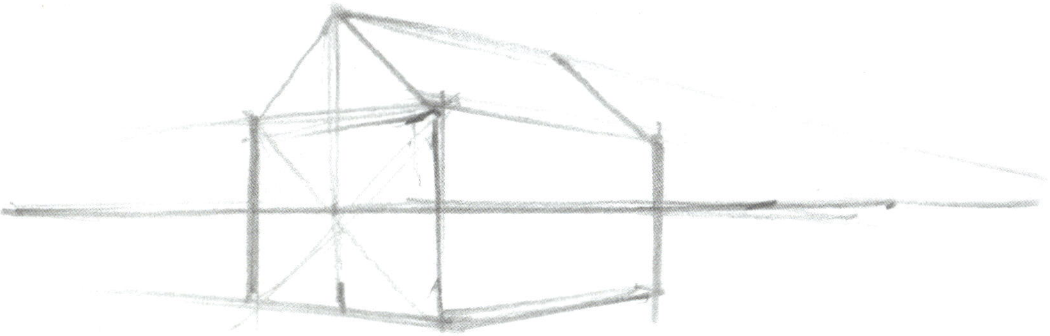

6 Join the Peak to the Wall

Connect the peak to the upper right and left corners of the front end wall. Then join the peak to the right vanishing point to establish the angle of the roof top. In order to keep this simple, match the slope of the roof to the line that joins the peak and right upper corner.

PLAYING WITH PERSPECTIVE

More Practice in Two-Point Perspective

Continue practicing two-point perspective by drawing a table with multiple vanishing points.

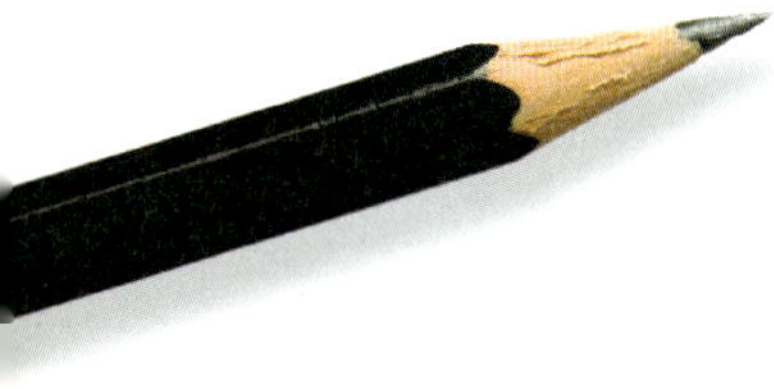

MATERIALS

Surface
acid-free art paper

Graphite
wooden or mechanical pencil

Other
kneaded eraser
masking tape
straightedge or T-square

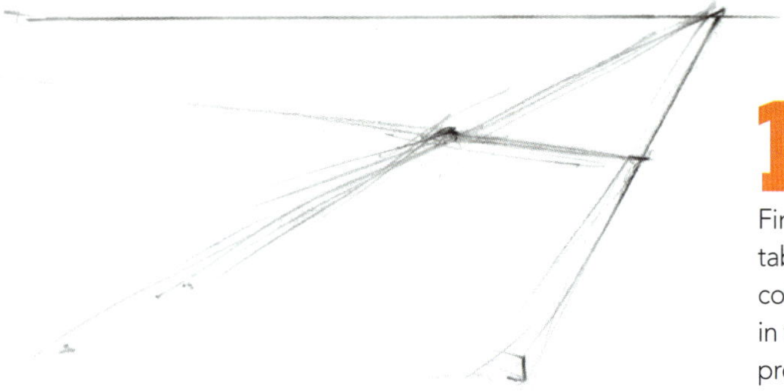

1 Find the Horizon and Rough In the Angles

Find the relation between the horizon and the coffee table. The horizon is always at eye level, and the coffee table should sit just below the horizon. Rough in the angles of the table freehand, then judge the proportions, comparing the length and width.

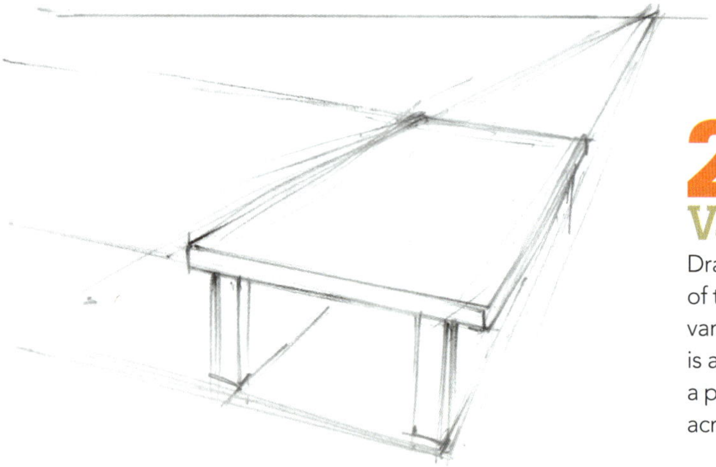

2 Sketch the Table and Project Lines to Vanishing Points

Draw vertical lines for the table legs and corners of the tabletop. Project all other lines to the vanishing points. Because the left vanishing point is a long way off the drawing surface, you can use a piece of masking tape to extend the horizon across your drawing board.

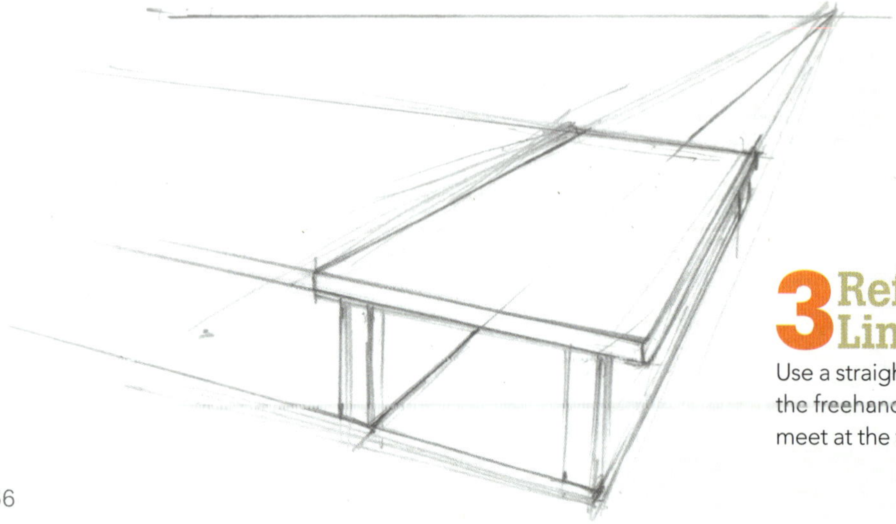

3 Refine Freehand Lines

Use a straightedge or T-square to refine the freehand lines so that they properly meet at the vanishing points.

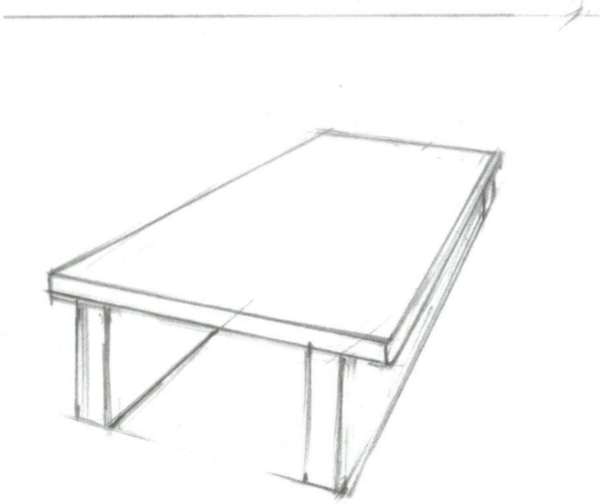

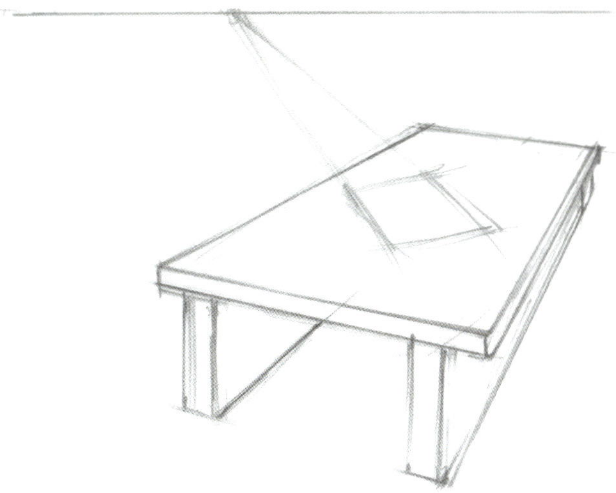

4 Clean Up the Drawing

Erase all the guidelines or trace the final lines and transfer your drawing to the desired surface.

5 Add a Book

Place a book on the table. If you were to use the same vanishing points as the table, the book would appear parallel to the edge of the tabletop. But if you want the book to appear more casually placed on the table, it will need to have its own vanishing points.

Rough in a shape for the book and extend lines from the sides of the book, making them meet on the horizon.

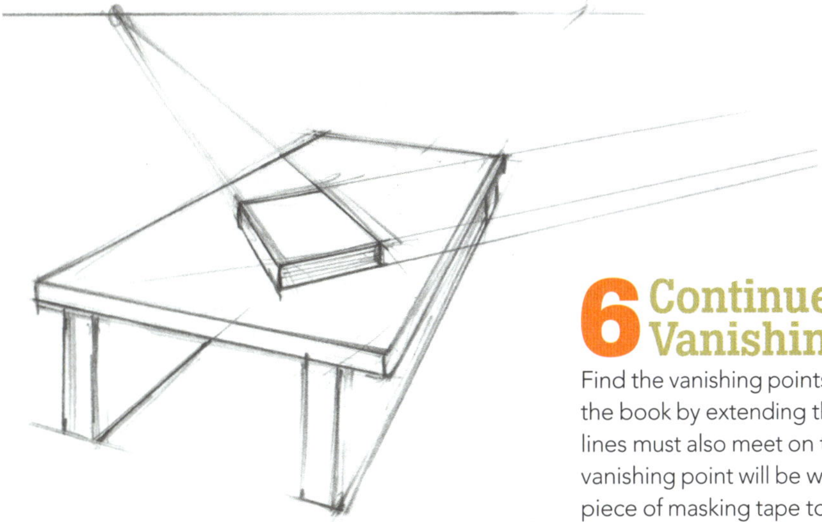

6 Continue Establishing Vanishing Points

Find the vanishing points for the top and bottom edges of the book by extending those lines to the horizon. Those lines must also meet on the horizon. Once again, this vanishing point will be well off the page. If necessary, use a piece of masking tape to extend the horizon.

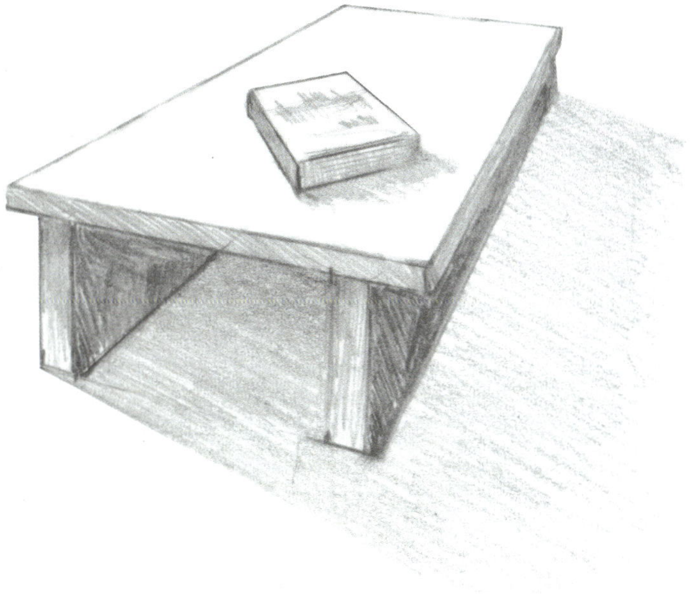

7 Erase Remaining Guidelines and Add Details to Finish

Erase the guidelines. You can protect the drawing during erasing by placing a piece of paper over the lines you want to save. Hold it firmly and erase right over the edge.

Add whatever tone and shading you like to finish the drawing.

Practice One-Point Perspective

Treat this project as a one-point perspective drawing even though the vanishing point is well off to the right side.

MATERIALS

Surface
acid-free art paper

Graphite
2H, 2B graphite sticks
HB, 2B wooden pencils

Other
kneaded eraser
straightedge

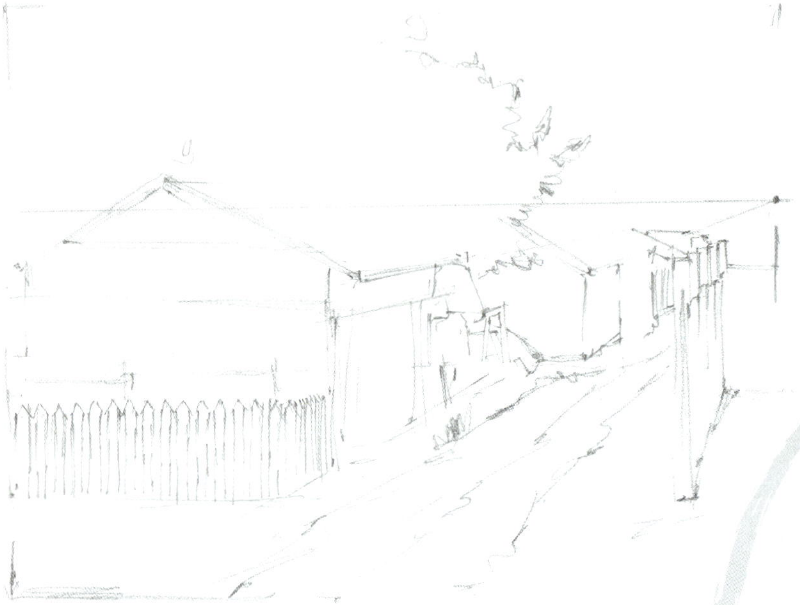

1 Rough In the Sketch

With a straightedge and an HB pencil, draw the horizon and place the vanishing point on the far right edge of the page. Draw a few light guidelines from the vanishing point to the key objects, such as the top and bottom of the main roofs and the fence on the right side. This does not need to be done with perfection because the lane will vary in level, causing the buildings to be less than parallel.

WORK LIGHT TO DARK

Most drawings that you plan to be a finished work should be rendered working from light to dark. There are exceptions where you may need to apply very dark values in the early stages, but this usually forces you to avoid that area throughout the course of the drawing. It also becomes hard to make changes to a value that is deeply embedded.

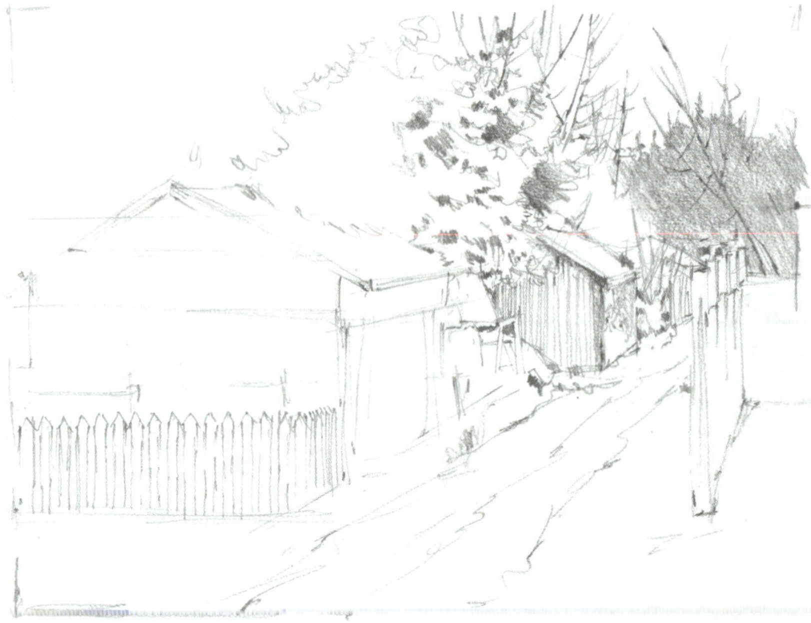

2 Begin Applying Tone

The distant trees are just a silhouette, so use the side of a 2B pencil to lightly skim the surface and leave some white paper texture showing.

Keep in mind the light is coming from the top right, so the left side of each building should be in shade.

Working from back to front (the most distant objects to closer foreground objects) will help to prevent smudging and allow you to start with the light values and progress to darker ones.

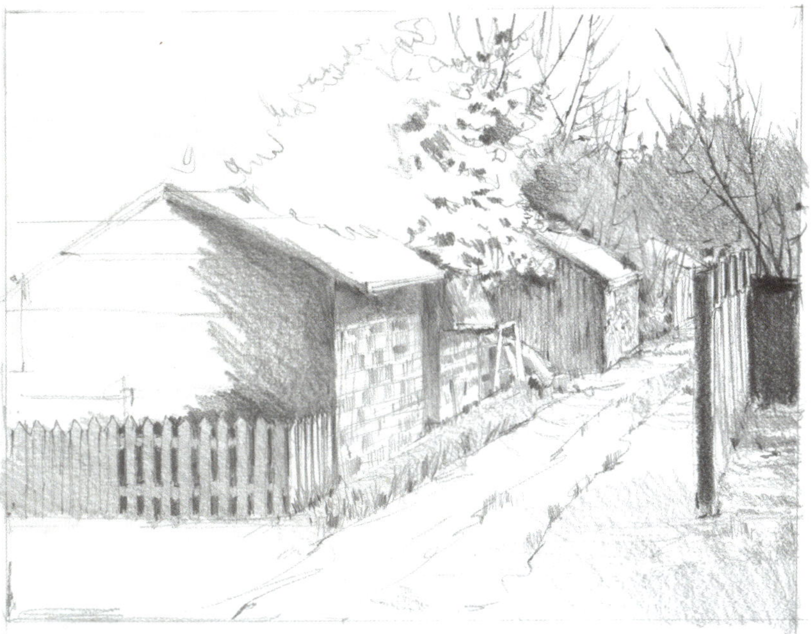

3 Add Tone to the Fence

Use a 2H graphite stick to apply the tone to the shadow side of the picket fence. Then use a 2B graphite stick to darken the areas between the pickets.

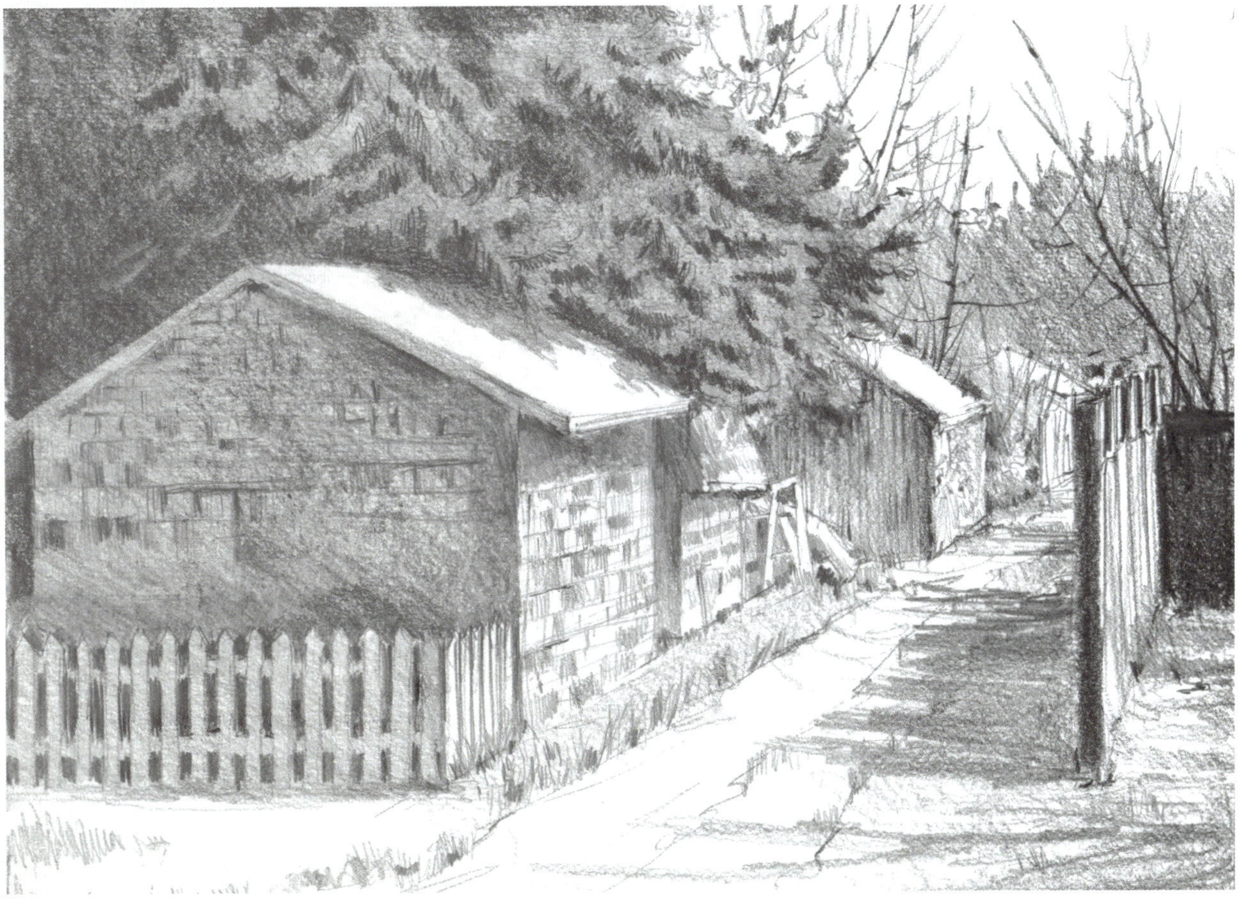

4 Finish Tone and Add Details

Use a plain piece of paper to protect the edge of the garage roof and apply tone to the overhanging trees with a 2H graphite stick. This keeps a clean, straight edge. Draw some branch detail right over top of this tone with the point of a 2B pencil.

CHAPTER 5

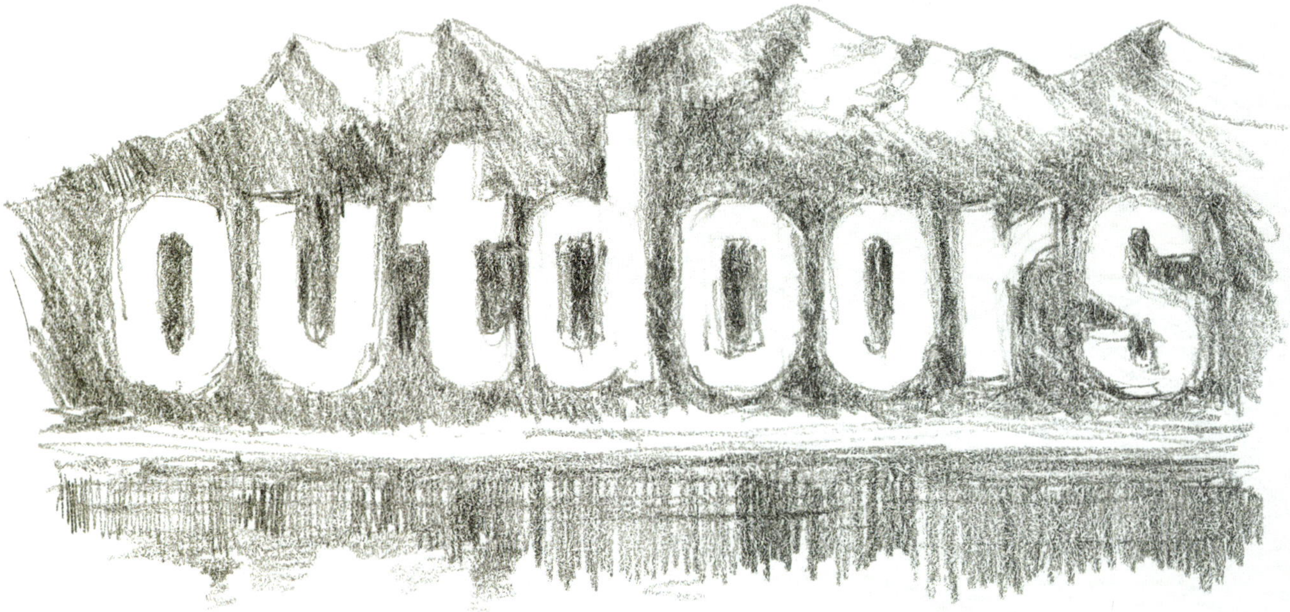

Plein air is the artist's elite term for working outdoors. It is beneficial to have first-hand knowledge of your subjects and to view them in a constant state of change. Feel the character of the subject and tell that story in the drawing. This is an important part of working on site. It allows you to make a connection that just cannot happen with a photograph.

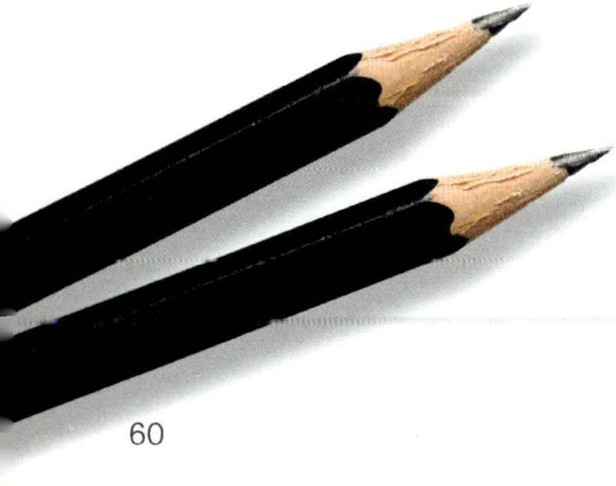

Drawing On Site

When working outdoors, the light is always moving so you will need to design your arrangement of light, dark and cast shadows very quickly.

Though some subjects, like buildings, remain still, others are in constant motion, such as water and anything that responds to the wind. This requires that we capture the essence of the elusive object, at least in a rough study. Your linework should reflect the spirit of the subject. It may need to be lively and full of motion, or quiet and refined.

Here are some drawings that I did on location close to home.

Separate Features From Surroundings

Separate the feature from the surroundings when sketching a busy subject like this boat in the marina. Eliminate all but the most important parts and simplify the background objects

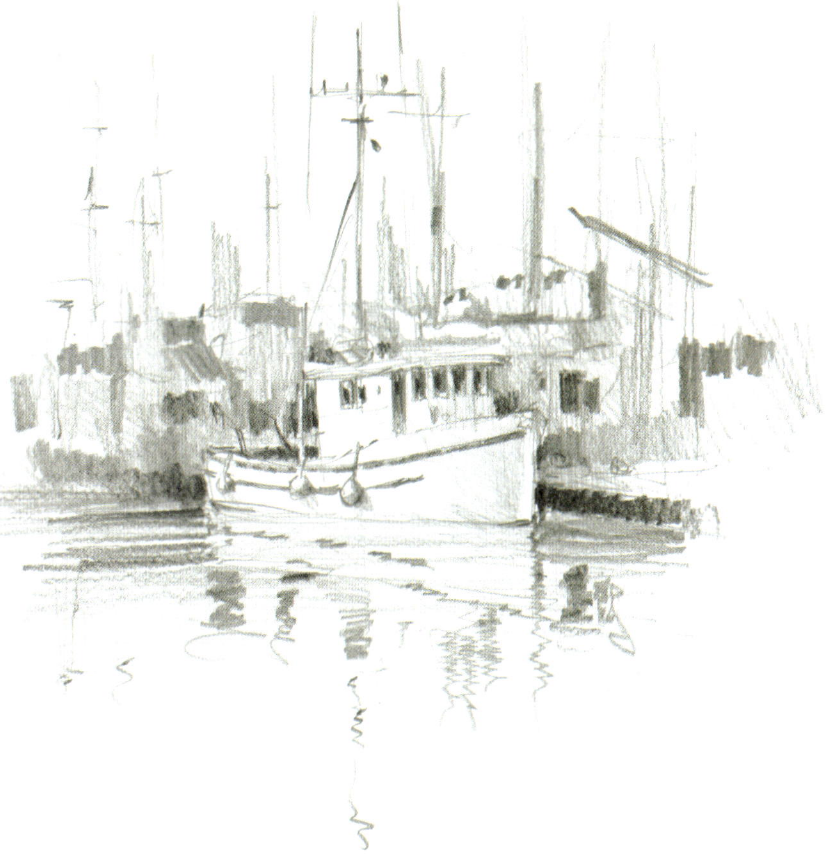

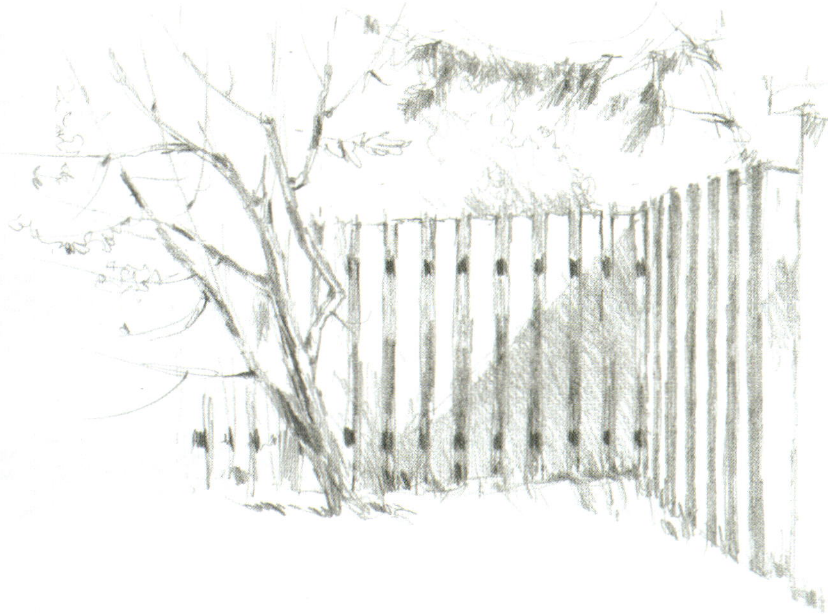

Work Backwards – Lighting First

This type of subject requires that you work backwards. Start with the lighting. The cast shadow on the fence will not be there in ten minutes so establish that first, at least in your memory. By the time all the pickets are drawn, the shadow can be added even though the lighting will have changed completely.

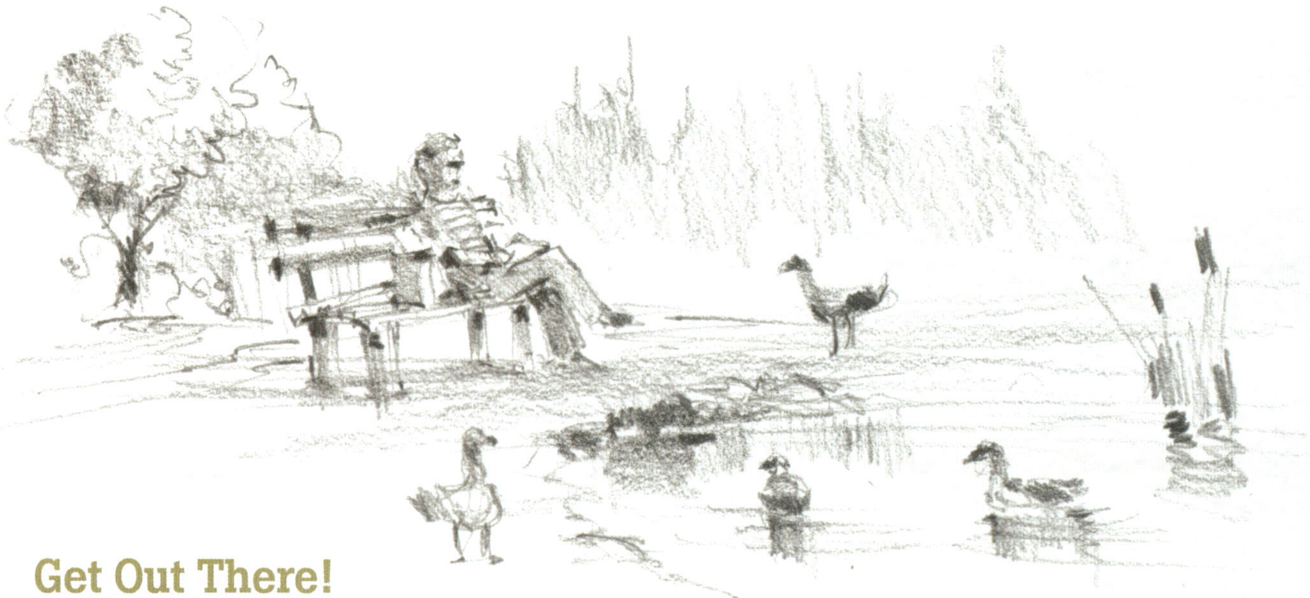

Get Out There!

Pack a lunch, grab your sketchbook and go to the park. Find a bench near the pond and practice your gesture drawing on the geese and ducks. They don't know the meaning of the word "pose," so you will be testing your short-term memory to the limit.

DON'T BE SHY

If you are new to working outside, you might be nervous about people watching. But even if you are not very experienced, most onlookers are impressed by anyone willing to draw. It often takes only one outing to overcome the fear of working in public.

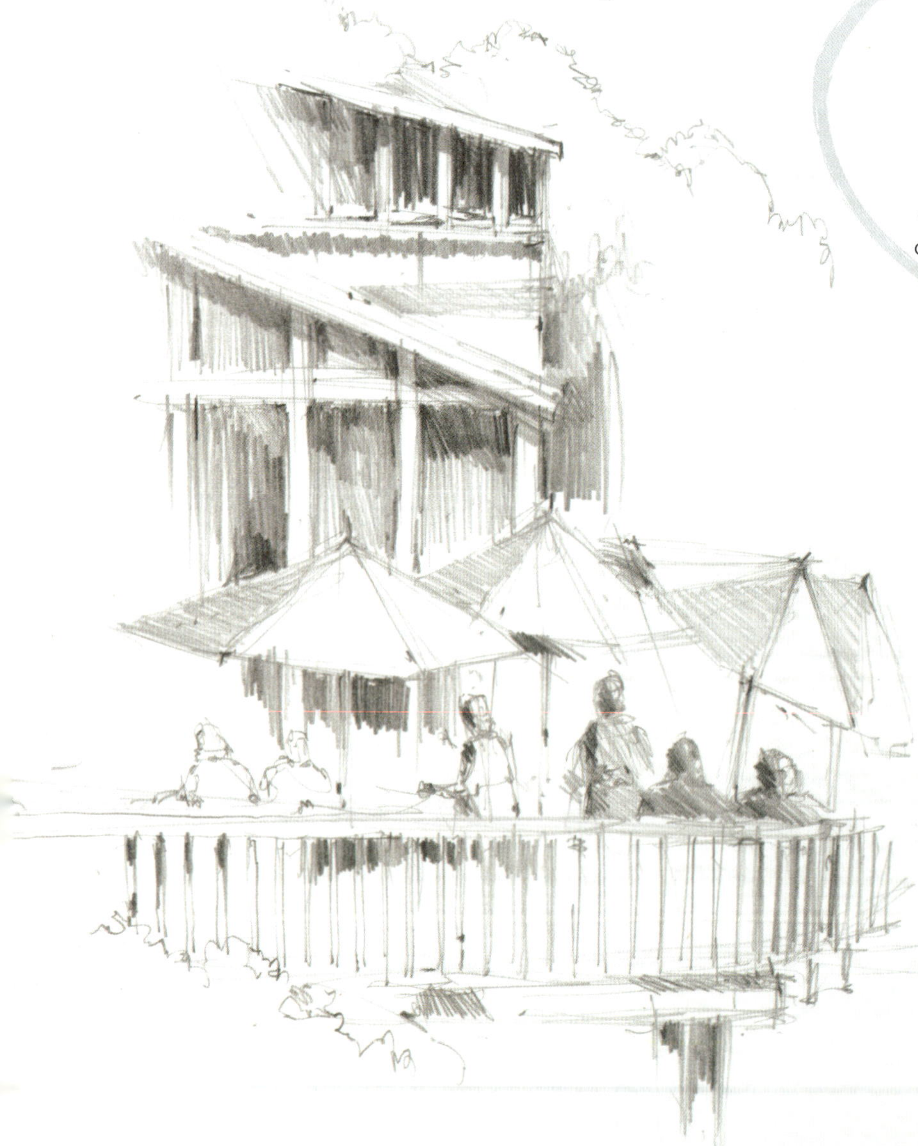

Quick, Before They Move

When working outdoors, capture the most fleeting elements first. Start by roughing in people and animals – they will not be there for long. The stationary objects such as buildings are not going anywhere and can be drawn in later.

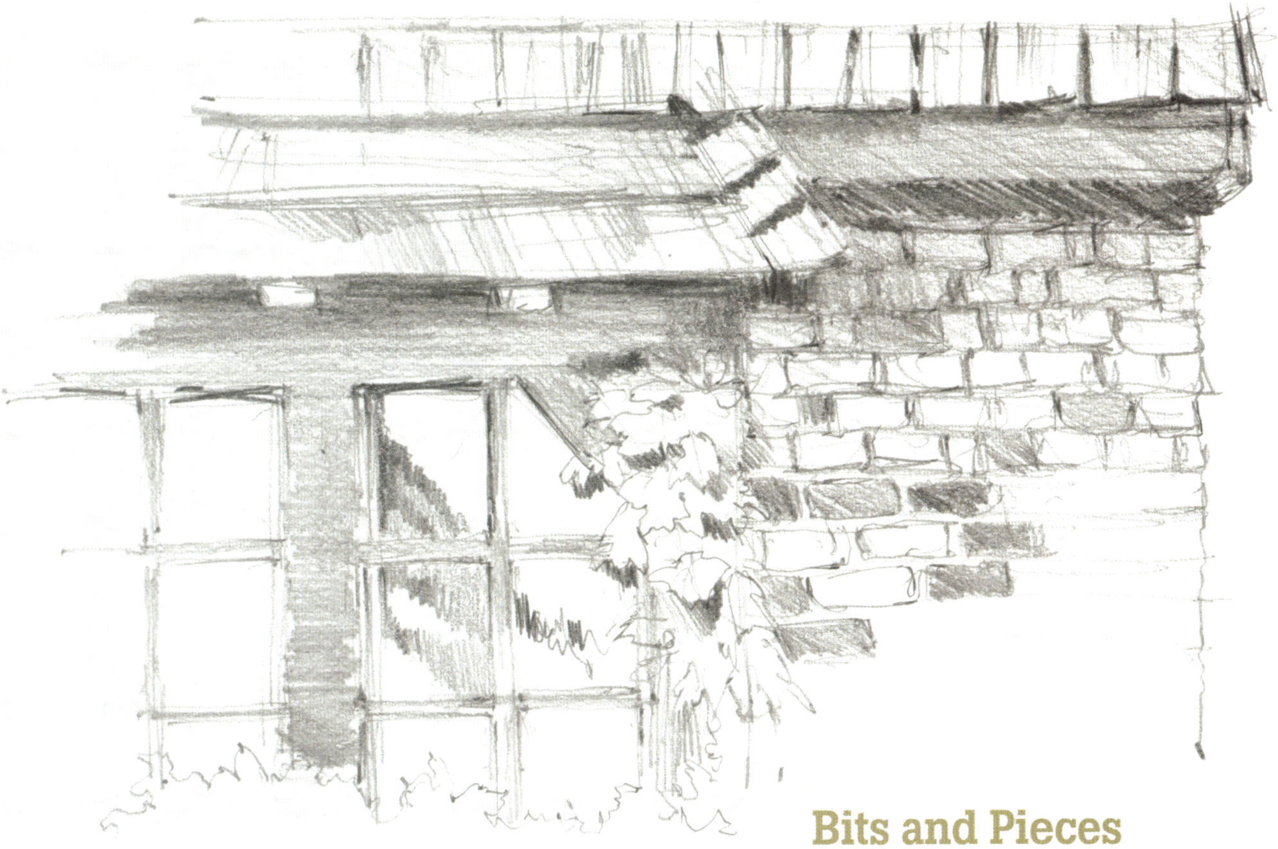

Bits and Pieces

It is also good practice to sketch parts of objects as opposed to trying to include the whole thing. Find the section of a subject that is the most appealing, then leave out the rest.

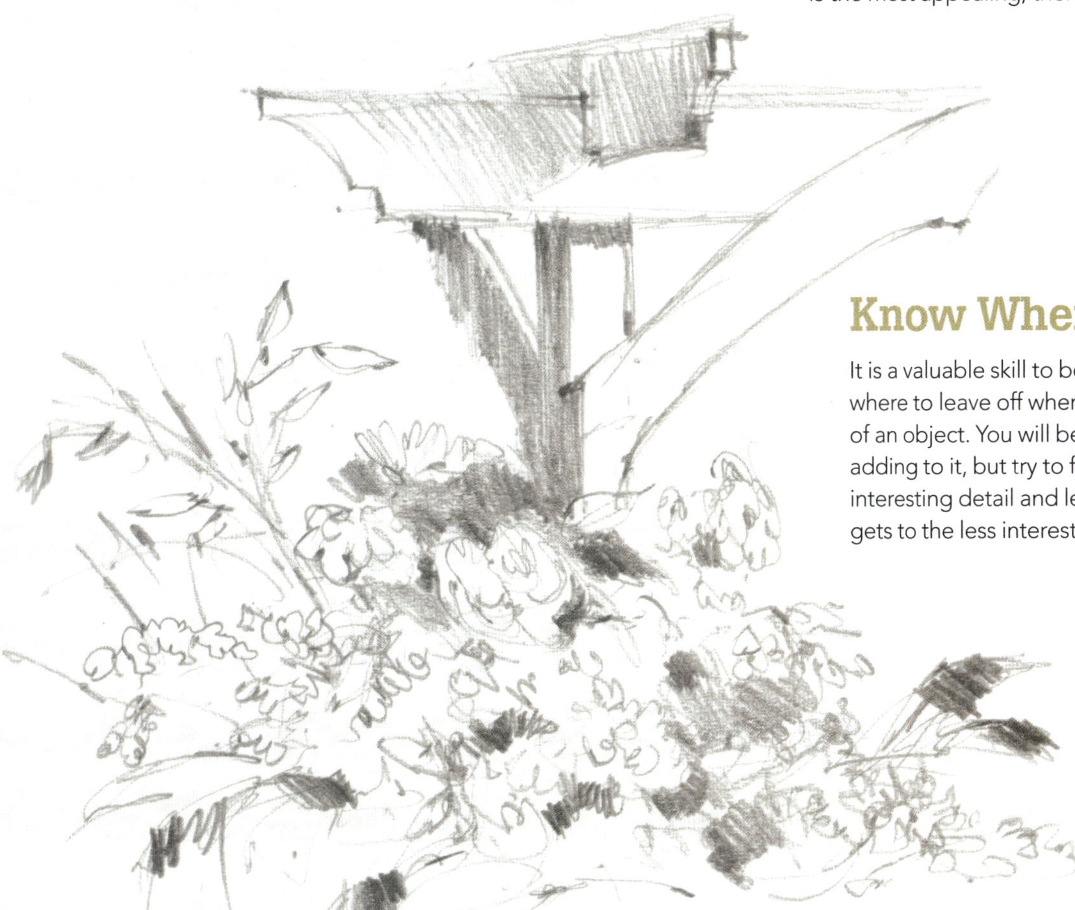

Know When to Quit

It is a valuable skill to be able to know where to leave off when drawing a portion of an object. You will be tempted to keep adding to it, but try to focus on the most interesting detail and let it disintegrate as it gets to the less interesting part.

THE GREAT OUTDOORS

Explore Tone and Texture

Although winter is not the best of seasons to be working outdoors, if you have a view from a window or car, there are spectacular subjects after a snowfall. This would be a good study for developing into a watercolor painting because it follows the "light to dark" method. The first values are light and become progressively darker with each layer.

MATERIALS

Surface
acid-free art paper

Graphite
HB, 2B wooden pencils

Other
kneaded eraser
stump (optional)

1 Rough In the Sketch

Use an HB pencil for the linear sketch. This subject may require you to redesign it a bit in order to make it natural and readable. You may need to reduce the clutter normally found in such places, otherwise it can be difficult to understand the picture.

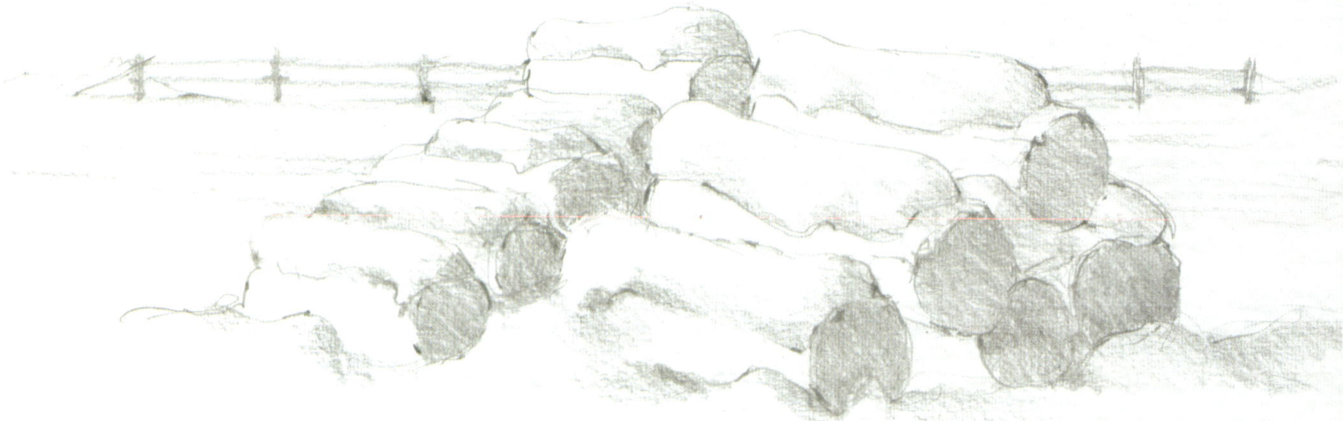

2 Apply Tone, Shape the Snow and Suggest the Fence

With the same HB pencil, begin applying tone to the shadow side of the logs. Use it very lightly to begin shaping the snow and suggesting the fence in the background.

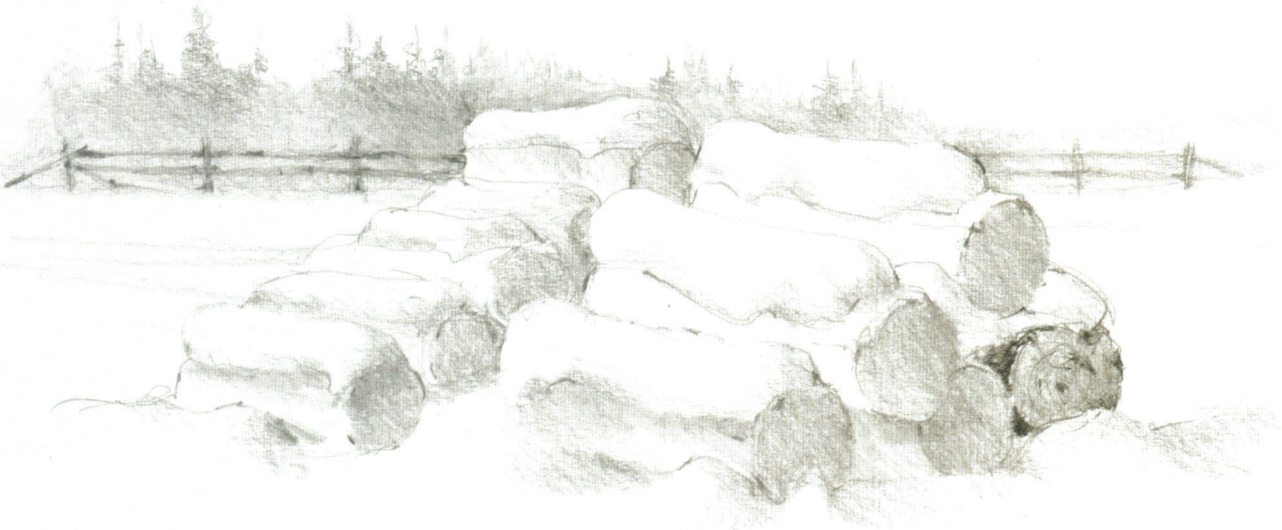

3 Add the Trees

Use a combination of the HB and 2B pencils to get variation in the distant trees. You can achieve this simply by changing the pressure on an HB pencil, but you will notice a change in the texture as well as the value if you use different pencils. Darken the fence to separate it from the trees.

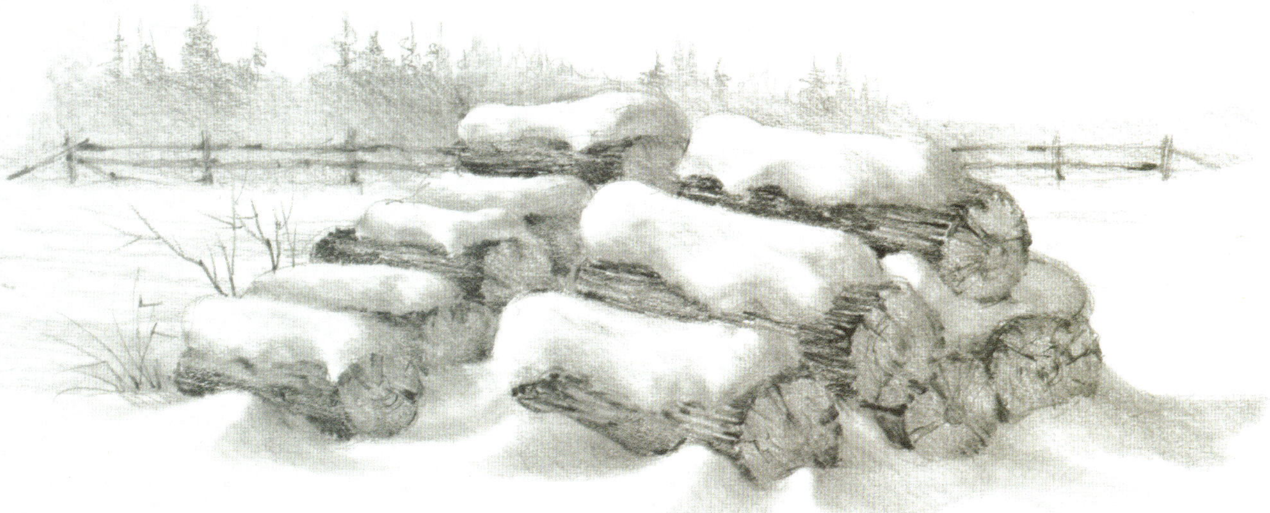

4 Add Tone and Texture to Finish

Add tone and texture to the logs. This can be done with the HB but for the very dark areas use the 2B to provide the finishing touch.

If you prefer a smooth finish, use a stump to blend the graphite. This will work particularly well to fade the shadows on the snow.

ON THE WATERFRONT

More Tone and Texture

The more you draw from live subjects, the more you will notice about nature. You will see shapes that don't look natural when you draw them exactly as they are. You will start to become very selective, choosing shapes that you like and altering others that seem too extreme.

MATERIALS

Surface
acid-free art paper

Graphite
2B graphite stick
2H, HB, B, 2B wooden pencils

Other
kneaded eraser

1 Sketch the Contours

Sketch the contours with an HB wooden pencil. Vary the size, shape and spacing of the rocks to avoid getting repetitious.

2 Add the Distant Shapes

Draw the misty shapes in the distance with a 2H wooden pencil.

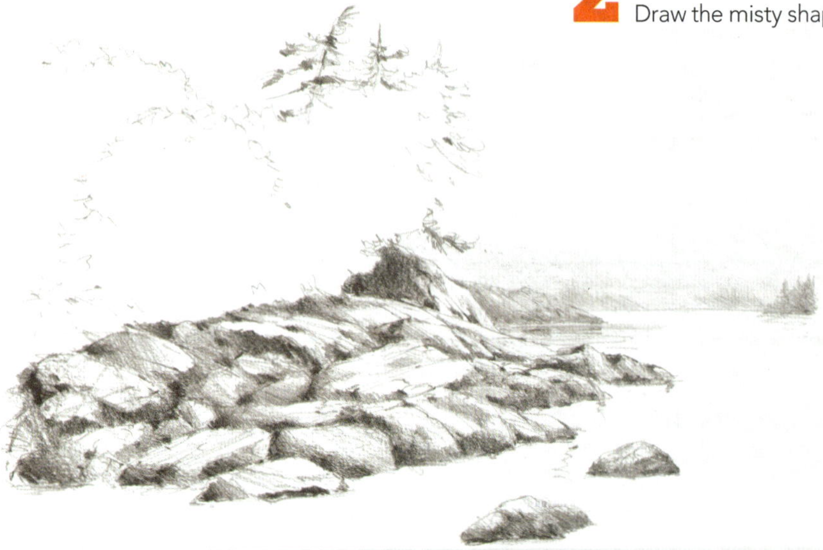

3 Add the Background

For the background, use an HB graphite stick. The side of the stick is good for broad areas, and the end works well for darker patterns in the water. To avoid accidental smudging, lace a paper towel under the hand you're holding the paper with.

4 Apply Tone to the Trees

Depending on how large you make this drawing, you may be able to use a graphite stick to put down the first layer of tone on the dark trees. Add variety into that tone with a 2B wooden pencil. Also use the 2B for the evergreen trees, which require a certain amount of detail.

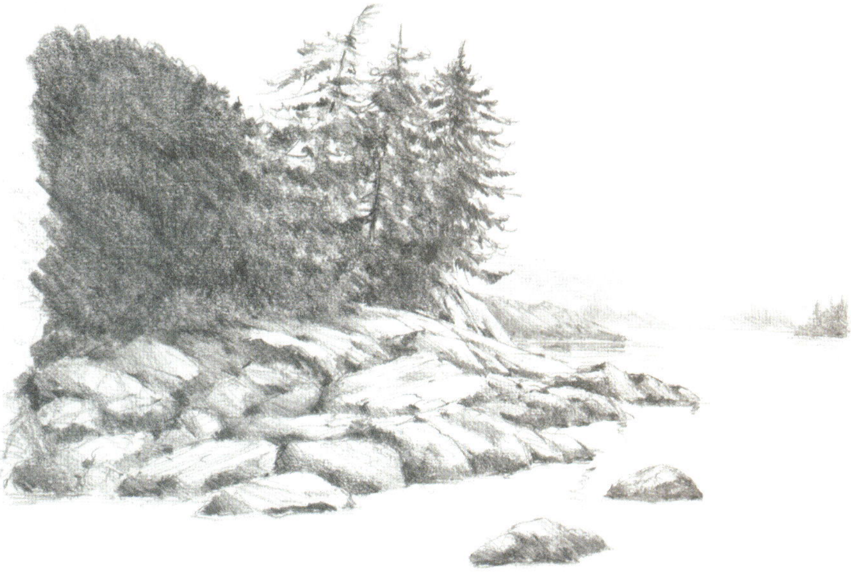

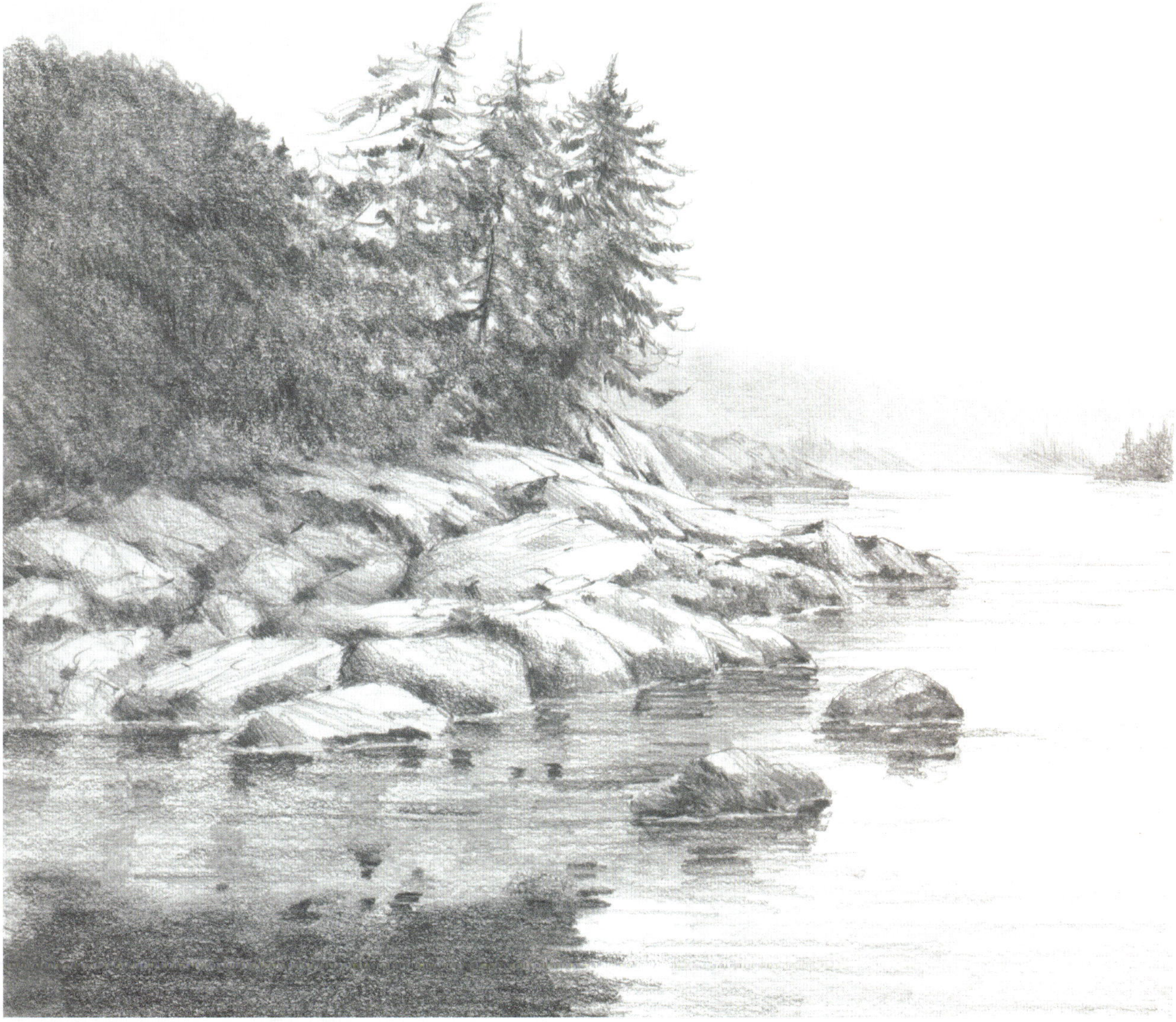

5 Render the Reflections

Use a combination of 2H, HB and 2B pencils for rendering the reflections. At the end of the drawing, use the side of a 2H wooden pencil to blend and darken the reflection of the rocks so it has a slightly lower value than the actual rocks.

ON THE WATERFRONT

Practice Cast Shadows and Reflections

This bumper tied to the wharf presented good challenges for rendering a convincing sphere with cast shadow as well as wood grain and reflections in water. The reflection is directly below the object, but it is distorted by the ripples in the water. Although photographs cannot replace the experience of drawing from reality, they can be very helpful when it comes to studying this type of reflection.

MATERIALS

Surface
acid-free art paper, heavy

Graphite
HB mechanical pencil
2H, HB, B, 2B wooden pencils

Other
kneaded eraser
reference photo (optional)

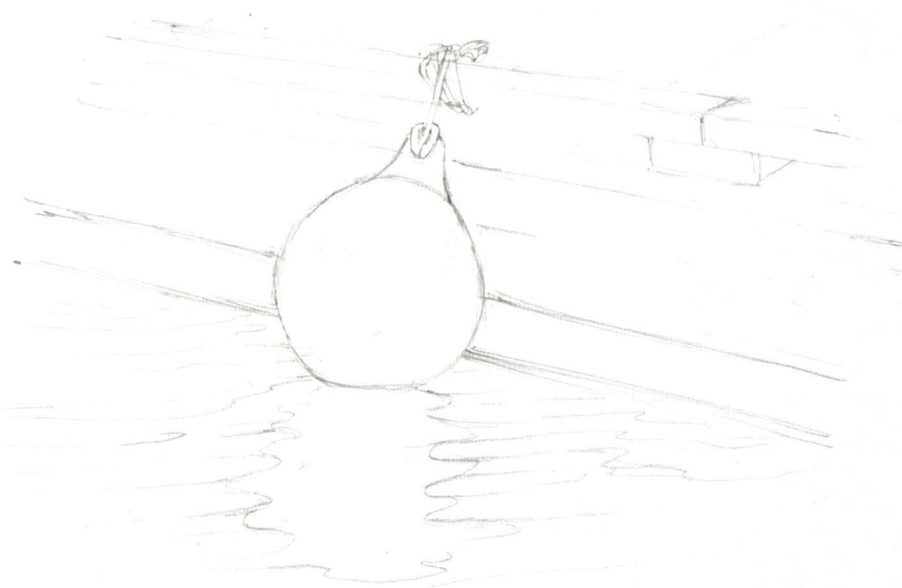

1 Sketch the Contours

Rough in the sketch with an HB mechanical pencil. Be sure to render your drawing on heavy paper, because you may need to use an eraser to get the oval bumper shape accurate.

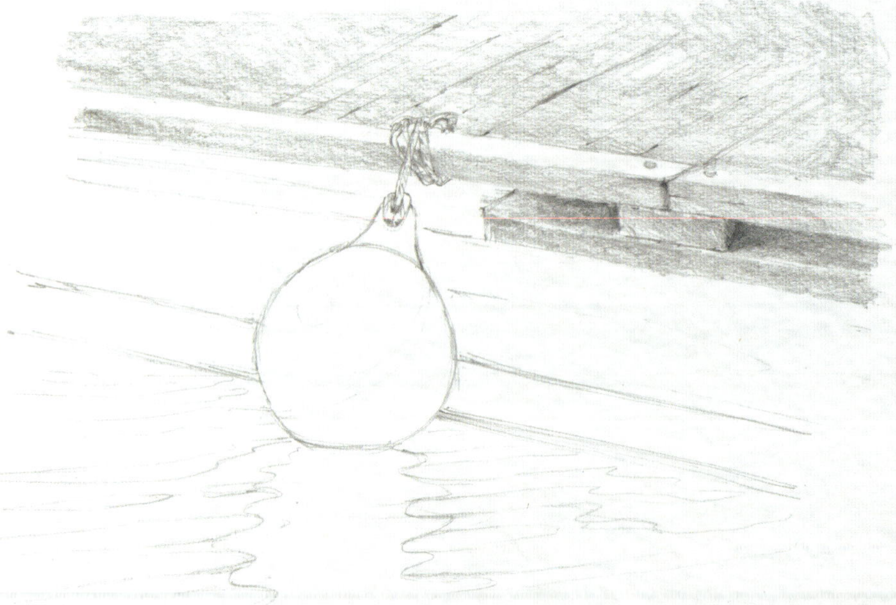

2 Add Tone and Suggest Planks

Add tone to the deck with a 2B wooden pencil. Avoid the top of the railing, leaving it white. Suggest a few planks for the deck, taking care to maintain the perspective. Don't draw all the planks because the pattern will be too strong and create a distraction at the top of the page.

3 Vary Pencil Weights

This is the point where switching between different pencil weights will be important. Use a 2H pencil for the light tone on the bumper and the wood grain on the face of the wharf. Render the darker end grain of the planks with a B pencil, and the black cap on the bumper with a 2B pencil. Finish the rope with an HB pencil. This will help get you familiar with the way these different leads behave.

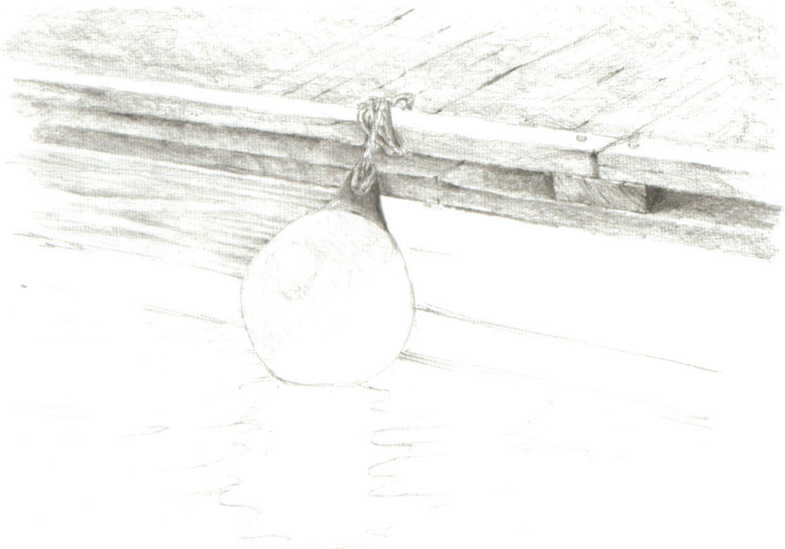

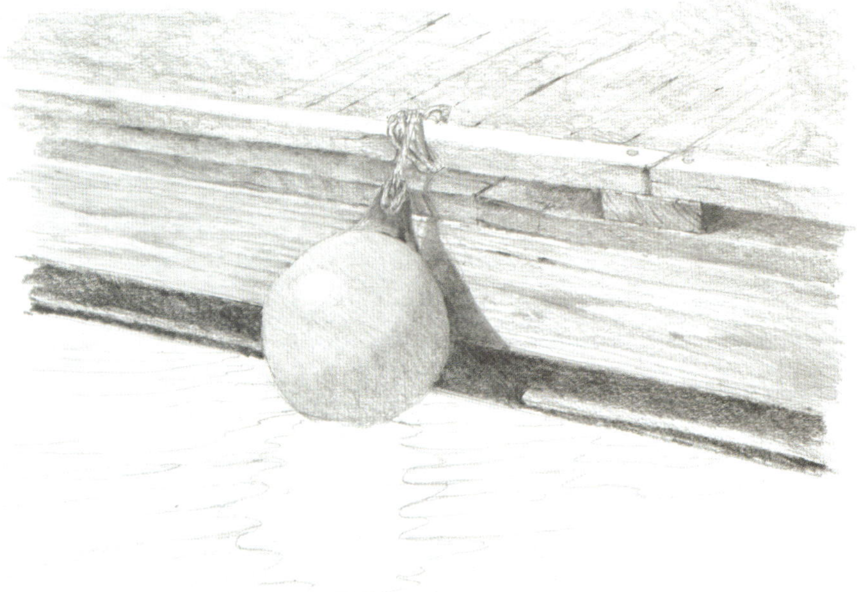

4 Continue Adding Tone and Apply the Cast Shadow

Continue drawing the dark patterns, such as the wood grain, with the B pencil, and then apply lighter tones on top with a harder pencil. This blends the edges slightly. For the cast shadow of the bumper on the wharf, apply the light tone first and add the darker values last.

5 Render the Reflections

Render the reflections in the water by working from light to dark, and then blend with a 2H pencil.

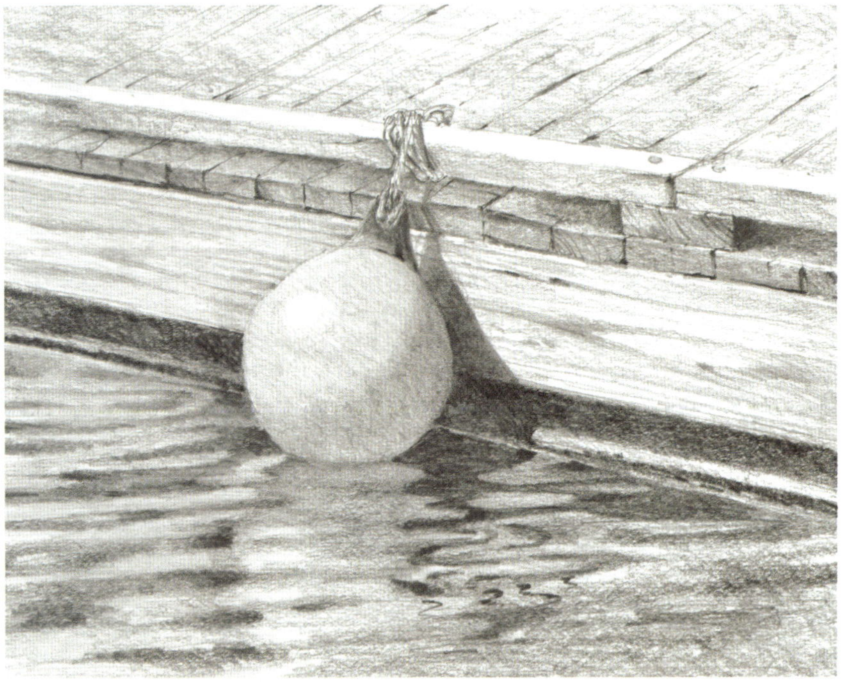

AROUND TOWN

Explore Soft Lines on a Hard-Line Subject

This demonstration is designed to help you experiment with using a few soft-line techniques when drawing a hard-line subject. However, the building here will not tolerate the same fluid-line movement as a moving figure, so the trick will be to find places where you can relax the line quality as opposed to where the lines must be tight and accurate.

MATERIALS

Surface
acid-free art paper, heavy

Graphite
HB, 2B wooden pencils

Other
kneaded eraser

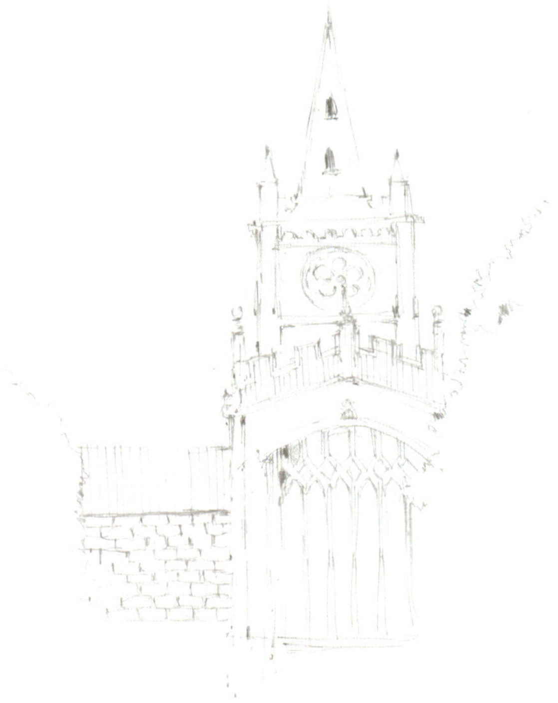

1 Sketch the Contours

Draw a fairly accurate contour using an HB pencil. Do not mark the borders of this image because it will remain a vignette.

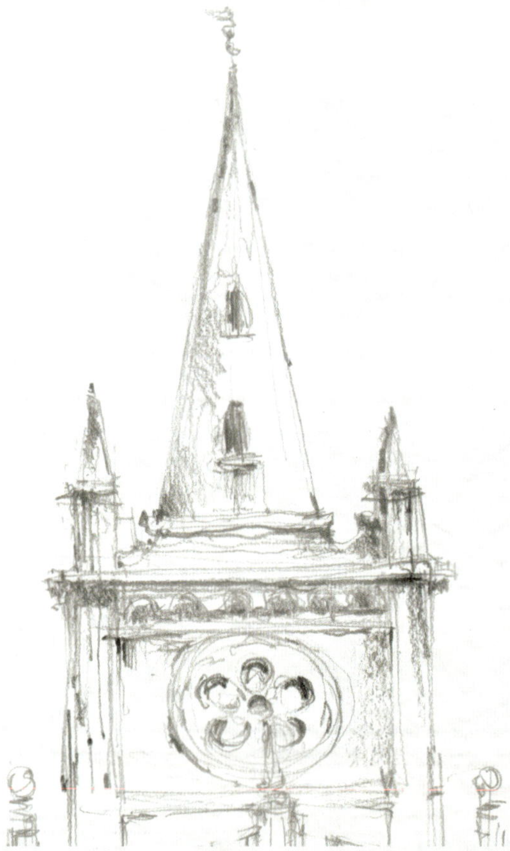

WORK ON SITE WHEREVER POSSIBLE

Ideally, you should draw from your own location site. Simply use the demonstrations in this chapter as a guide.

2 Focus on the Steeple

Switch to a 2B pencil for the rest of this drawing. This will force you to be less precise because the softer lead goes blunt quickly. Make the point on the steeple straight and sharp so that it doesn't look rubbery, but treat some of the ornamental work with a more casual line. Duplicate some lines and darken others by increasing the pressure on the pencil.

Don't worry if it takes two or three tries to find the right place for a line. An honest searching character in the line will add to the richness of the work.

3 Apply Tone and Add Details

Use the side of the pencil for a broad application of tone, and the sharp tip of the pencil when rendering details like the bricks of the building.

Try to keep the pencil on the paper for as long as possible rather than jumping from place to place. This will result in a more continuous line, and the whole drawing will hold together better.

4 Add Trees and Shrubs

Frame the fine detail with dark, unfinished trees and shrubs. This arrangement of light and dark areas will direct the viewer's attention towards the ornamental architecture.

These design considerations are important even though this is just a vignette.

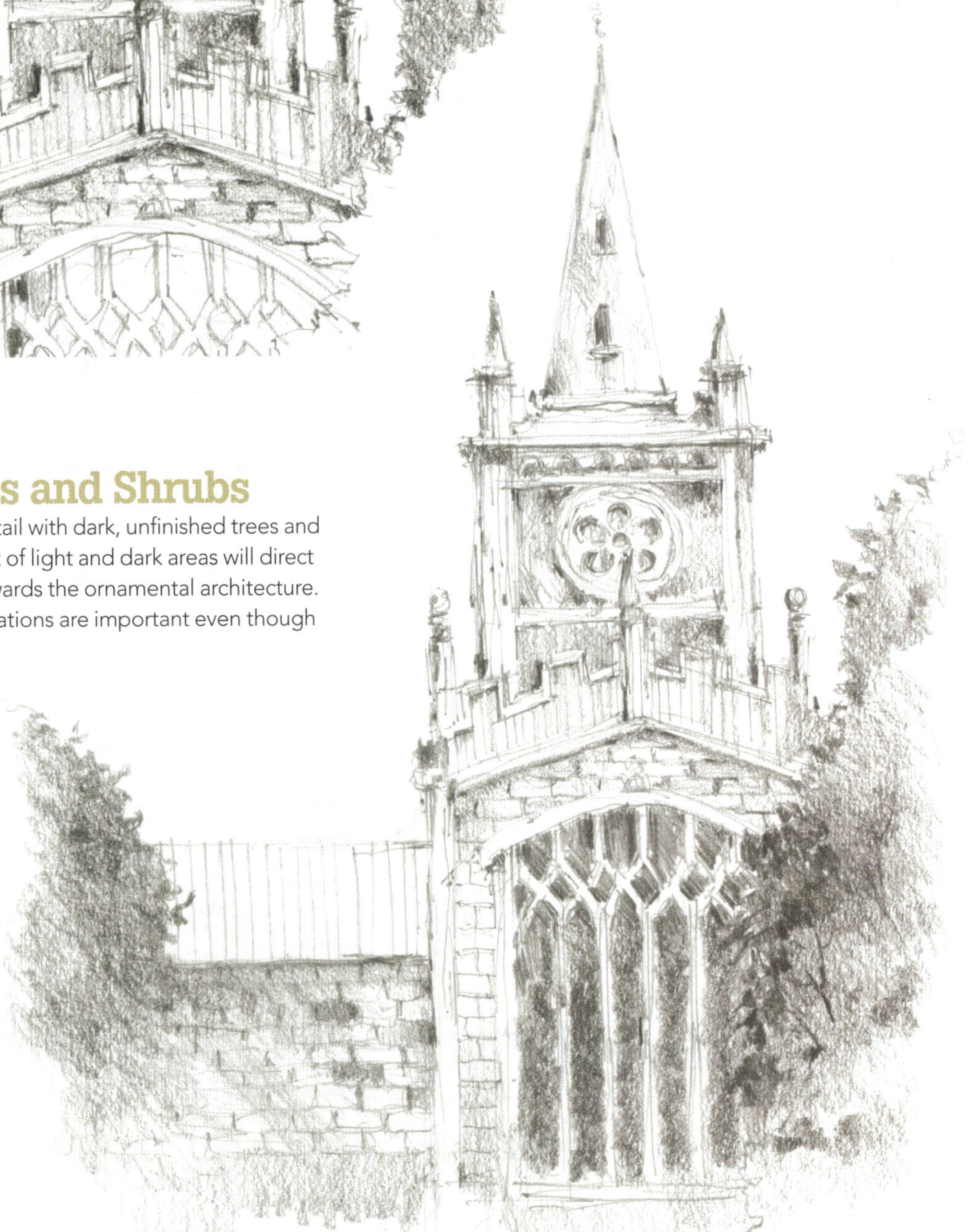

AROUND TOWN

Draw a Street Scene in One-Point Perspective

This will be another one-point perspective drawing but from the street level with a single vanishing point.

MATERIALS

Surface
acid-free art paper

Graphite
2H, HB, 2B wooden pencils

Other
kneaded eraser
reference photo (optional)

1 Rough In a Sketch

Use an HB pencil to rough in the sketch. It is not necessary to draw the horizon line because it will be obscured by other elements of the cityscape. The key lines are the top of the wall on the right and the sidewalk.

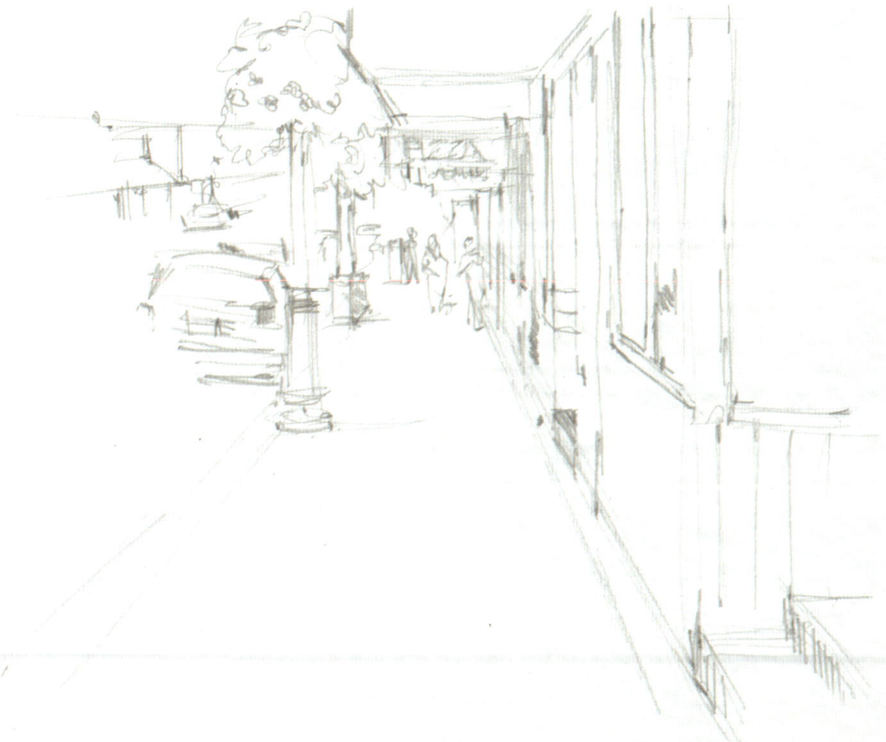

2 Draw the Storefronts

Make the storefronts compressed as they are being viewed from an extreme angle. Do not make many of the doorways and windows much wider than a pencil line.

Try to keep the pencil on the paper as long as possible and use a fluid motion on shapes that are not rigid structures.

3 Draw the Cars and Apply Tone

Draw the cars and then begin adding tone to the shadow side of the cars with a 2B pencil. It's easier to get a feel for the final product when the drawing starts to take on a more three-dimensional look.

Have some reference photos of objects you want to include in the drawing. It is too difficult to draw complicated objects from memory. In this case, you'll need some photos of cars taken from the same angle as the street.

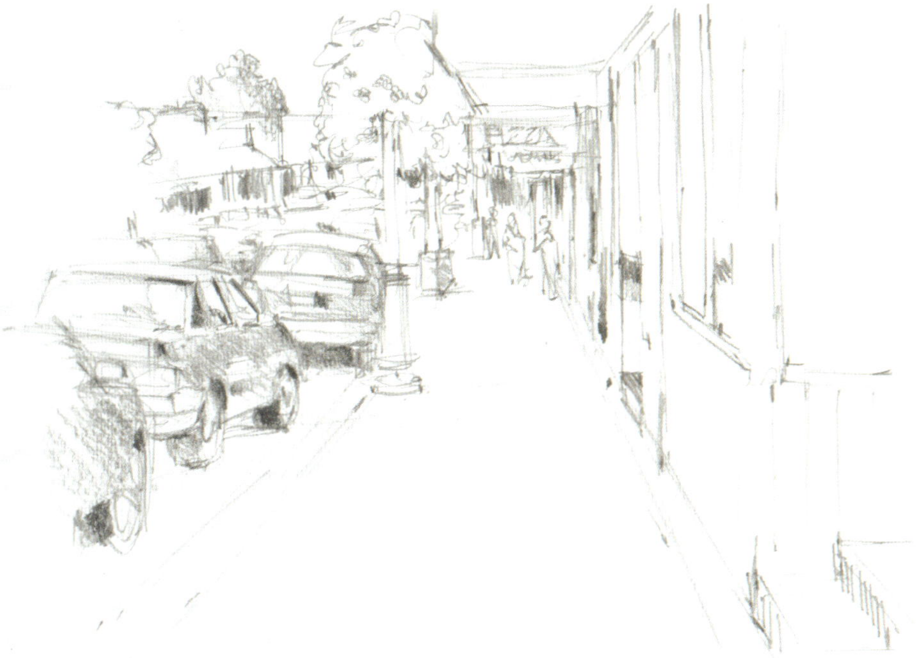

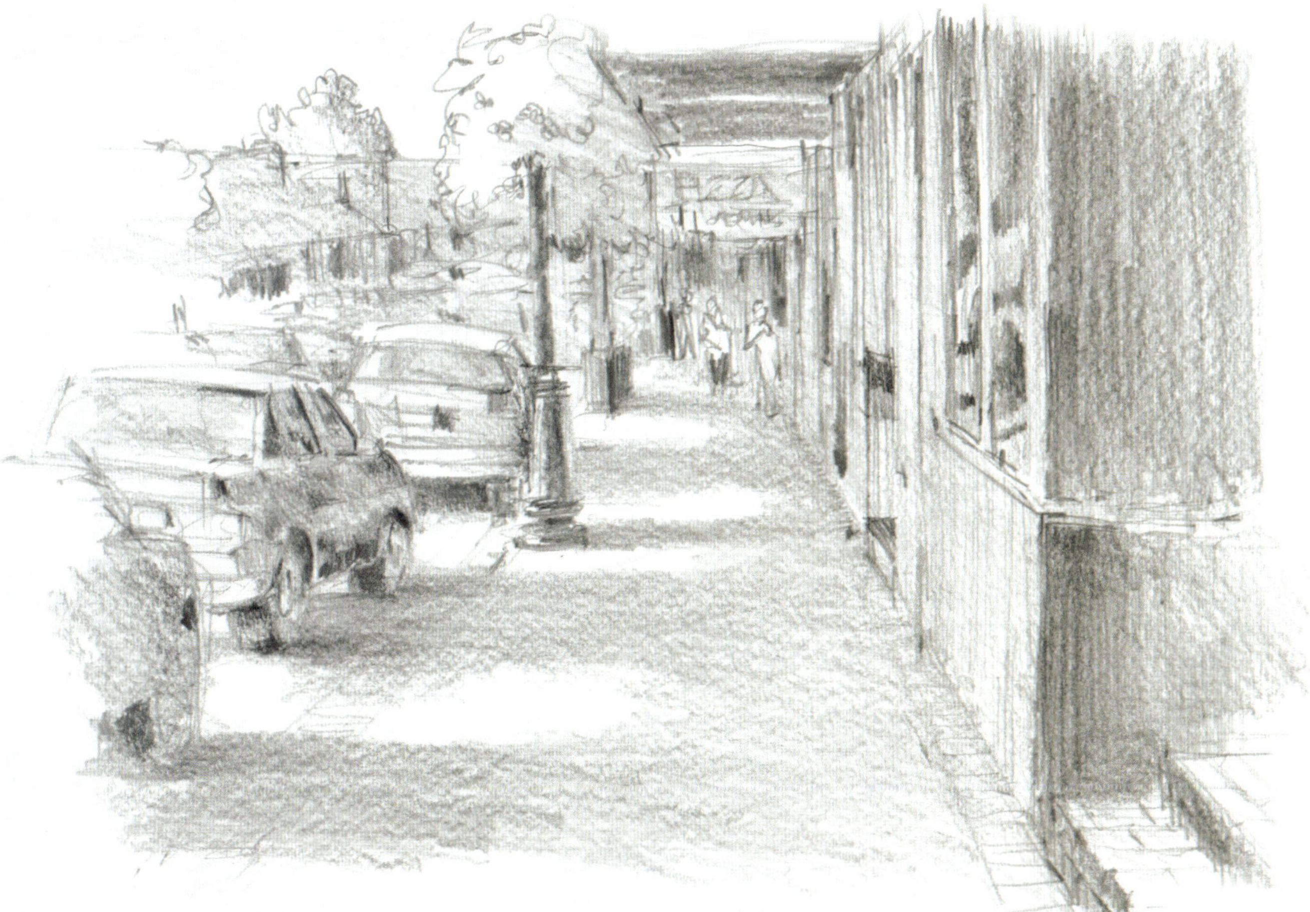

4 Smooth the Texture to Finish

Go over the tone with a 2H pencil in order to smooth the texture in the shadow areas.

AROUND TOWN

Draw a Street Scene With Multiple Vanishing Points

The purpose of this exercise is to capture a fairly complex subject with as little work as possible. This will be a one-point perspective drawing with the exception of the angled roof on the tower, which will have its own two vanishing points.

MATERIALS

Surface
acid-free art paper

Graphite
HB mechanical pencil
2H, HB, 2B wooden pencils

Other
kneaded eraser
straightedge

1 Rough In a Sketch

Establish the vanishing point. With an HB wooden or mechanical pencil, start with the most interesting structure and roughly position it in the composition. Decide on the cropping. (Note the marks indicated by the arrows. This is where I planned to crop my image.)

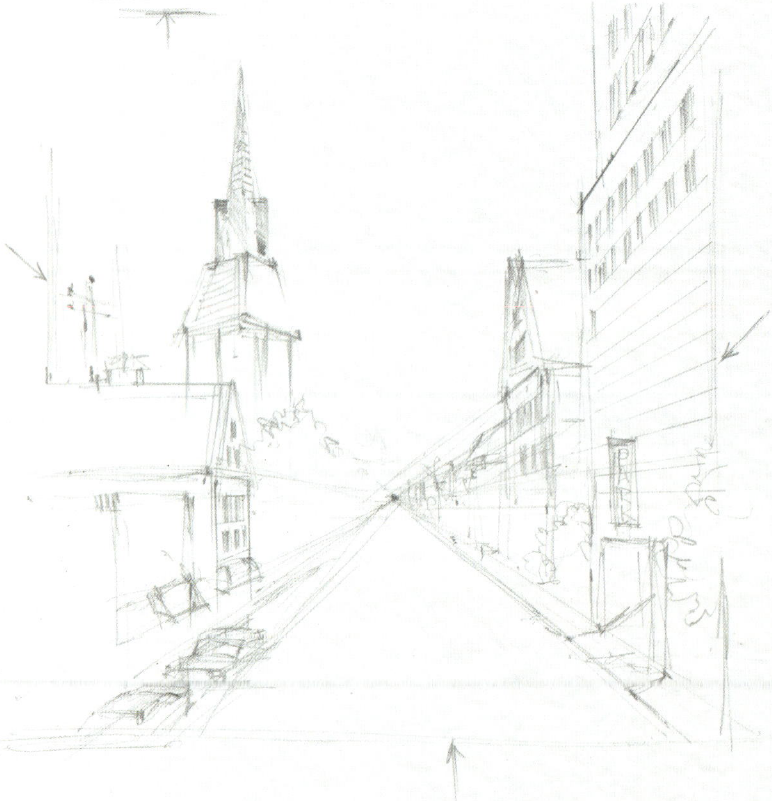

2 Create a Series of Guidelines

Use a straightedge placed on the vanishing point to create a series of guidelines. Some angles are so extreme that it is hard to get them correct without a straightedge.

Suggest a few windows and other size-related elements. From this steep angle, the windows should not be much more than a pencil line wide.

3 Develop Details

Develop some of the more interesting details while letting other parts of the picture remain unfinished. Keep the small objects very simple.

Erase the guidelines as you go. This will help you avoid smudging later.

PREVENT UNWANTED SMUDGING

Get into the habit of keeping a piece of plain paper or a paper towel under your drawing hand while working. This will prevent unwanted smudging and save you having to constantly clean up with an eraser.

4 Add Tone to Finish

Use 2B and 2H wooden pencils to apply the tone. You can add as much or as little tone as you like. I chose to keep a rough, unfinished look to this subject because it leaves more to the viewer's imagination.

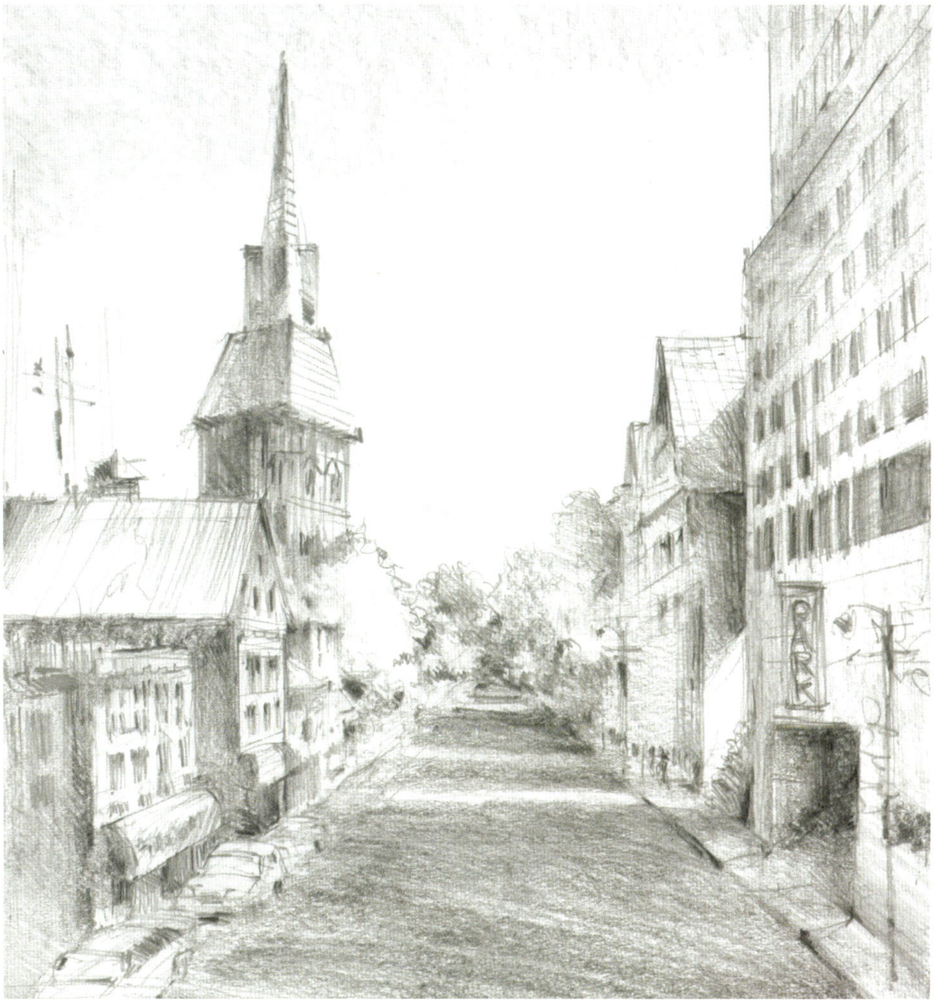

AROUND TOWN

Estimate Vanishing Points

This demonstration will help you practice how to guess at the position of vanishing points. The buildings are very large, so the vanishing points will be well off the page. Establish the horizon and use your best guess to line up the left and right vanishing points.

This exercise is another chance for you to explore soft lines on a hard-line subject.

MATERIALS

Surface
acid-free art paper

Graphite
HB, 2B wooden pencils

Other
kneaded eraser

1 Rough In the Sketch and Establish Key Angles

Use an HB wooden pencil to rough in the sketch. Choose one angle, say the top of the left roof, and use that to relate the other top lines. Find the bottom of the walls and project them to the left vanishing point. Make any line that falls directly on the horizon horizontal.

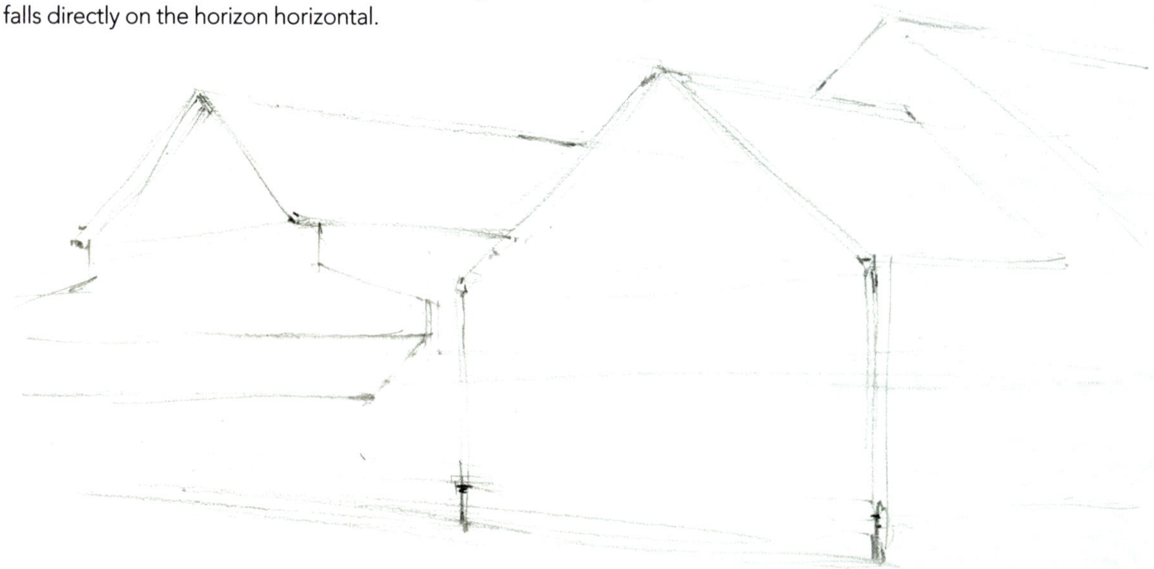

2 Add Details With Varying Line Speed and Weight

Once the key angles are correct, you can take great liberties with the other elements in the picture. With a 2B pencil, use a wandering line with lots of variation in speed and weight as you begin adding details.

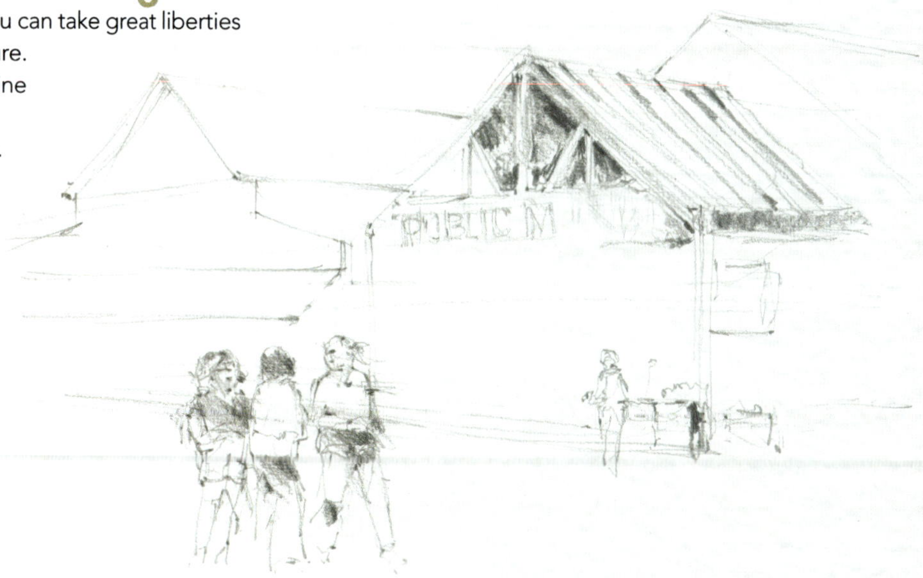

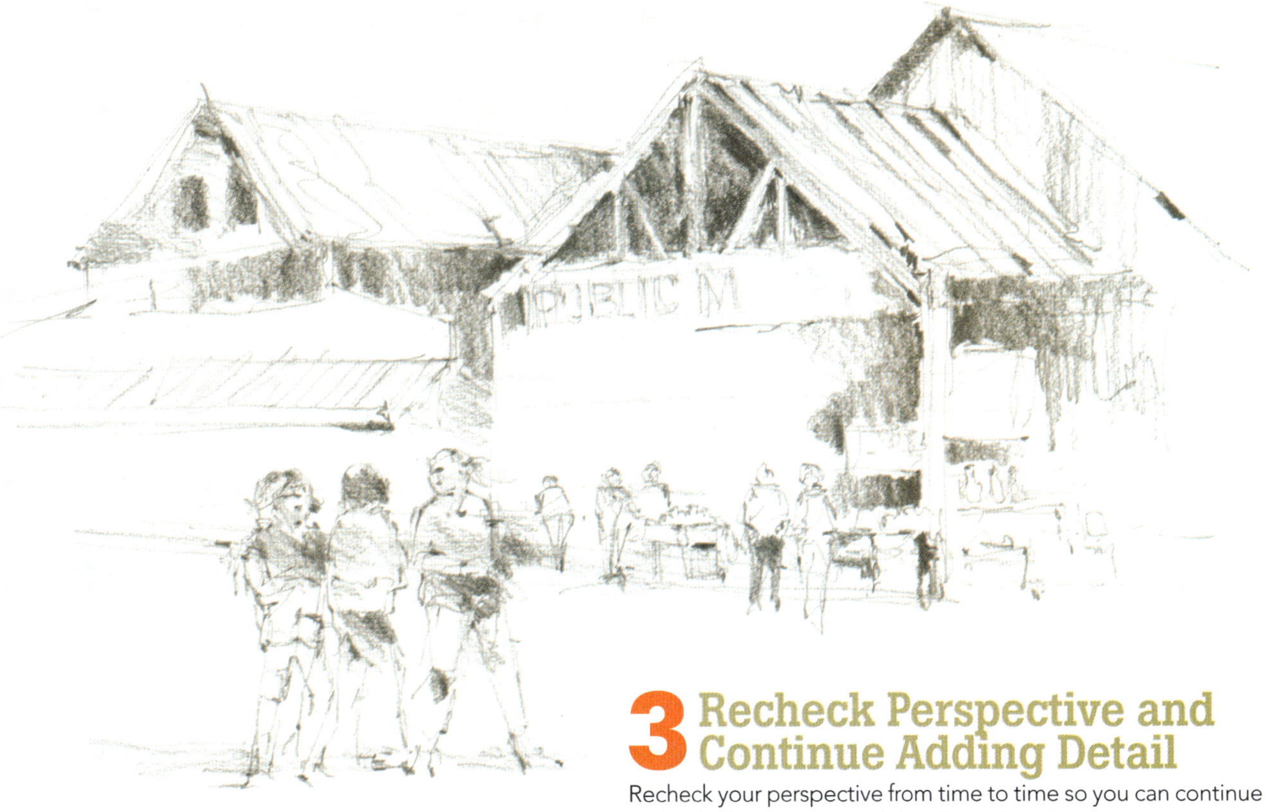

3 Recheck Perspective and Continue Adding Detail

Recheck your perspective from time to time so you can continue to make the buildings look old and weathered without appearing to be falling down. Practice a few figures and other objects on a scrap of paper in order to get the knack of suggesting detail without really having to render it.

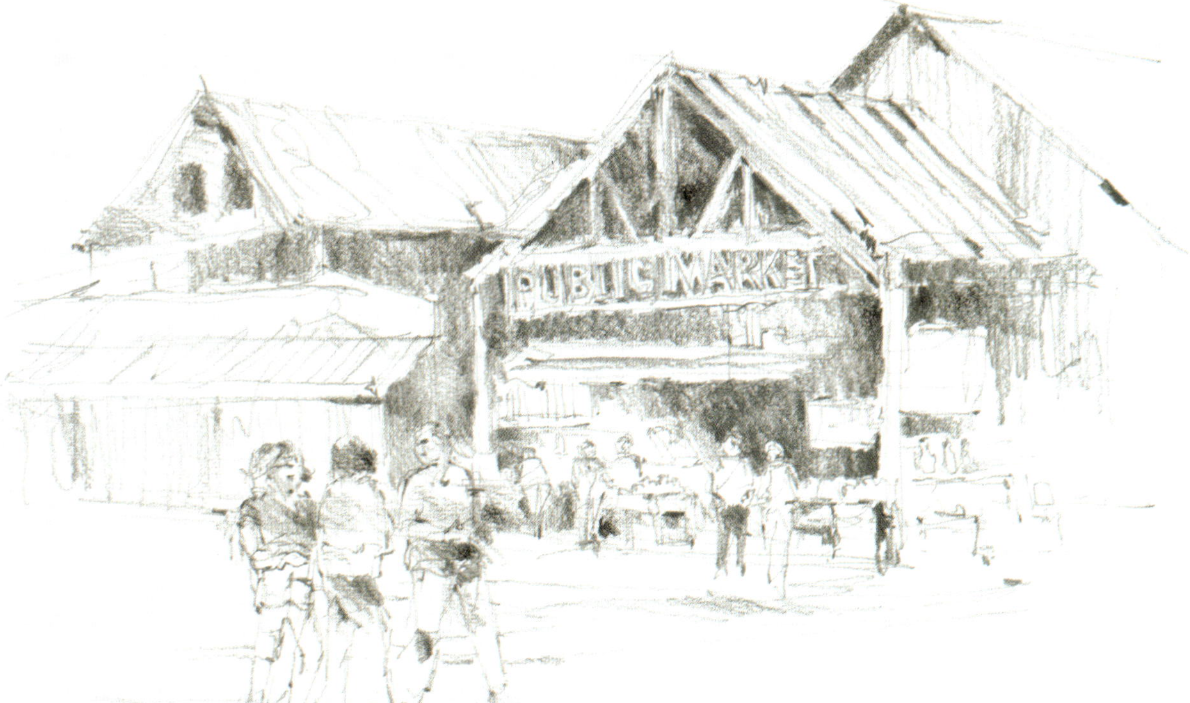

4 Add Tone to Finish

Turn the line into a flat tone by switching from the point of the pencil to the side. This is more like painting with a pencil rather than a basic drawing.

This is another case where I will leave the drawing as a vignette. This casual treatment lends itself to the unfinished look.

CHAPTER 6

faces and figures

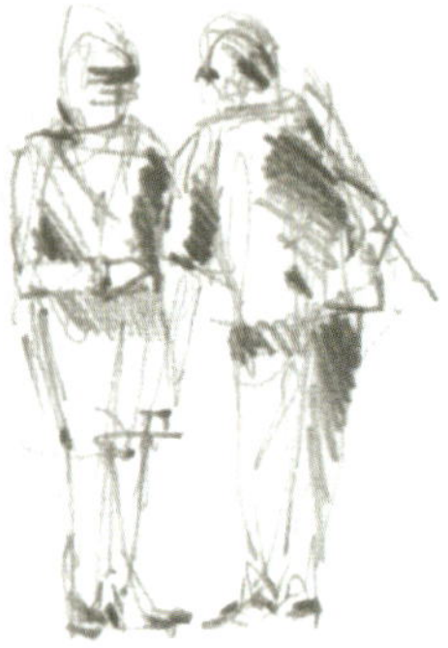

Many artists agree that faces are the most challenging subject. A brilliant artist and good friend of mine once said, "A portrait is a painting of someone with something wrong with the nose." He meant that someone always finds something wrong with the likeness in a portrait. But knowing that in advance should free you up to create a likeness that suits you, the artist. Every face is different, but if you know the average facial shapes and proportions, you have a basic standard and can compare specific features to the average. Portraits demand a certain temperament of the artist because you cannot make mistakes that you might otherwise get away with when drawing a rock or tree. But if you like this type of challenge, you will eventually enjoy a wonderful feeling of accomplishment.

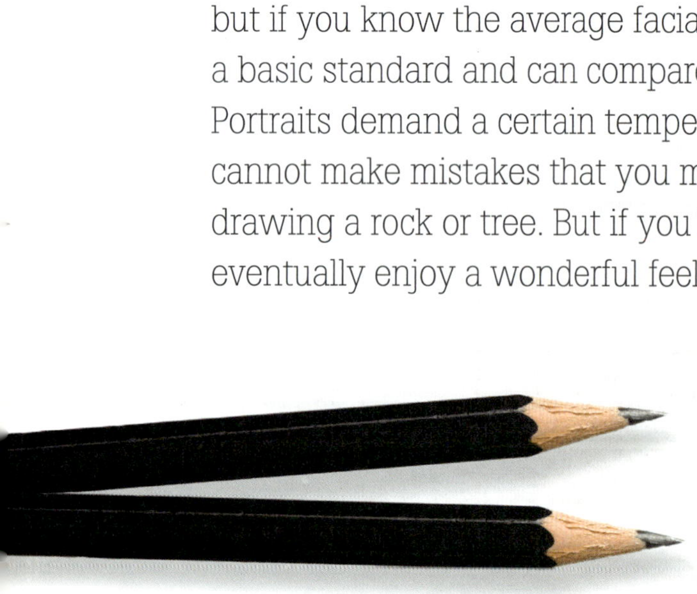

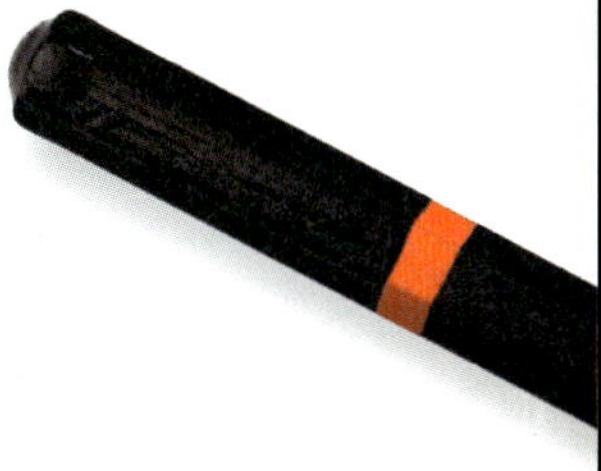

Facial Anatomy

Facial Anatomy Simplified

Use this simplified version of facial anatomy to aid in establishing good proportions.

- The eyes are halfway between the top of the head and the chin.
- The center of the upper lip is halfway between the eyes and the chin.
- The width of the mouth is the same as the distance between the pupils.
- A horizontal line drawn through the center of the eyes should be parallel to a line drawn through the center of the mouth. Otherwise the face you draw will be twisted and distorted.

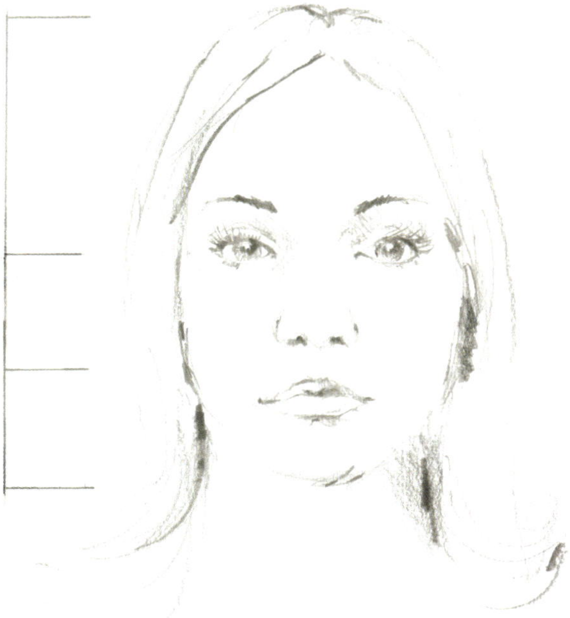

Use this as a norm, and look for variations when drawing a specific portrait. For example, is your subject's nose longer than this average or shorter? Is

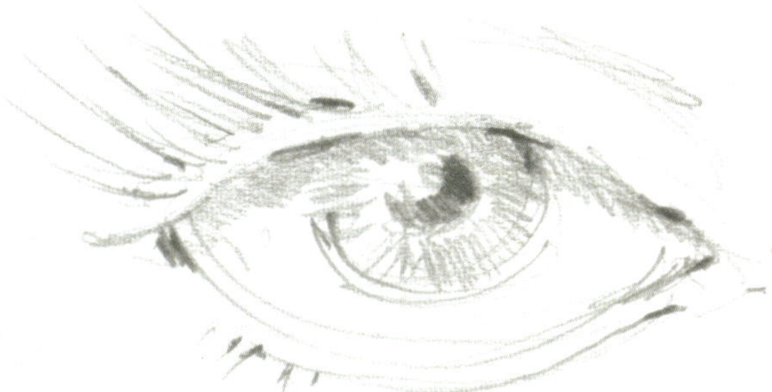

Expressive Eyes

Because the lower eye lid remains stationary and the upper lid opens and closes, the top part of the eye shows less than the bottom. When drawing your subject, take notice of how much of the eyes are showing. More of the top makes the expression look surprised, less creates a sleepy appearance.

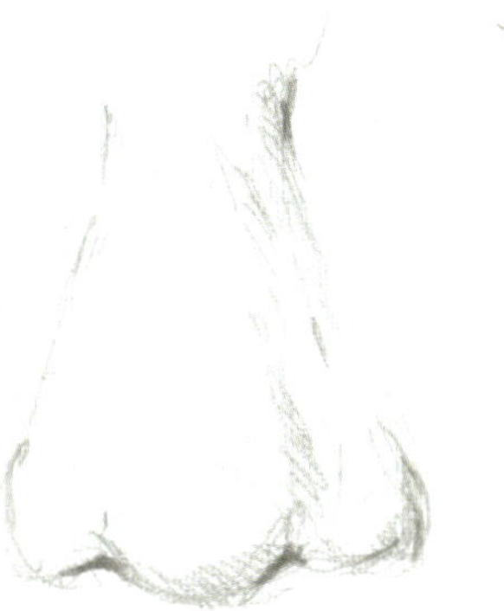

Study Lip Muscles

There are three muscles in the top lip, two in the bottom. Study your subject to see how noticeable these shapes are. Some will be barely visible but still important enough to show in your drawing.

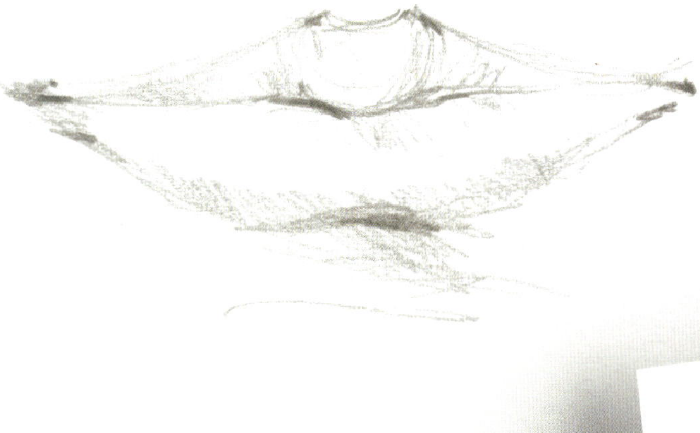

Be Aware of Subtleties

The bottom half of the nose is cartilage and muscle. The ridge of the skull stops slightly below the eyes. It may be subtle or prominent, but if you know it is there you can look for it.

Sketching Facial Contours

Angle, lighting and cast shadows will all have an effect on the expression of a model. Changes you make in size and position of facial features will also alter the expression. Sometimes you will want a neutral expression and other times a more dramatic look. Experiment with different lighting and perspectives to achieve the look you want.

Incorporating Tone

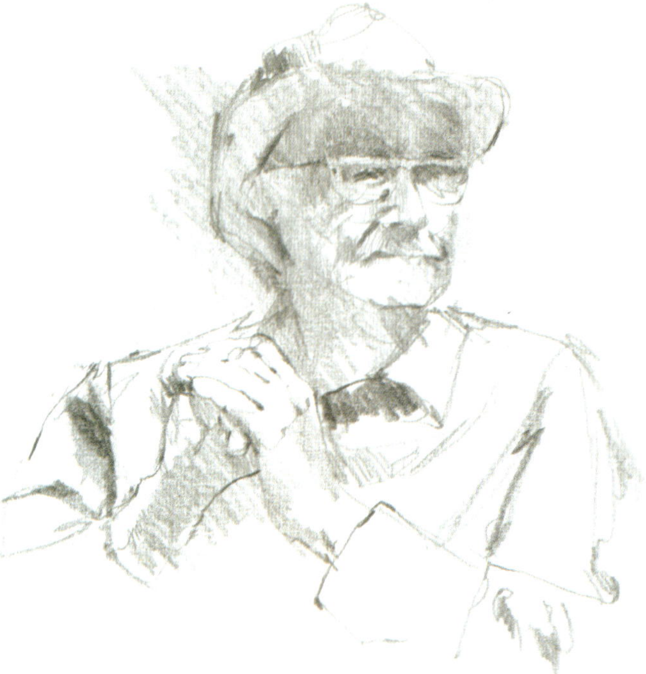

Photo Reference Is Useful When Applying Tone

Once you are comfortable with contour drawing and have a grasp of proportions, start to apply tone to the drawing. The light source is important here. If you can, set up a photo portrait to use as reference – it will be very helpful. Most commission portraits are done this way. It is a rare occasion when you hear of someone actually sitting for a portrait drawing.

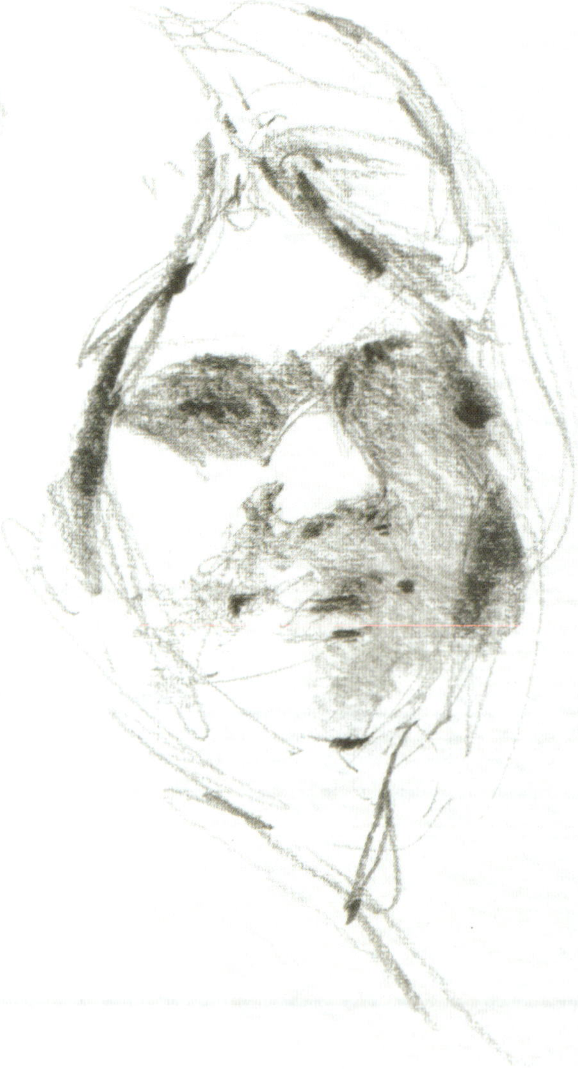

Practice a Simplified Light and Dark Treatment

Break the tones into as few values as possible. Try to do a sketch that tells the story with only two or three values.

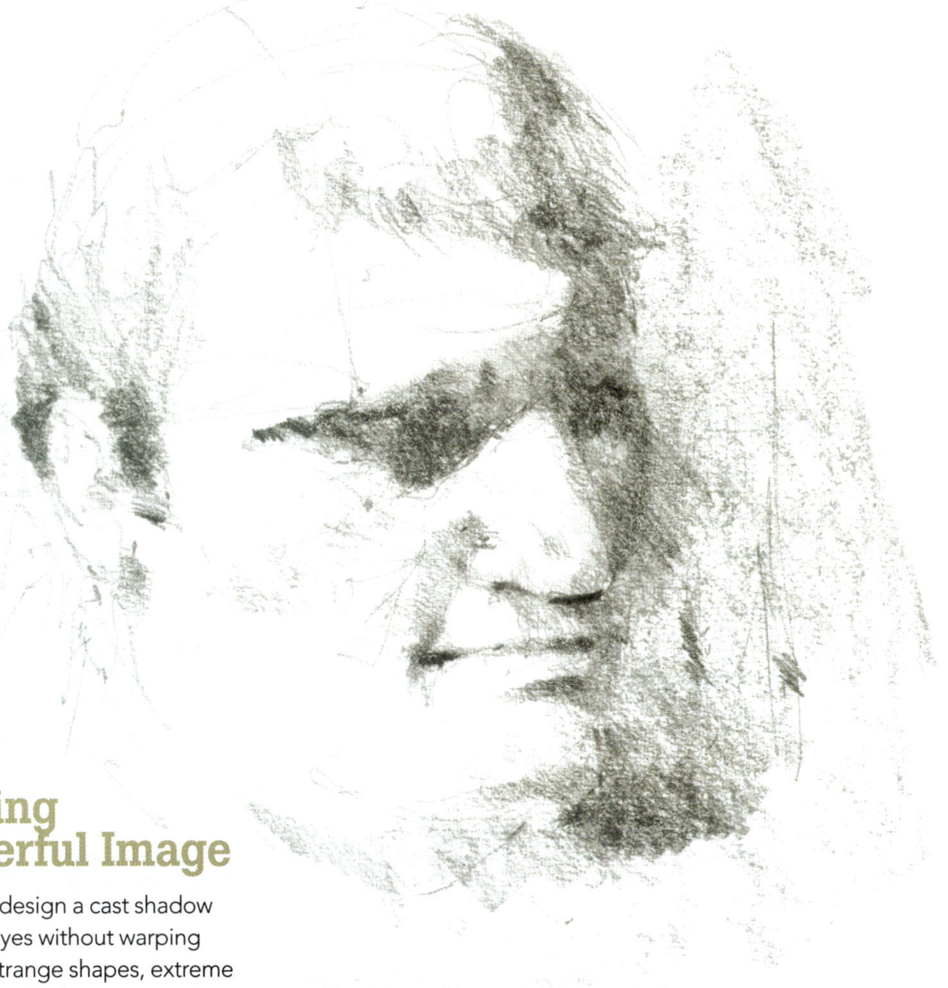

Extreme Lighting Creates a Powerful Image

While it can be a challenge to design a cast shadow that obscures details like the eyes without warping the face or creating new and strange shapes, extreme lighting creates a powerful image and commands a lot more attention than flat lighting.

TRY BLIND CONTOUR DRAWING WITH FACES

Head shapes vary greatly, so you may find it useful to try blind contour drawing with this subject. There will be distortion in that exercise, but you'll see more expression and convey more character in your line work.

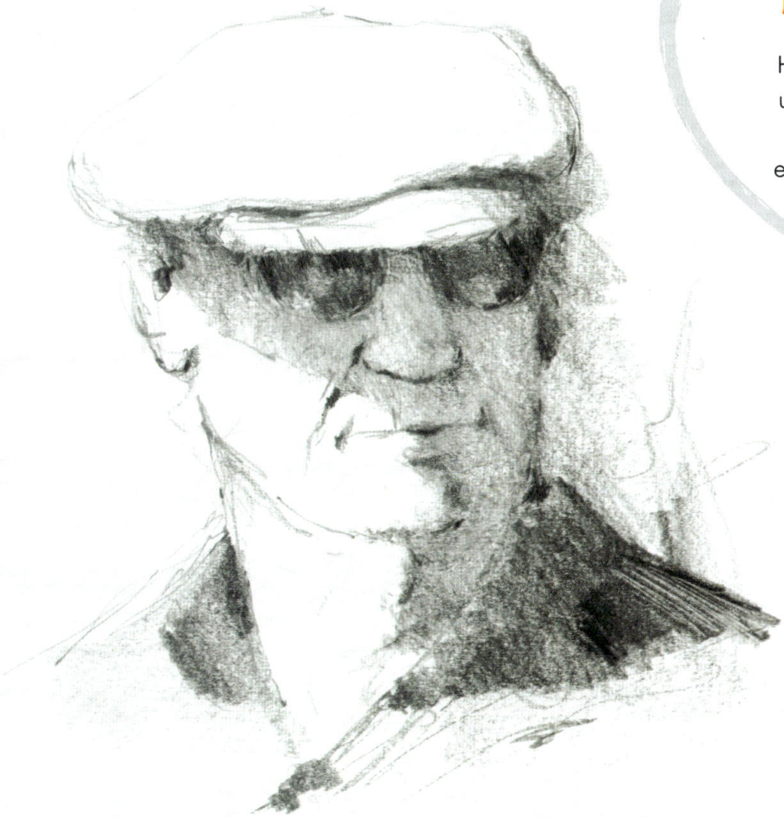

Contrasting Tones and Shapes Contribute to Overall Form

Notice the contrast of the bright highlight areas against the dark values. The shape of the shadow, the cap and the shirt all contribute to the form of the face. These accessories are as important as the proportion of the features.

Changing Perspectives

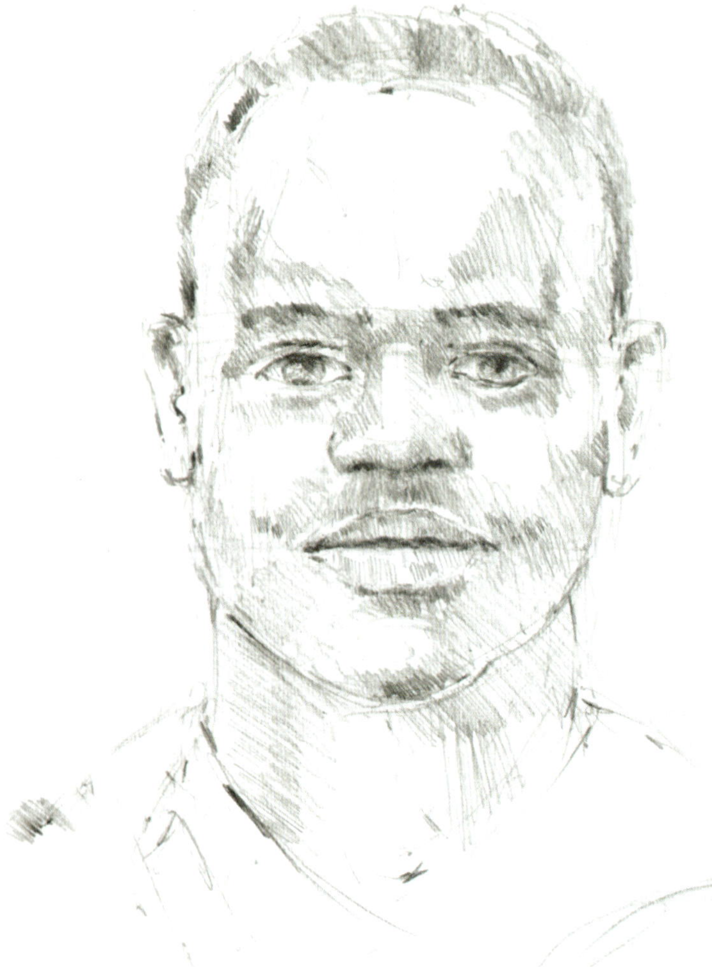

Profiles Can Be Challenging

Profiles are challenging because the slightest distortion will change the whole structure. If you are a beginner, use vertical guidelines to help judge how far the nose and chin protrude. The angle from the base of the nose to the chin is critical and will be different for each portrait.

Relationship of Features From a Straight-On Perspective

All the usual rules apply here, such as the distance between the top of the head and chin, etc. This angle is good for practicing how to balance each side of the face.

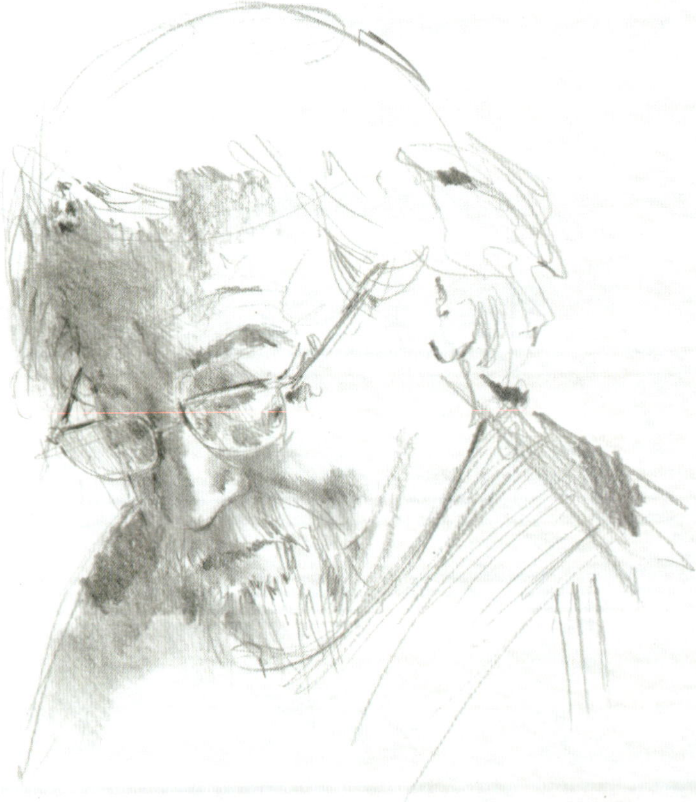

Angled Perspectives Take More Practice

It is harder to line up the facial features when the head is on an angle like this. It may help to turn the paper to a more familiar vertical position in order to check your work. Eventually you will be able to visualize how the features change in perspective as the head turns and tilts. Practice working quickly like this, even if the subject is difficult. Mistakes look better if the drawing is done with confidence.

When Is It Finished?

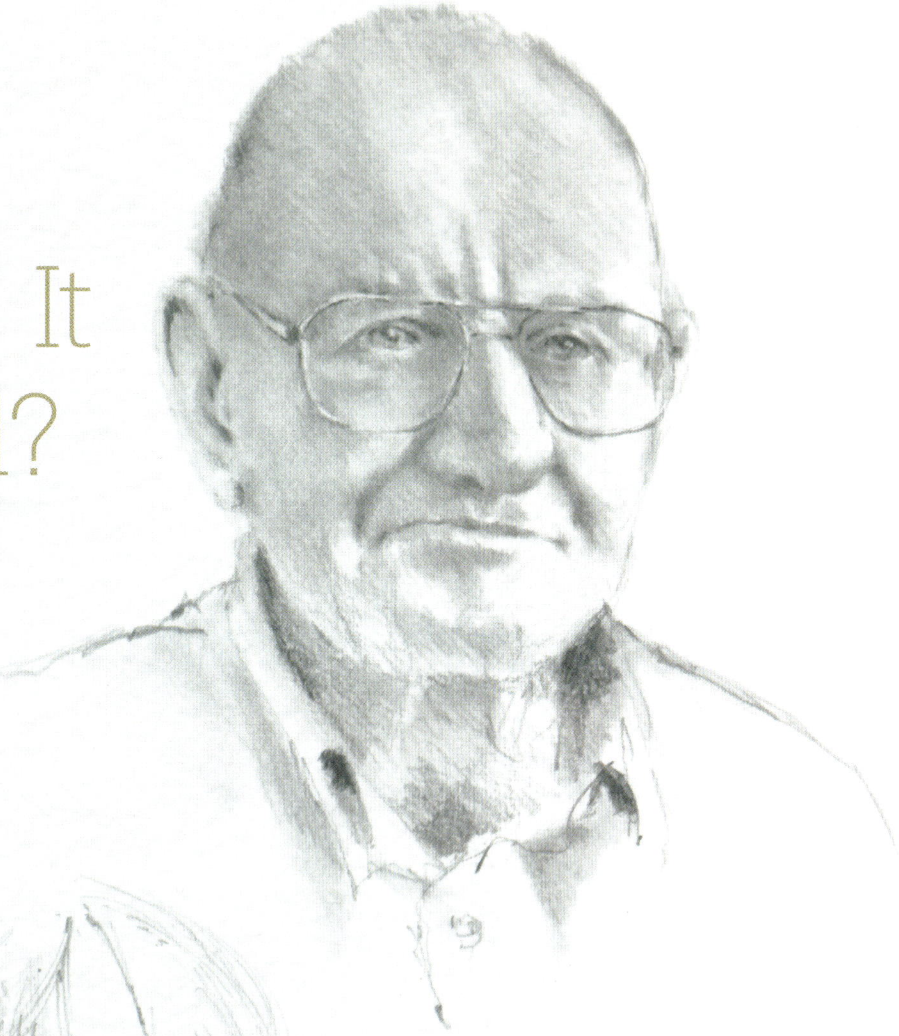

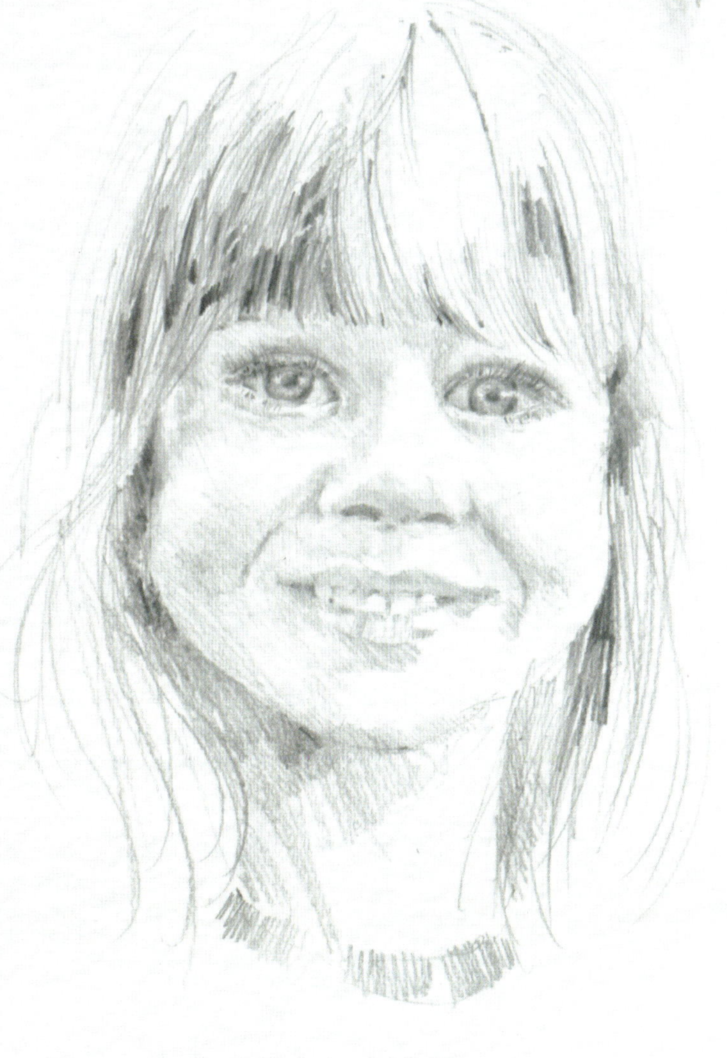

Different Drawings May Feel Complete at Different Stages

I consider both of these drawings finished even though they stopped at different stages of completion. Some subjects require a high level of polish and some are captured in just a few strokes.

As soon as you become unsure of what to do next, the answer is always "stop." Put the drawing aside for a while. If it requires more work, you will soon see the next step.

FACES

Sketch a Character Study

If you plan to develop as a portrait artist, you will need to do many character studies. Quick sketches like this will help you see how facial features can vary from the basic rules, giving each subject a unique personality.

MATERIALS

Surface
acid-free art paper, heavy

Graphite
HB, 2B wooden pencils

Other
kneaded eraser

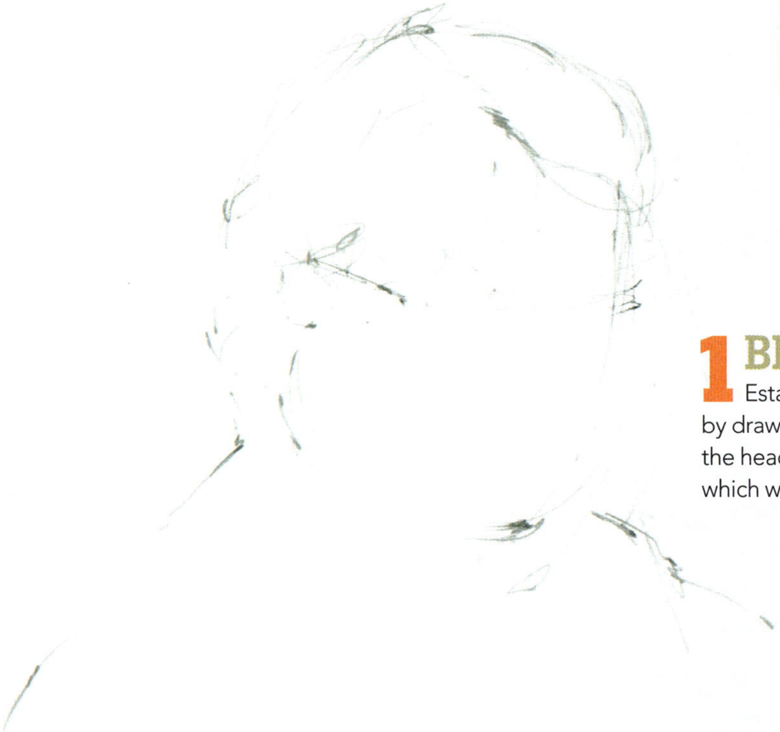

1 Block In Basic Shapes

Establish the size and placement of the portrait by drawing a light oval with an HB pencil. In this case the head is fairly circular. Start to sketch the glasses, which will help you to find a halfway point.

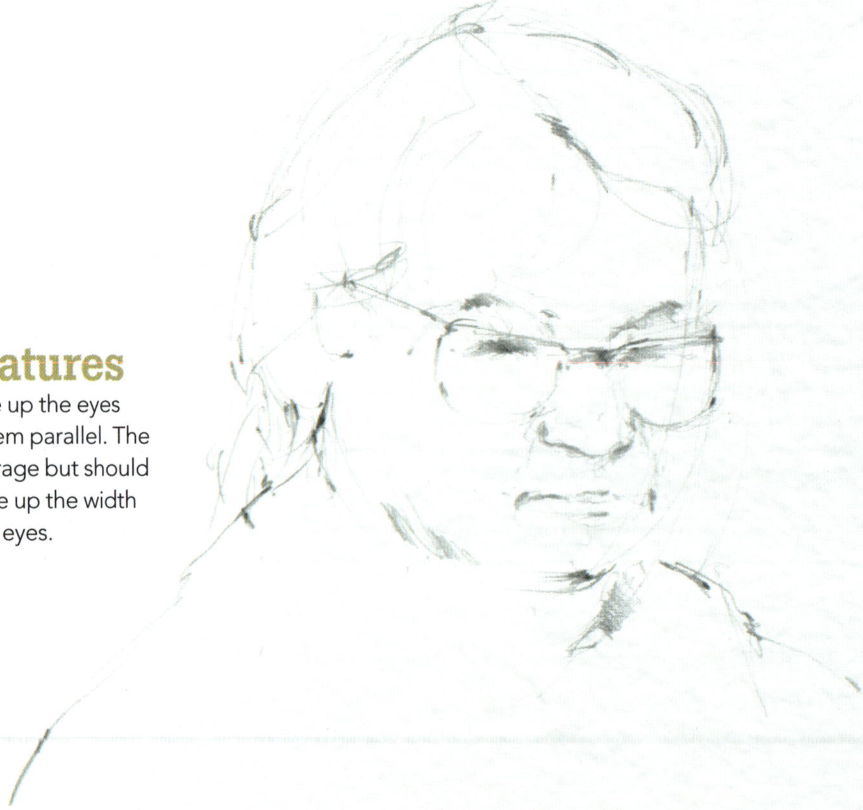

2 Sketch the Features

Draw the facial features. Line up the eyes and mouth, taking care to make them parallel. The features are slightly wider than average but should still be in relation to each other. Line up the width of the mouth with the center of the eyes.

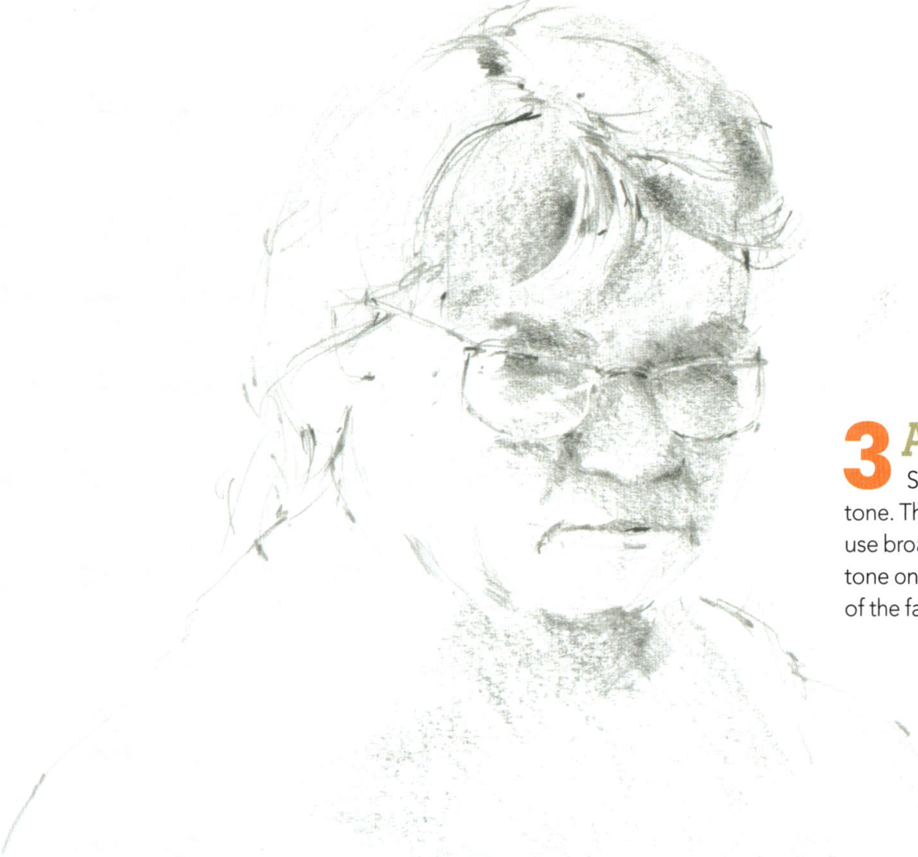

3 Apply Tone

Switch to a 2B pencil and add the tone. This is just a sketch, so it's fine to use broad strokes for blocking in some tone on the shadow side. Note that most of the face is in shadow here.

4 Continue Adding Tone and Define the Hair

Use a 2B pencil for the darks and some definition in the hair. Do not draw each hair separately. Suggest the hair by drawing just a few strands.

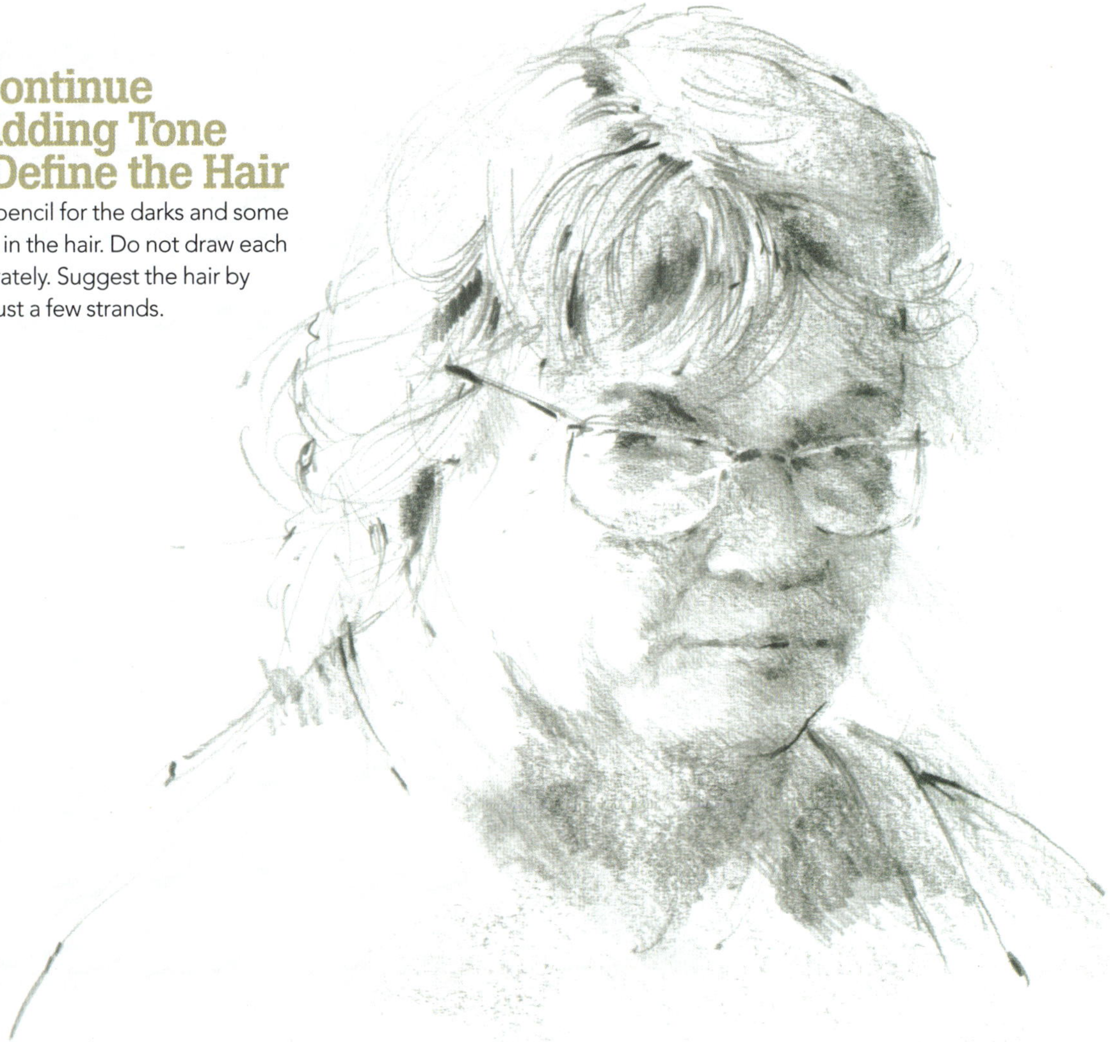

FACES

Plan a Portrait

When you are sketching a plan for a painting, it is important to give some consideration to the background. It is not necessary to have an elaborate surrounding but it helps to explain the circumstance of the model by introducing a location. Should the model be standing, sitting or reclining? Should he be posed or candid? These ideas can be explored in a sketch.

MATERIALS

Surface
acid-free art paper

Graphite
HB graphite stick
HB, 2B wooden pencils

Other
kneaded eraser

TAKE CARE WHEN ADDING PROPS

Sometimes glasses or sunglasses add a certain drama to a portrait, but getting a good result is equally as difficult as drawing eyes. So don't think you're avoiding trouble with props like hats and glasses.

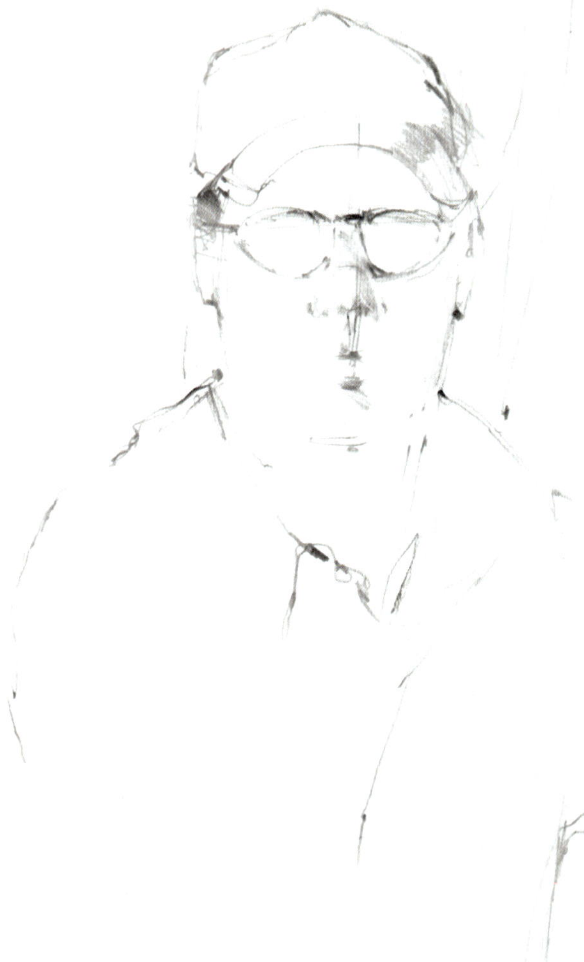

1 Rough In a Sketch

Rough out a linear sketch with an HB pencil. Think about how you want to arrange the values.

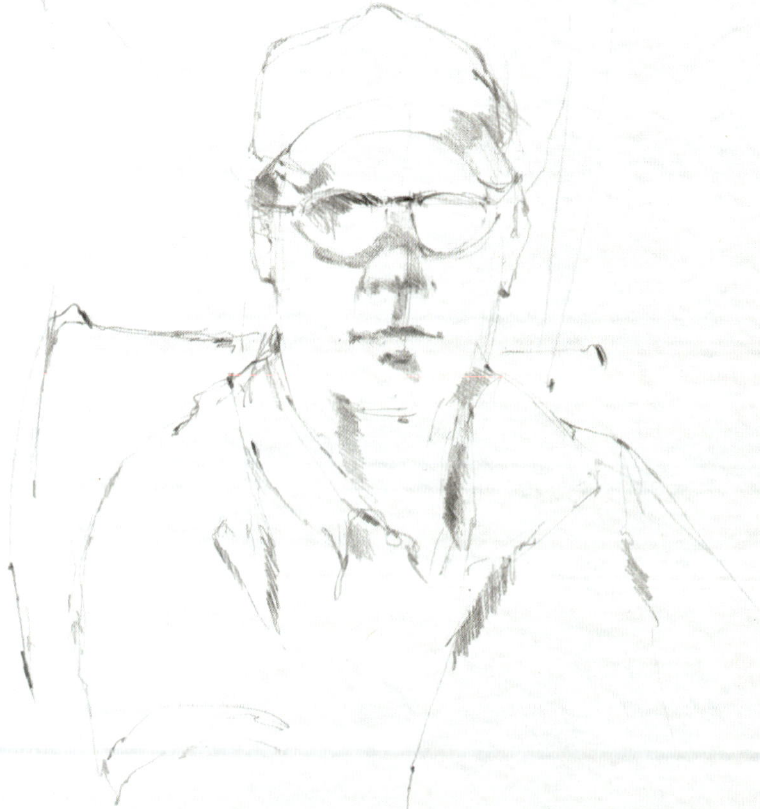

2 Begin Applying Tone

Once you have decided on how to break the design into light and dark, apply the lighter tones with an HB graphite stick. Use a 2B pencil for the finer dark areas.

3 Add the Background

With this type of project, the surroundings don't need to be very detailed. In fact, the more abstract the better because you want the focus to be on the impact of dramatic lighting, not objects that could be distracting.

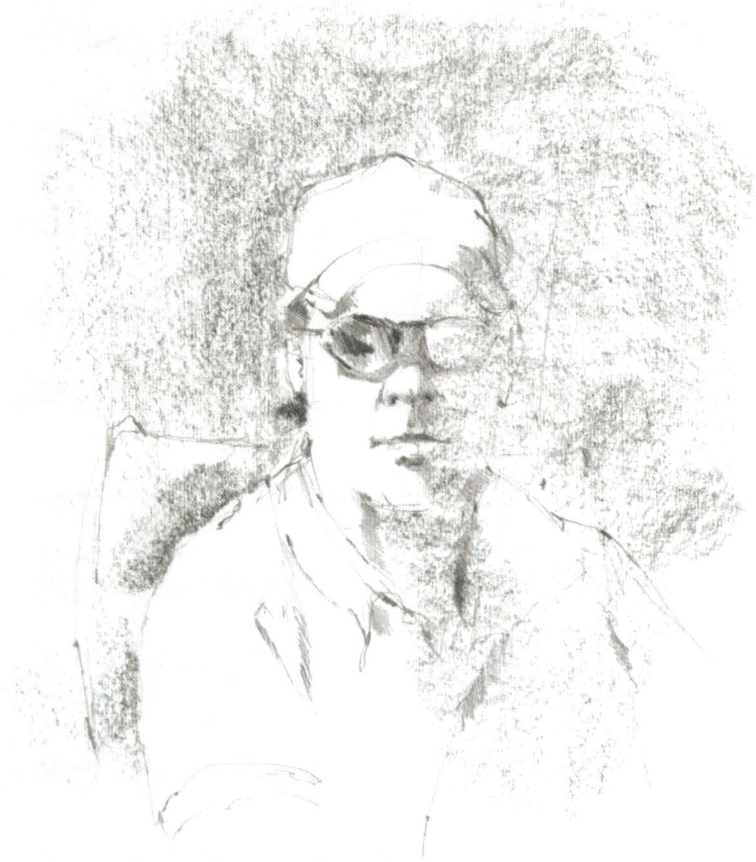

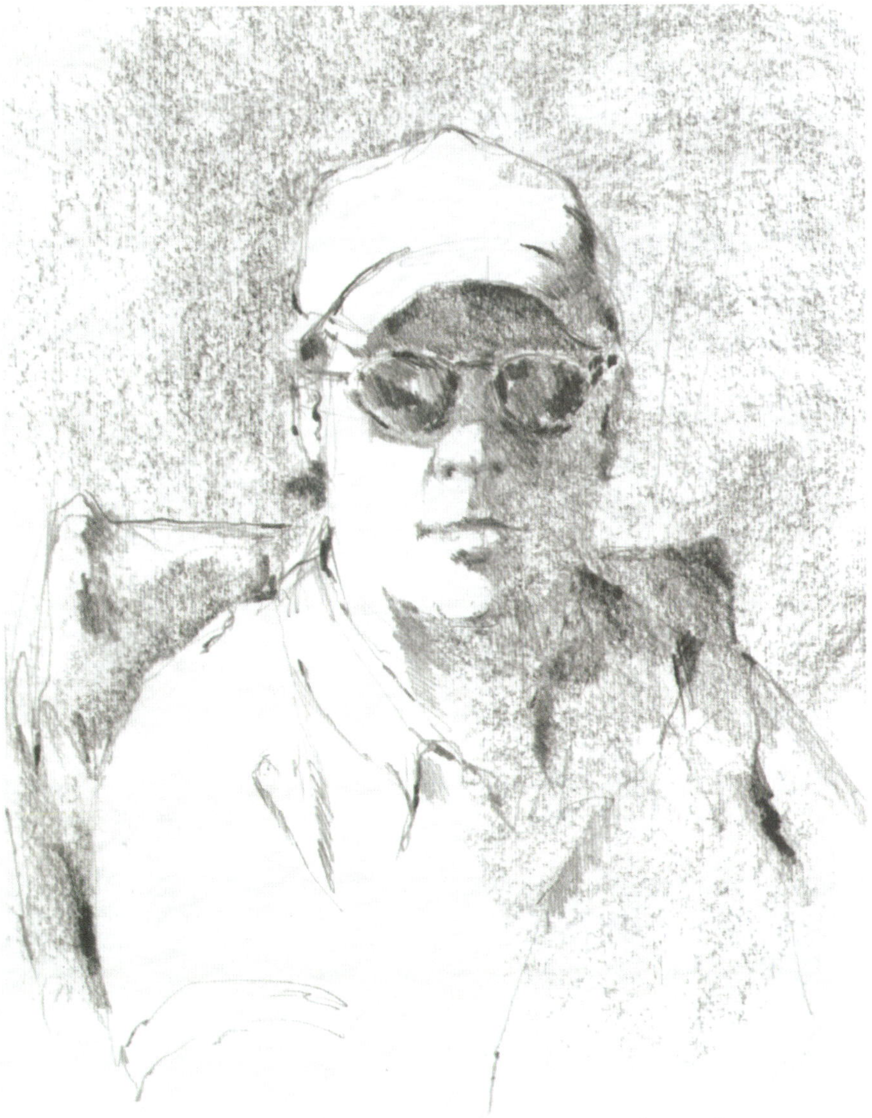

4 Add More Tone to Finish

Think in terms of the three main values and keep it loose and simple. Do not be concerned with telling a whole story here, just create an attention-getting arrangement of light and dark.

Figures

Practice observing and memorizing the most striking qualities of a particular image. Sunlight often plays a significant role in creating the impression, but look for other things as well. If you are nervous about working in public, practice from these examples until you get more comfortable. See what it feels like to make marks like the ones shown here. It will be necessary to move the pencil fast, which requires some rapid decision-making.

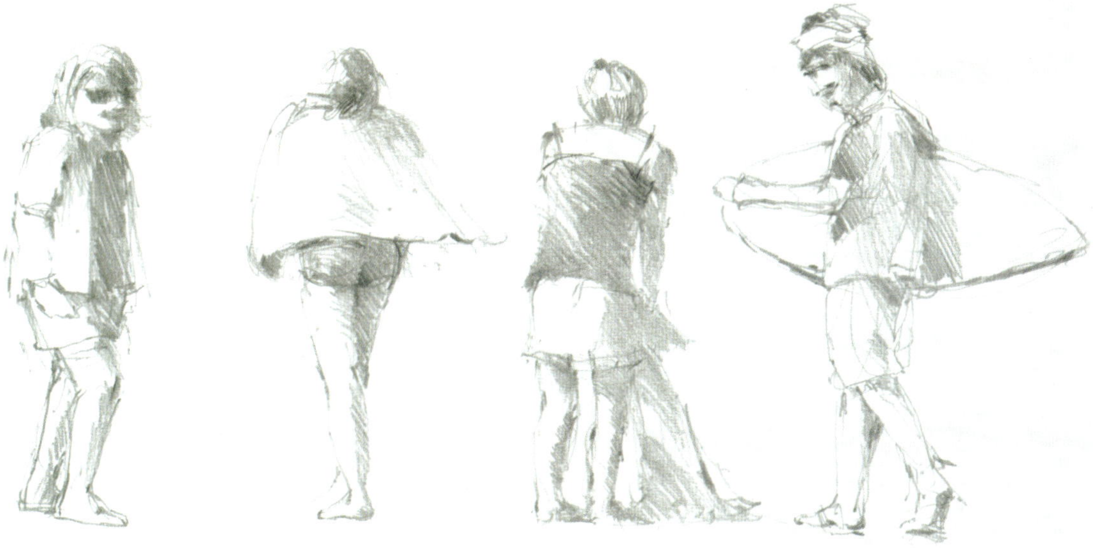

Start Slowly

At first, rehearse the moves slowly, gradually speeding up as you learn where the pencil needs to go. Soon you will pick up speed as you learn the way.

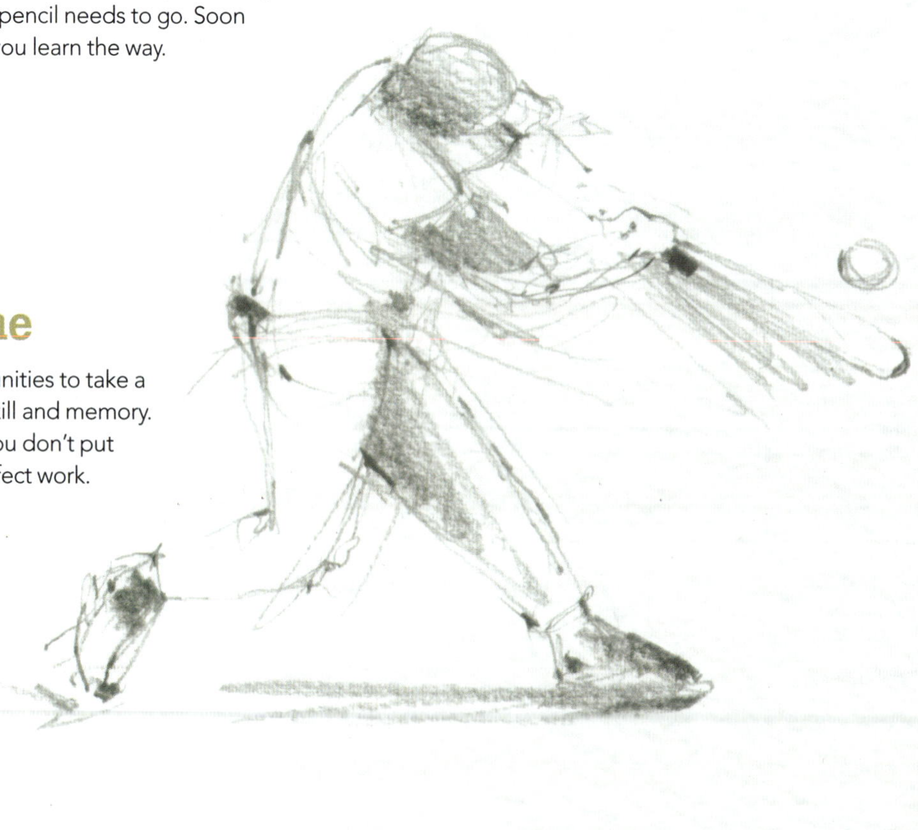

Get on Your Game

Sporting events are great opportunities to take a sketchbook along and test your skill and memory. This can be good fun as long as you don't put pressure on yourself to create perfect work.

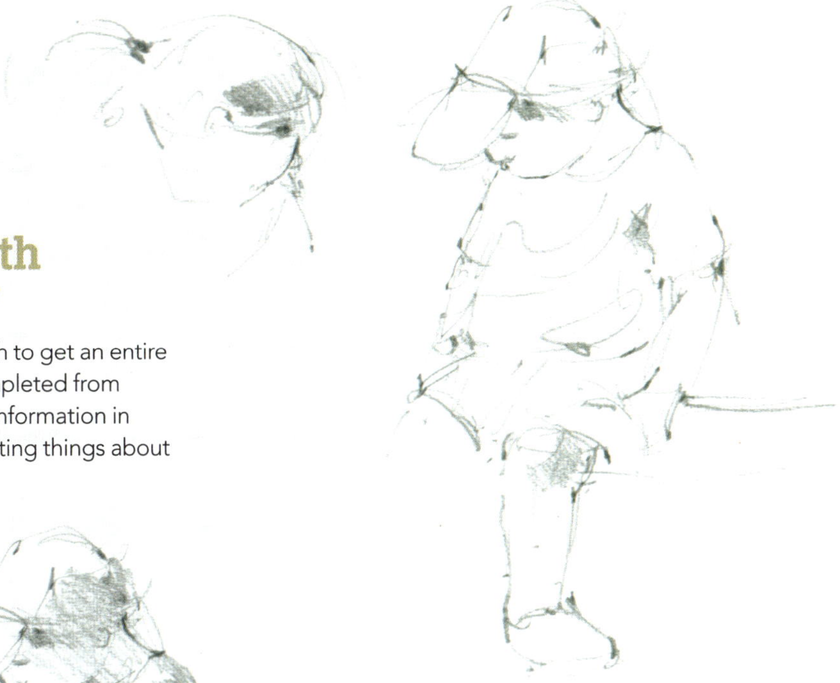

Get Comfortable With Relying on Memory

People do not usually sit still long enough to get an entire drawing done, so much needs to be completed from memory. Your memory will gather more information in time, and you can focus on the more fleeting things about the image.

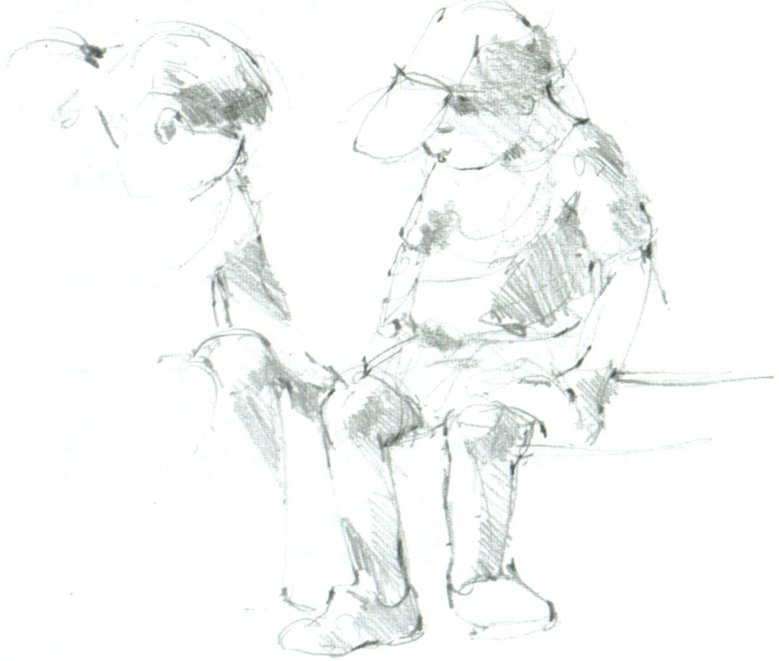

Sketch Important Positions First

In this case the angle of the heads was important, as well as the position of the arms. I drew those first and established the position of the shoulders relative to the heads. The position of the girl's knees and the boy's feet are also important to the drawing.

Fill In Details From Memory

The shirts, hats, legs and hair were all done from memory, so a quick glance to get an idea was all that was needed. You can often get ideas for completing the sketch by looking around at other figures after your main subjects are no longer there.

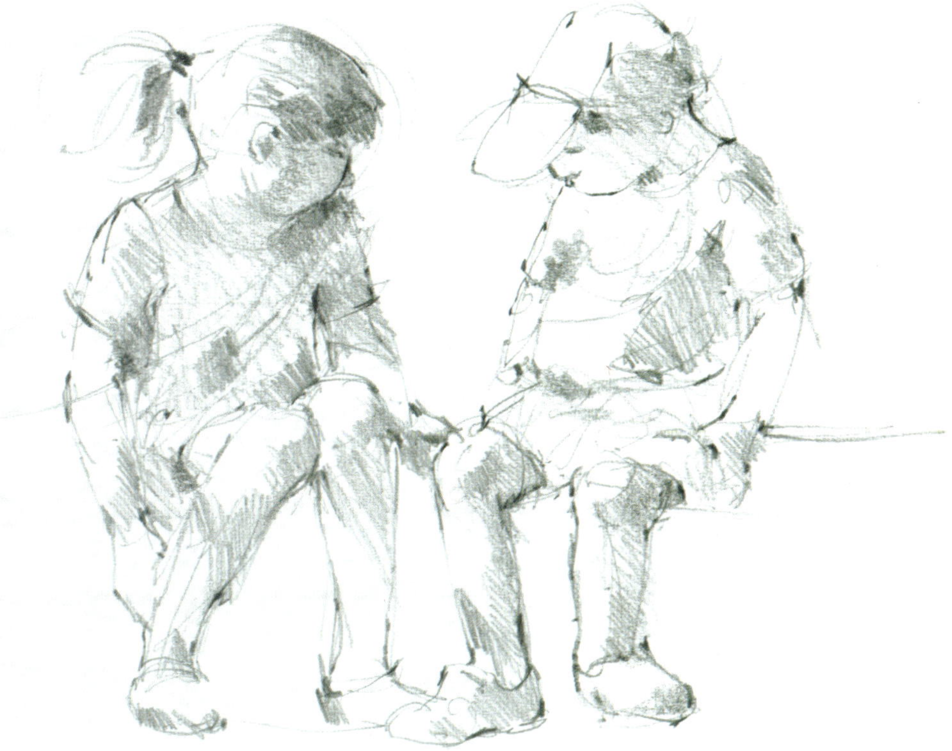

Gesture Drawing

Gesture drawing is the term used to describe quick suggestions, usually of figures. Gesture drawings can be done in a life-drawing class or outdoors in public locations.

All the sketches in this section started as quick gestures, but the more stationary poses allowed me to finish them later. They represent various drawing speeds, some very fast, others a little slower. Use them as reference to practice. Try to mimic the linework. This will require using both the point of the pencil and the side, plus various leads and different pressures. Have fun exploring!

Still Subject

Sketching this fisherman was fairly easy because he sat motionless for a long period of time.

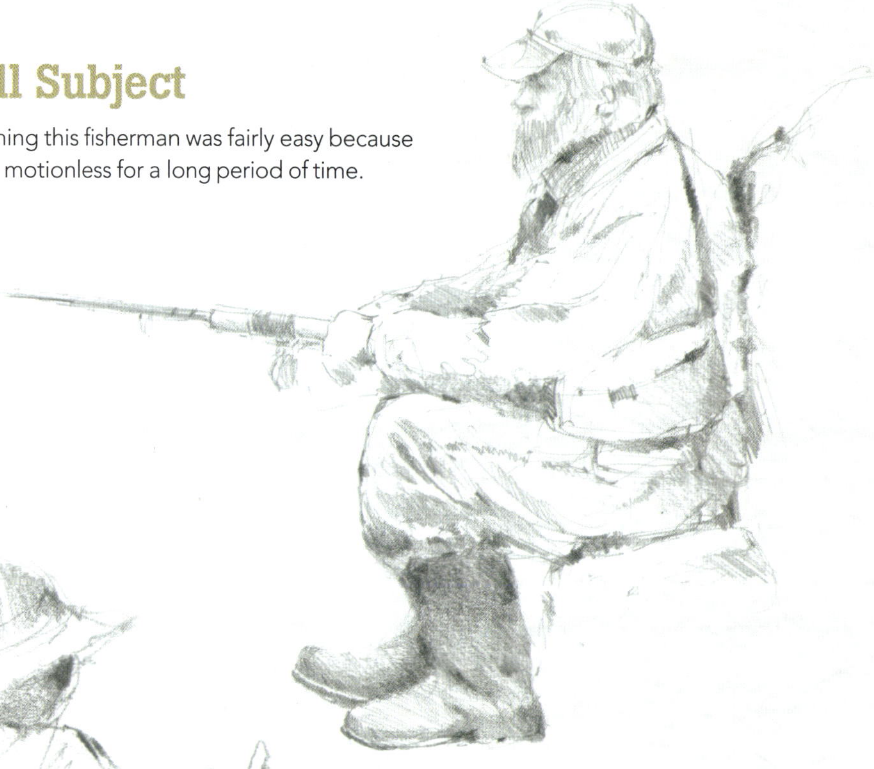

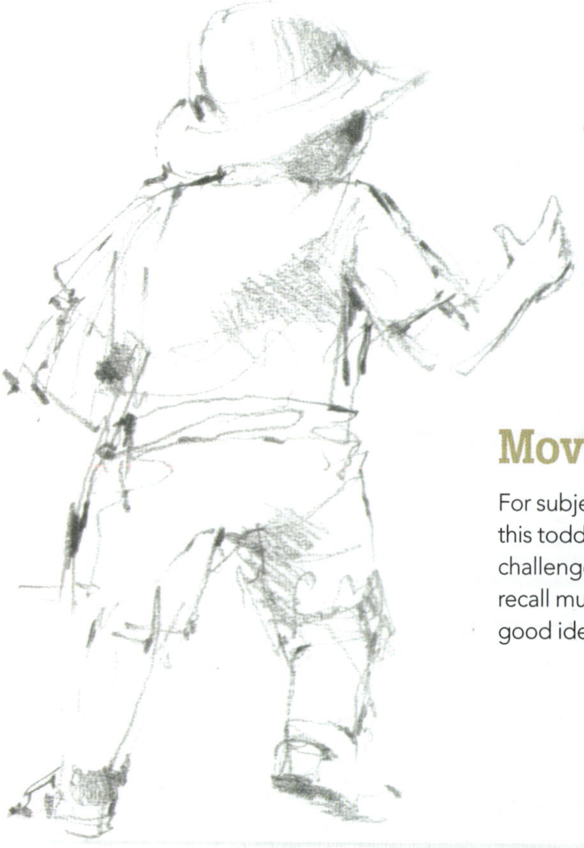

Moving Subject

For subjects that move about more frequently, such as this toddler, I pretend my eye takes a picture and then I challenge my memory to re-create that moment. I can't recall much detail, but I can get a feel for the pose and a good idea of where the lights and darks were.

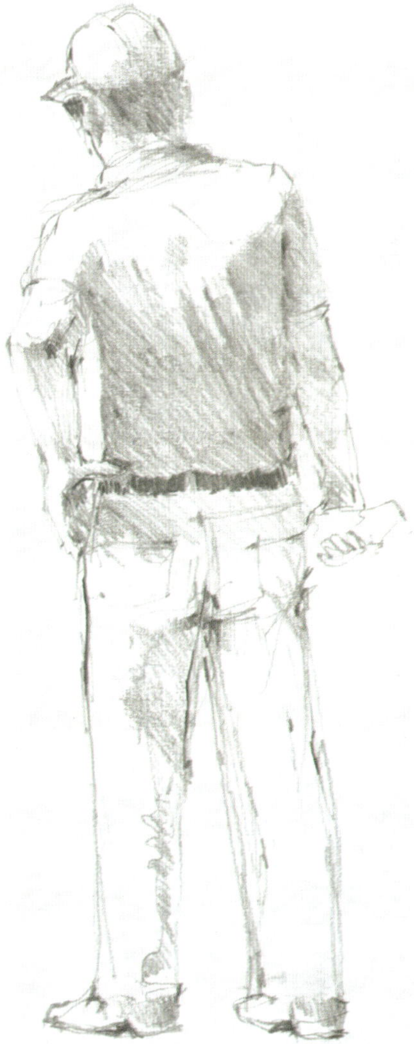

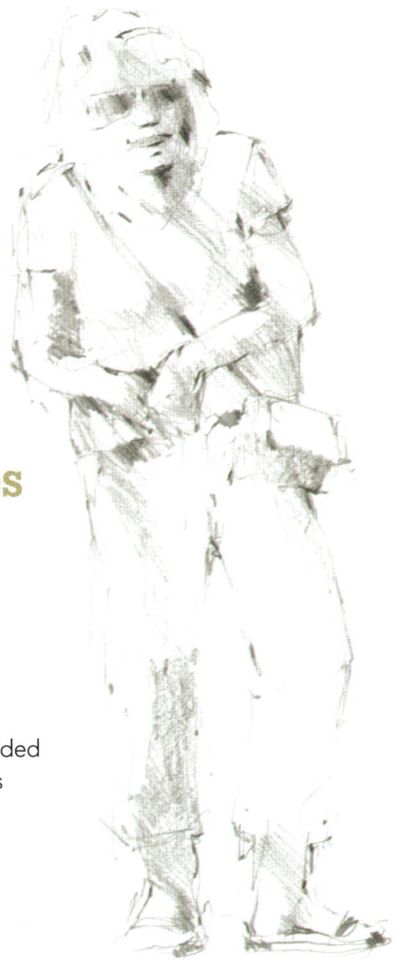

Accessories Can Be a Challenge

The woman's arms and handbag made establishing the proportions here a bit more challenging. I added a few darks and details from memory to get a better-looking sketch.

Establish Proportions First

The back view of a standing figure is fairly easy to render. The height and width, as well as the waist line were established first. Finishing tone and detail were added later.

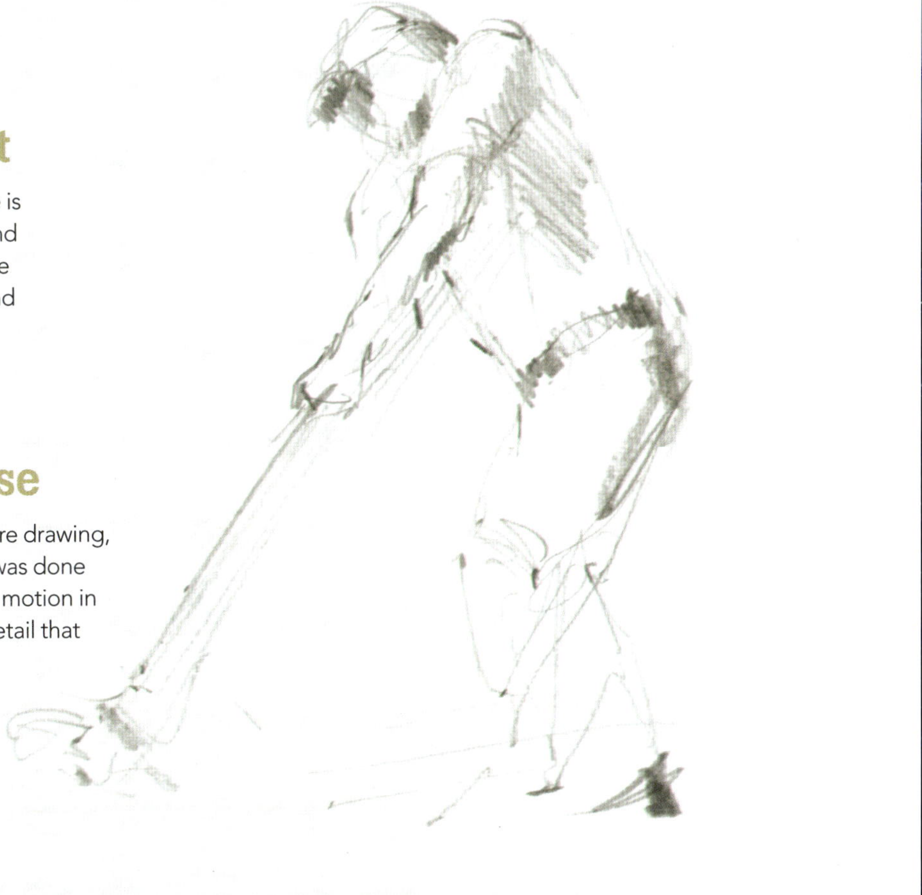

It's All In the Pose

The golfer is more of a true gesture drawing, even though most of this sketch was done from memory. I tried to retain the motion in this figure and avoided adding detail that might stiffen the pose.

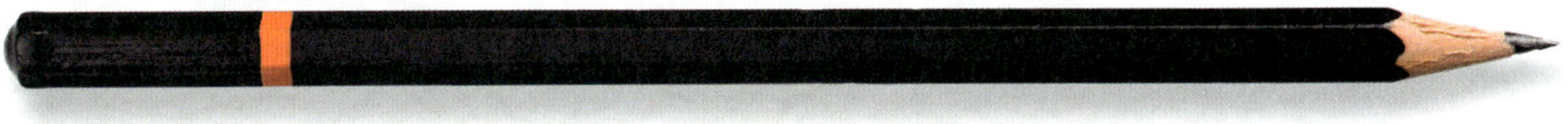

CHAPTER

7

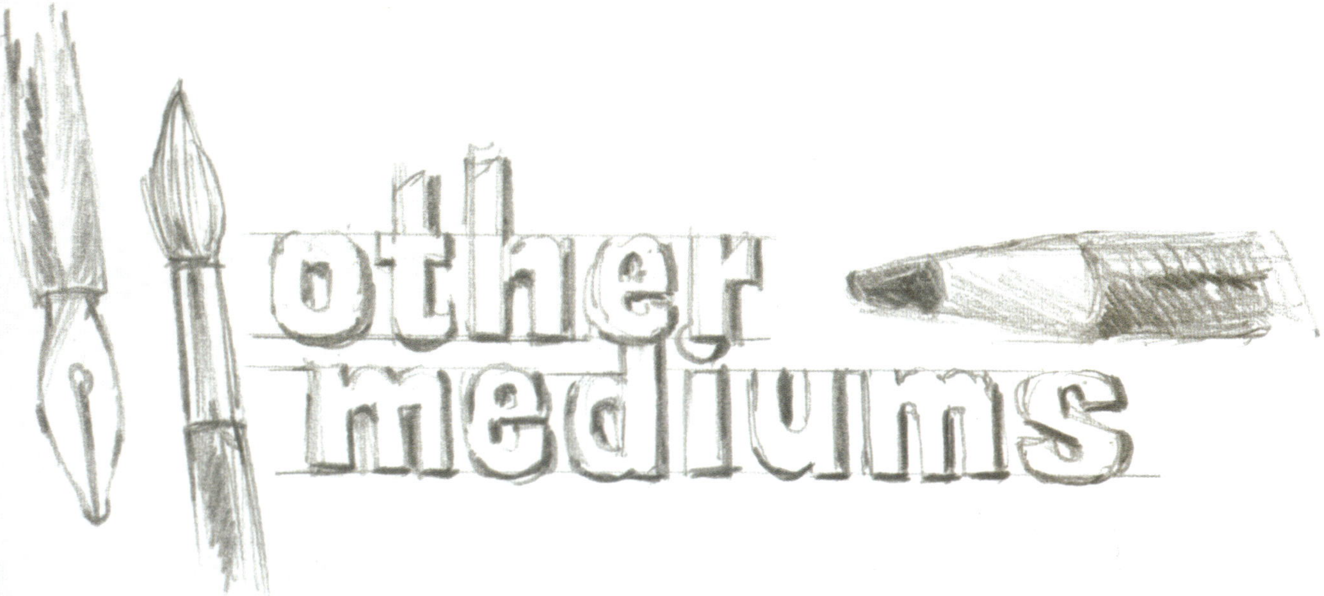

other mediums

The other mediums we'll explore in this chapter have one major difference from graphite – they are not forgiving. Ink and watercolor wash are not easily removed. Charcoal is very black compared to graphite. It does not erase easily but can be smudged, creating a lighter version of the original marks. Wash drawings require exploring new papers that are designed for use with water. There are also papers made specifically for pastel and charcoal that can hold the powder these mediums deposit.

Although they can be more of a challenge than simple graphite, it is well worth trying these other mediums. The more you experiment, the more you'll learn. In the process, you may find a medium that suits you perfectly.

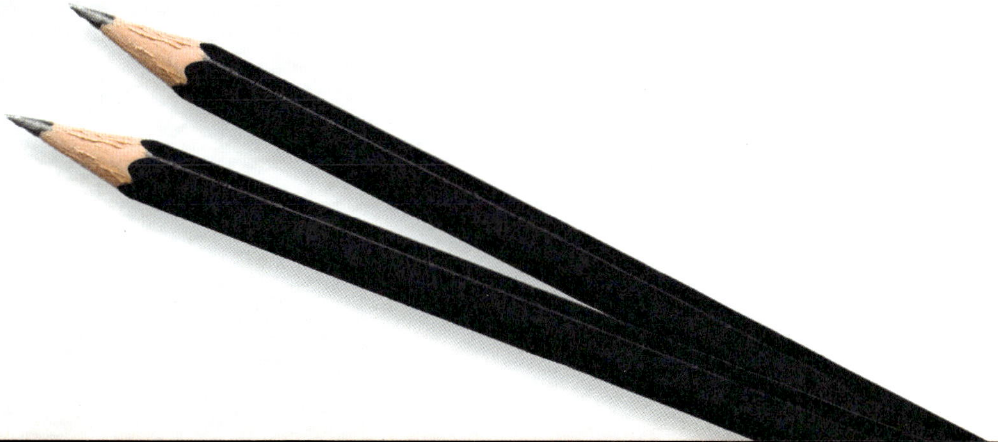

Pen & Ink

Many different design applications are possible with pen and ink. Once you have explored some of the possibilities, you can begin to specialize.

The following pen-and-ink renderings were done with a lightfast and permanent nylon-tip pen. Many pens are labeled "permanent" but that refers to the non-smear property, meaning they dry fast and do not dissolve with moisture. This, however, does not mean they can resist fading from sunlight – those pens are labeled "lightfast". They come in various tip sizes such as fine and ultra-fine.

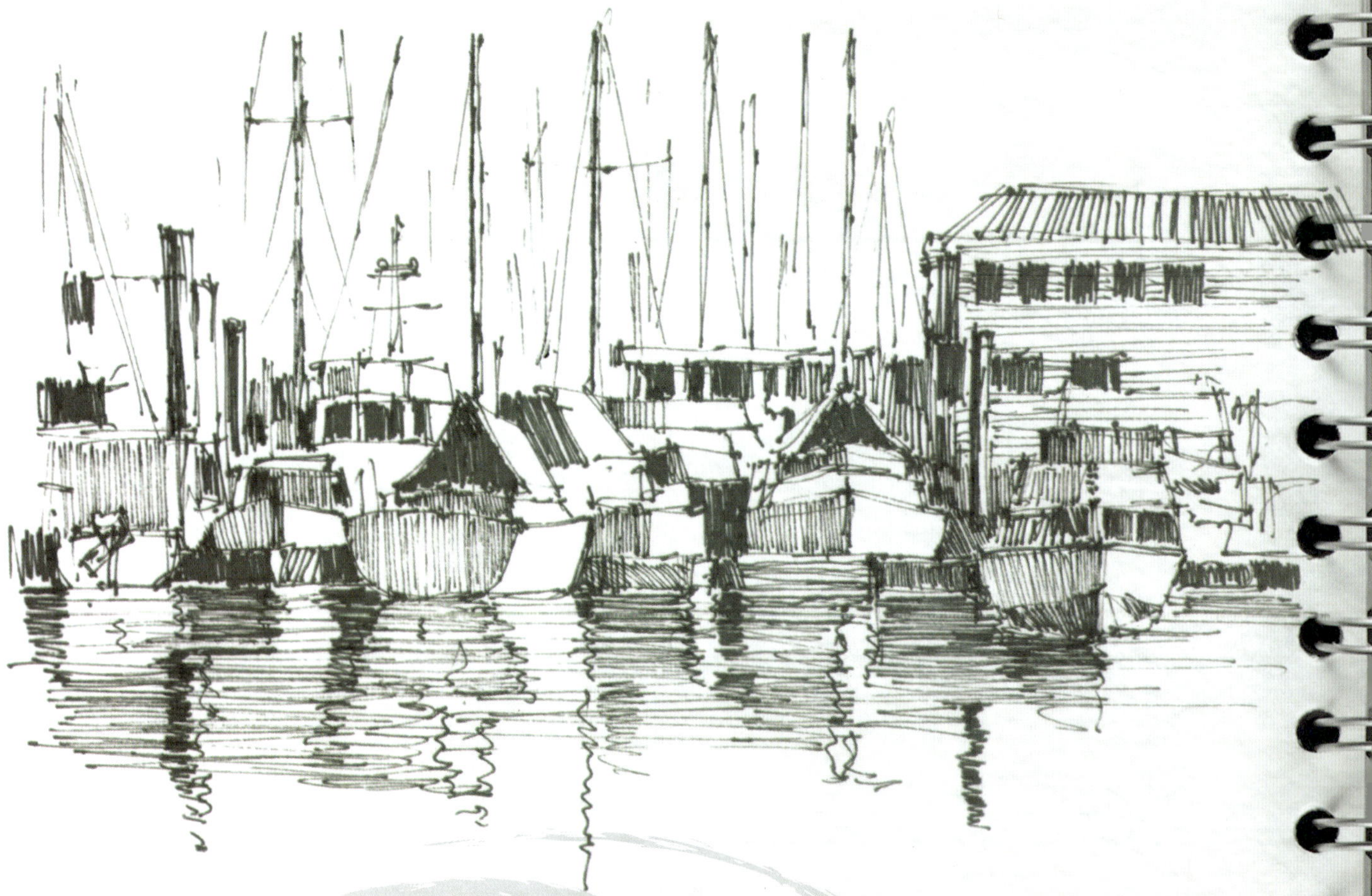

USE HATCHING AND CROSSHATCHING TO APPLY TONE WITH PEN AND INK

Fine art subjects such as the marine scene here can be quite successful with pen and ink, but the usual tone application as done with graphite will not work with ink. Other means must be used to suggest a value other than black. This is where hatching, a series of close parallel lines, or crosshatching, a series of crisscross lines, are used to create a three-dimensional appearance. Small dots made with the pen at varying densities will also work to make tonal values.

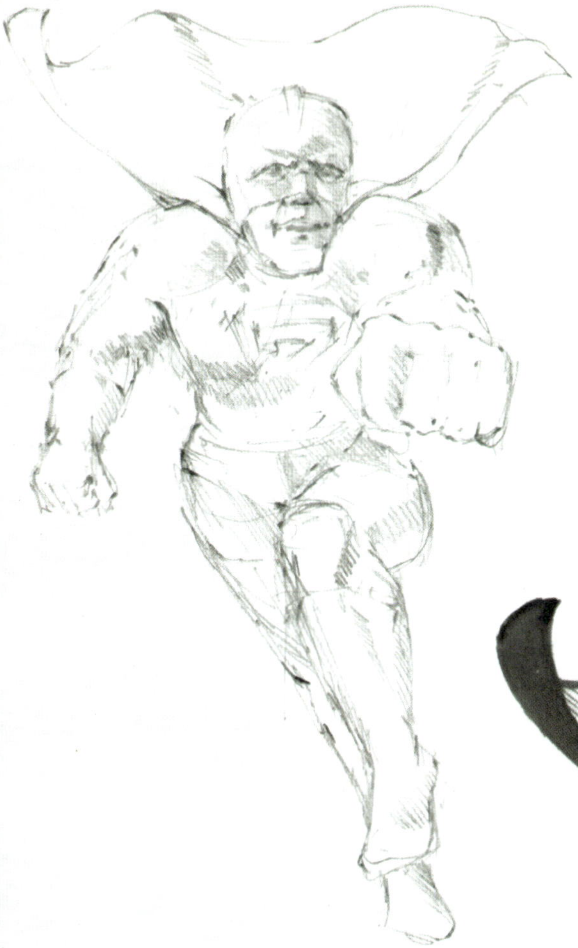

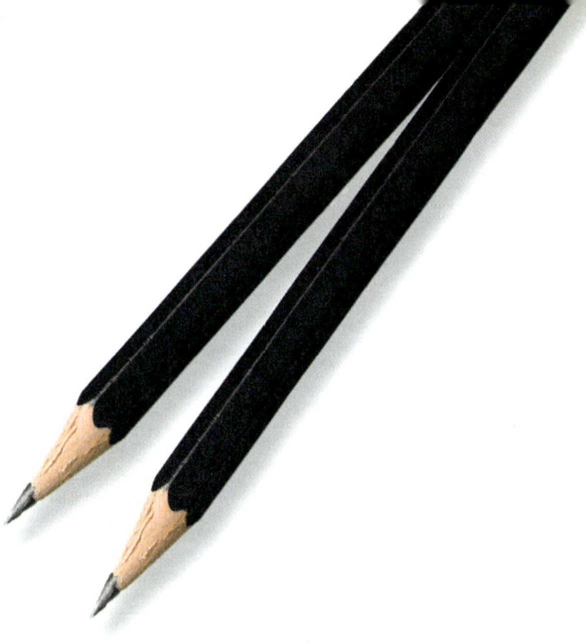

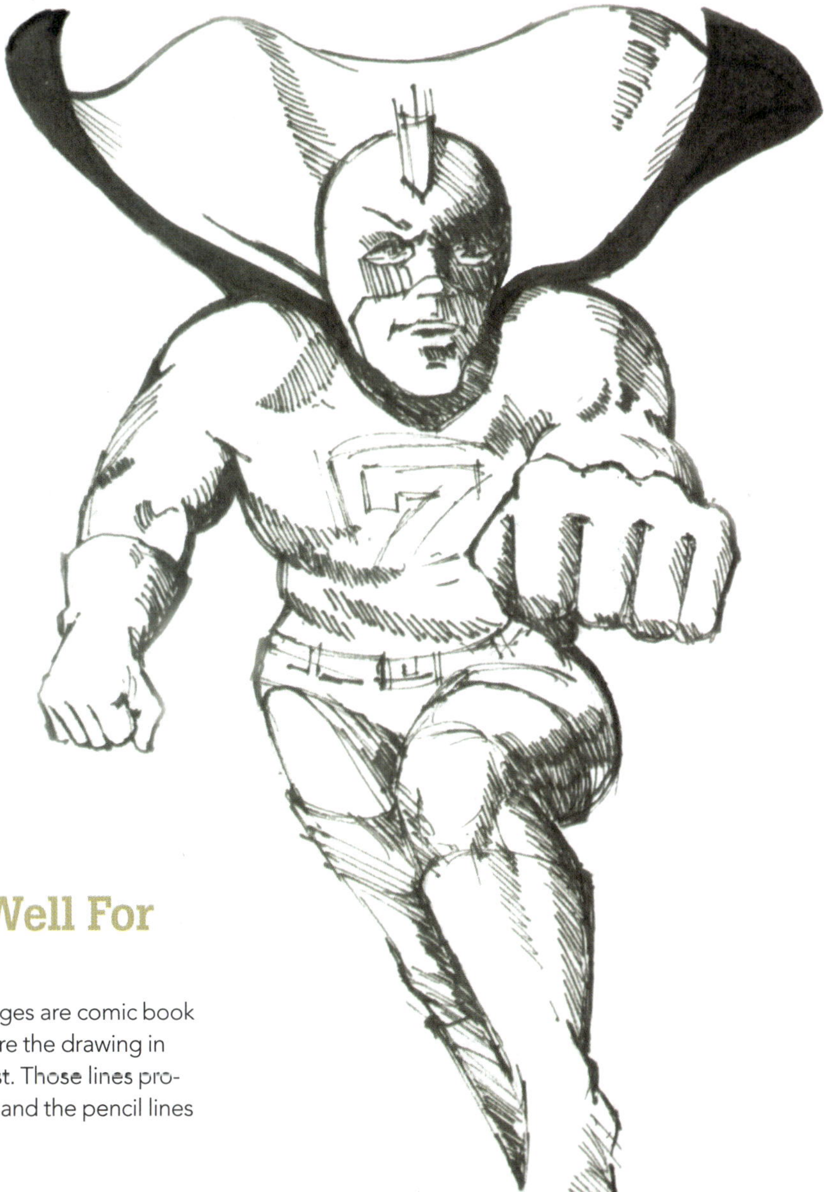

Pen and Ink Works Well For Comic Characters

Some of the most familiar pen-and-ink images are comic book characters. Invent your own, but first prepare the drawing in pencil. An HB with light pressure works best. Those lines provide a good guide for confident pen work, and the pencil lines can be erased later.

Charcoal

Charcoal is much different than graphite. It is basically burnt wood. It comes in stick form, which is made by heating wood in the absence of oxygen and then compressed in pencil form. I prefer working with pencils because they are more consistent. The texture of sticks often varies from soft to hard abruptly and can scratch the paper. But they are usually a larger diameter than pencils and can be great for larger-scale work.

No graphite pencil is needed prior to using charcoal. Although charcoal does not erase well, it is possible to make very light marks to use as guides.

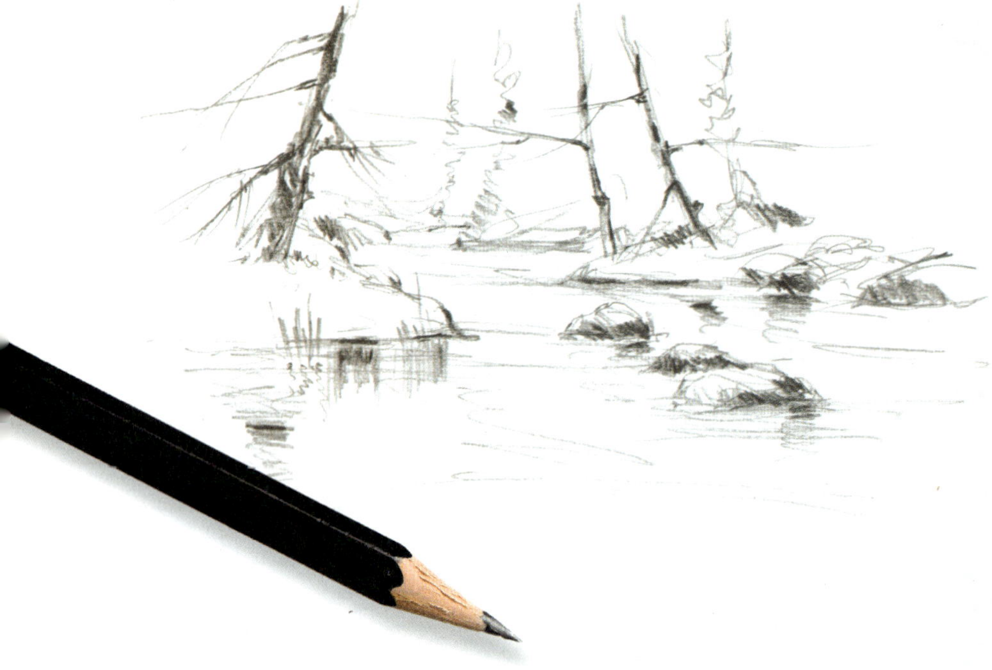

Avoid Smudging When Getting Familiar With Charcoal

Charcoal smudges easily, so it's best to practice drawing several sketches using only linework without intentional smudging. This control is important because later you will want to explore the effects of smudging, but only in desired areas. For now, though, start with clean, pure linework and take the time to get comfortable with avoiding accidental smudging.

Explore Smudging Effects Later

Once you have command of drawing with charcoal, begin exploring the various effects smudging creates. It can be used to suggest motion or to smooth a transition of form. It can make edges disappear so objects blend in places and separate in others. You can draw, smudge and draw again on top. This process can be repeated until you are happy with the results.

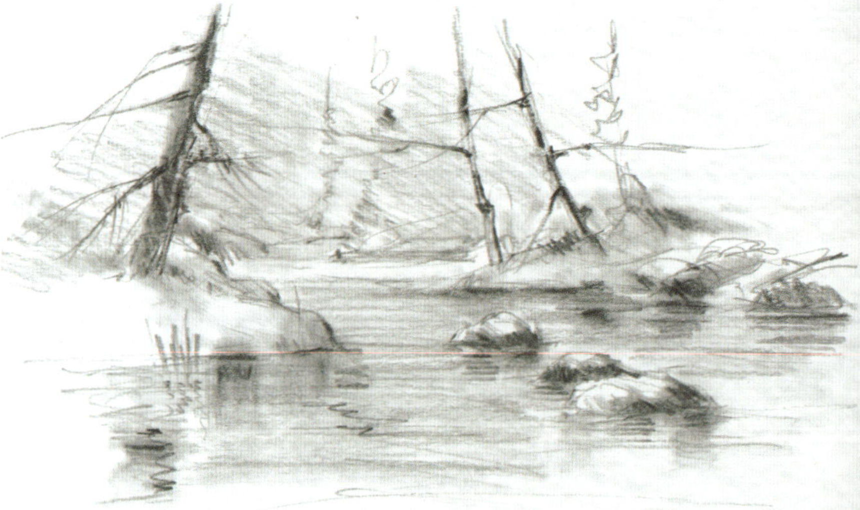

Exploring Charcoal

Draw a Deer in Charcoal

This project will help you practice getting the right balance between drawing and smudging to add texture and dimension to your work. Try copying these images at first, then work with a photo of your own, maybe a pet. You may find it necessary to use a grid (like the one demonstrated for the scaled car drawing in the Proportion chapter) to achieve accurate and balanced proportions in the deer's face.

MATERIALS

Surface
medium-texture illustration board

Other
charcoal pencil
kneaded eraser
paper stump
paper towels

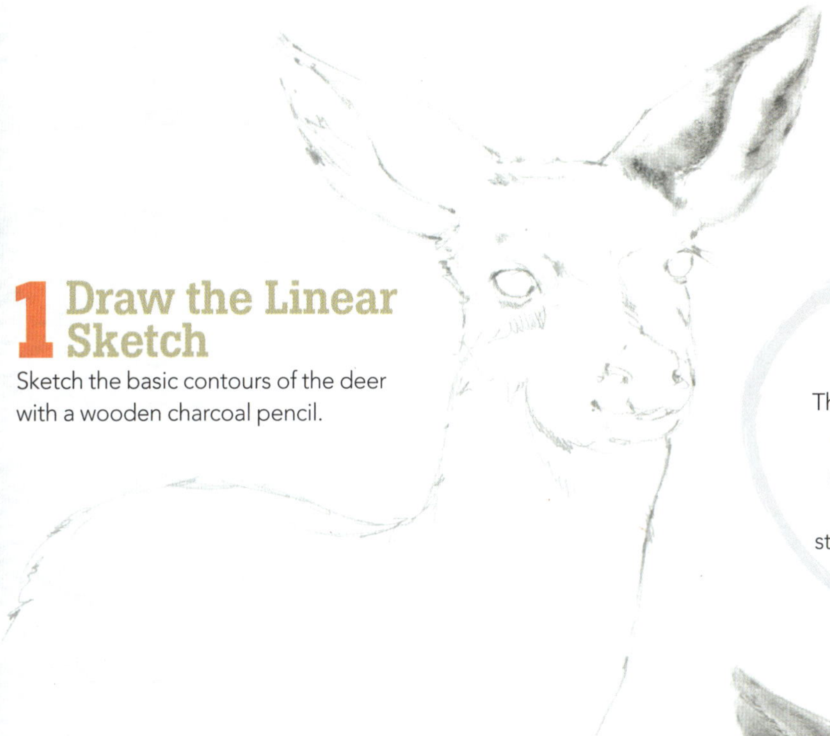

1 Draw the Linear Sketch

Sketch the basic contours of the deer with a wooden charcoal pencil.

MAKING THE GRADE

The charcoal pencils I use are not graded. Some manufacturers try to emulate the grading of graphite by calling their charcoal 2B or other such designations. There is no consistent standard, however, so you will likely have to buy a few and experiment with them.

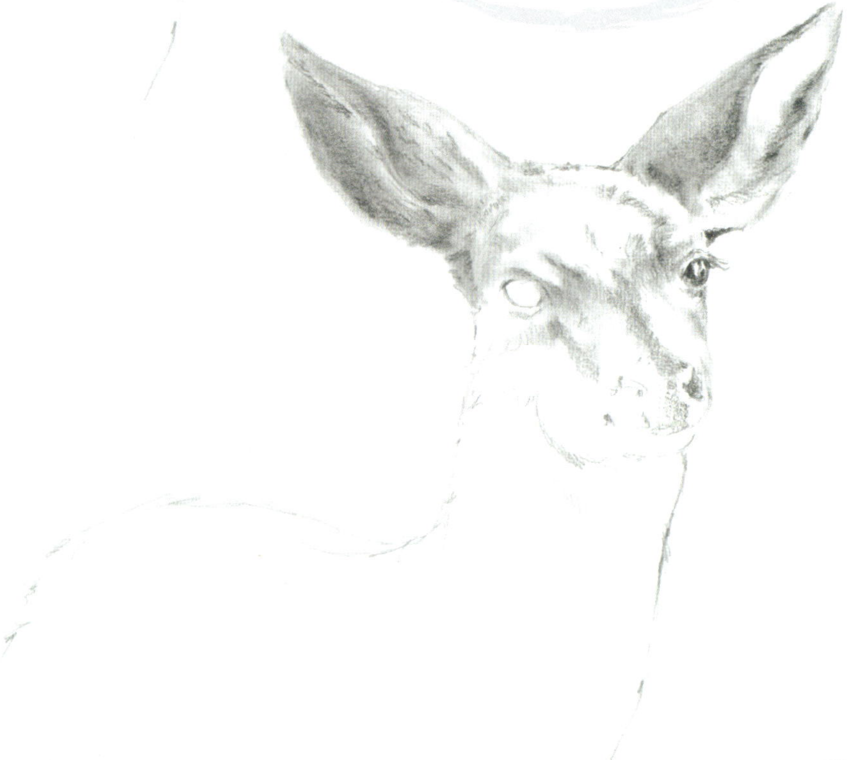

2 Build Texture

Alternate between drawing and smudging to build up dimension and soft texture. Place a paper towel under your hand to avoid unintentional smudging of the linework.

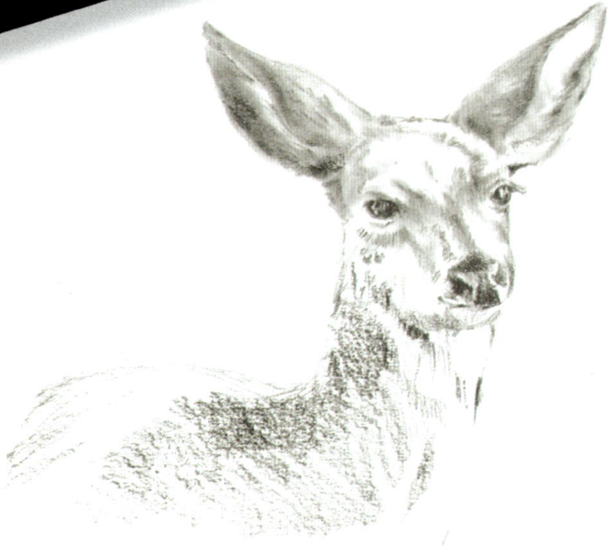

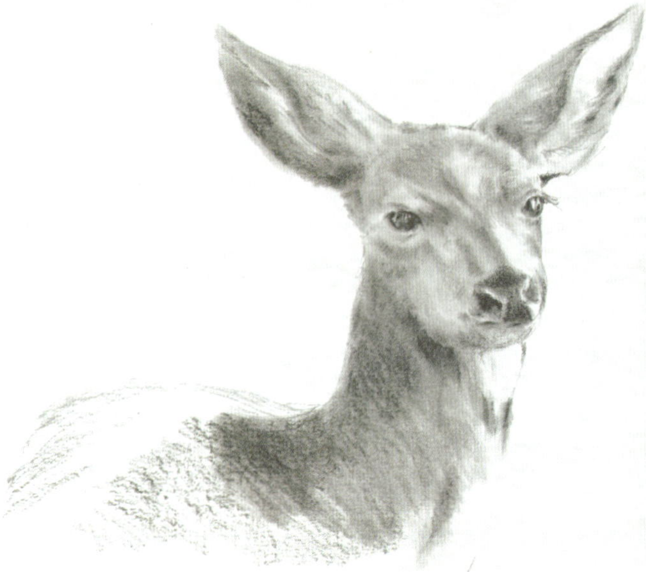

3 Begin Smudging Into the Light Areas

Apply the charcoal to the darkest part of the subject and smudge it into the light area with a paper stump. This is much easier going back and erasing to achieve the highlights later. (If absolutely necessary, erasing in a smudged area will lift a certain amount of charcoal, but you will soon see it is the least desirable option.)

4 Continue Blending

Continue blending with the paper stump, but do not attempt to eliminate all the evidence of drawing texture from the original application of charcoal. You want to clearly see the marks and lines as they mingle with the halftone blending.

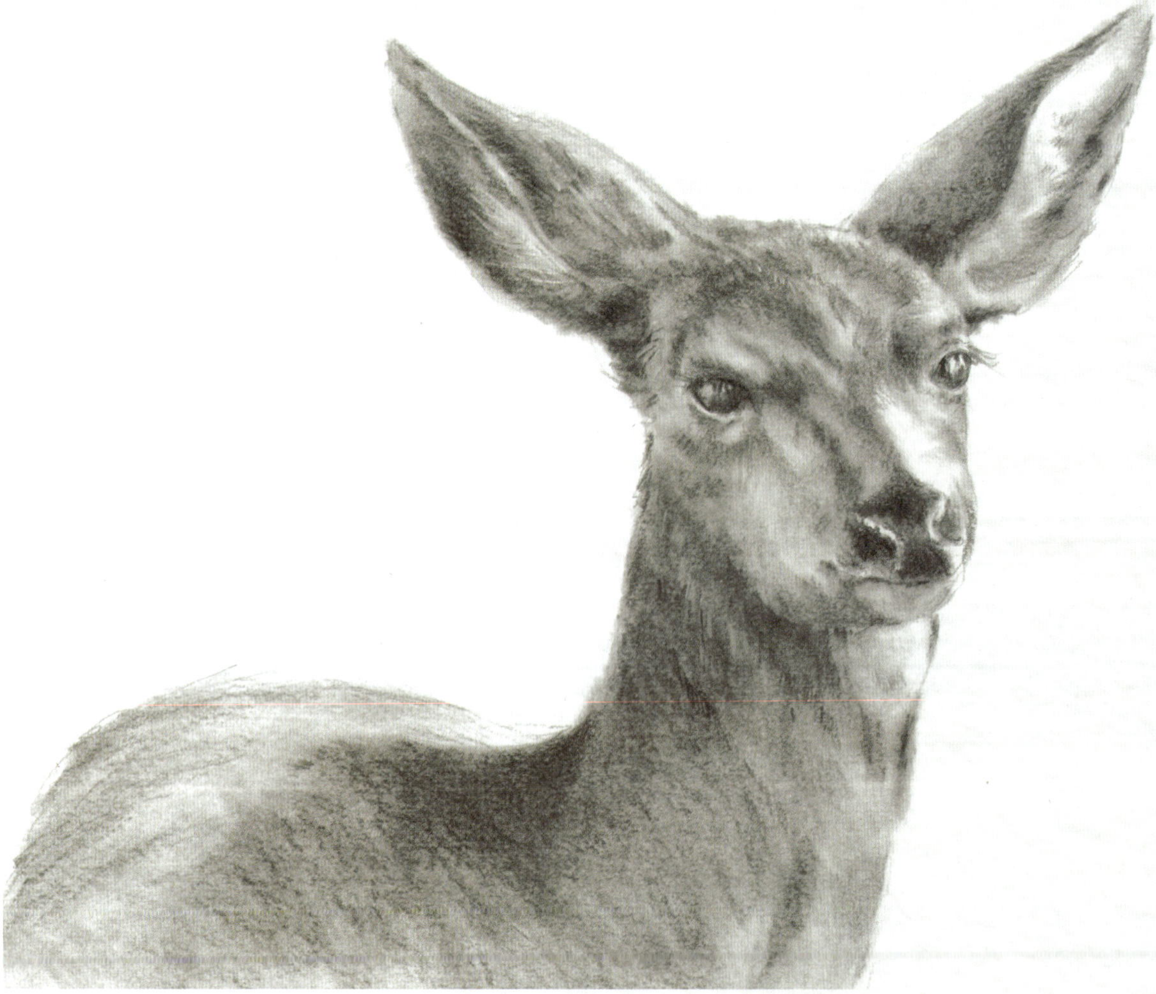

Wash Drawing

Wash drawings are a combination of graphite and watercolor. They are usually one color, creating a monochrome scheme. The pencil drawing can be completed to a reasonably finished product before the wash is applied, or it can be a rough sketch.

Drawings become something unique when the drawing tool switches to a brush. It is important to keep the tempo and feel of the drawing when making this changeover. Practice drawing with the brush as opposed to treating it like a paintbrush. The more you explore this, the more exiting the results become. You'll discover new marks and shapes, sometimes quite by accident, but usually through study and effort.

This begs the question, When does it become a painting rather than a drawing? Although I tend to think of the whole process as drawing whether I'm working with graphite, chalk or a paintbrush, I will concede it is fair to call it a painting when the original graphite work is no longer visible or a contributing factor.

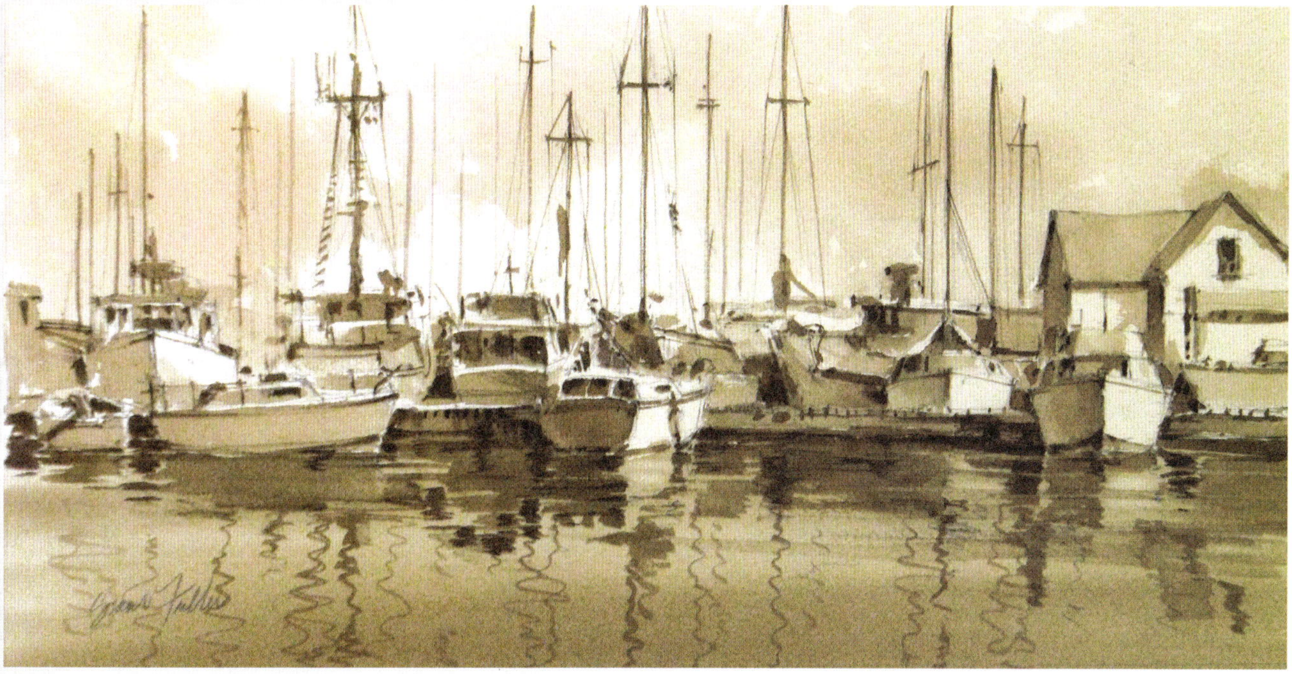

Many Factors Affect Stages of Completion

The nature of the subject and the amount of time available to do the work will likely affect your decision whether to leave it as a sketch or vignette, or complete the design as a piece worth framing. This piece was not done on location, but from a photograph. Consequently, I had more time to plan and finish it as a painting.

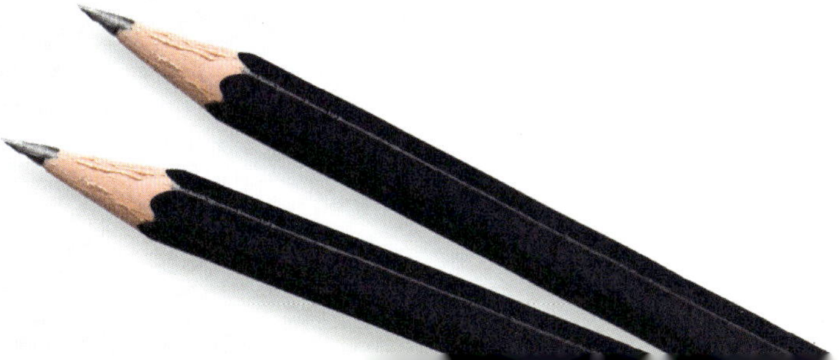

Wash Drawing

Mix and Apply a Wash

Wash drawings are often referred to as sepia drawings because traditionally the wash was made from sepia pigment. Any color can be used, however. I like to mix a combination of Burnt Sienna and Raw Umber so the brown is a bit more variable. Alternate pigments for this project would be Burnt Umber, Payne's Grey or Brown Madder.

MATERIALS

Surface
200-lb. (425gsm) rag watercolor paper

Brushes
no. 8 synthetic round

Graphite
HB mechanical or wooden pencil
Sepia Pigments
Burnt Sienna, Raw Umber

Other
blow dryer
scrap paper
water
white saucer

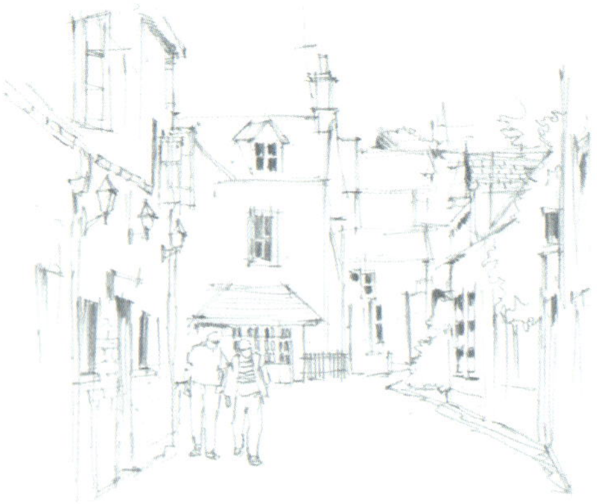

1 Sketch the Line Drawing

Sketch in your line drawing. Be sure to make the linework dark enough to be visible through the first wash.

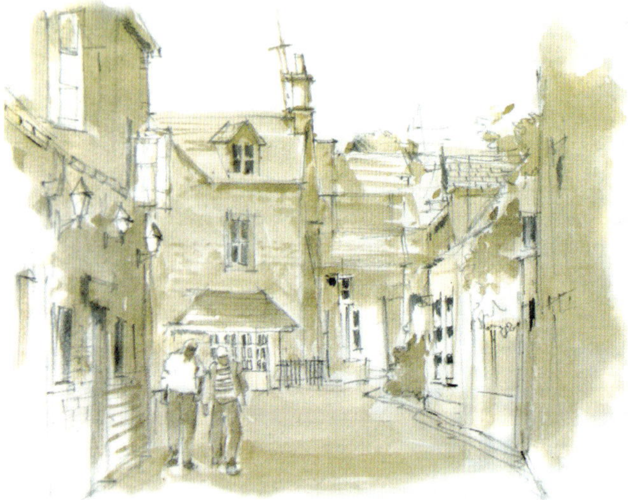

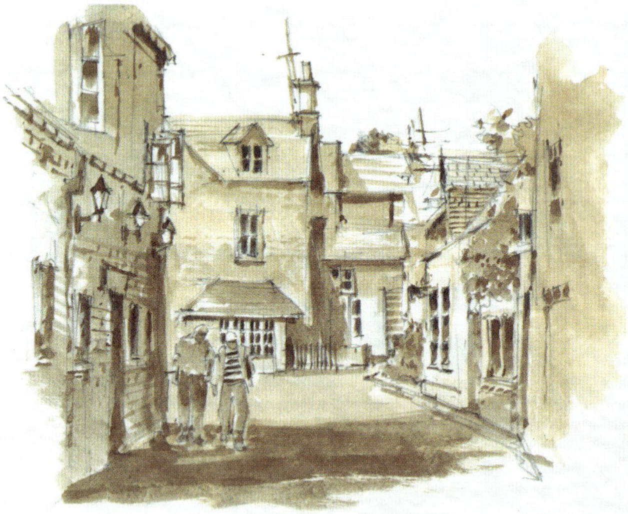

2 Mix and Apply the First Wash

In a small white saucer, combine Burnt Sienna, Raw Umber and water to mix up a wash. Test the strength of the pigment versus the water on a piece of scrap paper. Use a light value for the first wash (or glaze). Apply a broad wash, avoiding dark areas that have more graphite, like the windows. Paint those last when the paper is dry. A small amount of smudging is acceptable, but be careful to avoid damaging the lines with the brush.

3 Apply the Second and Third Washes

Make sure the paper is completely dry. A blow dryer is handy for speeding up the drying time. Add a second layer of the same wash to darken the image. The paint will bleed into the paper if it is still damp from the previous wash. When the paper is dry, the brushstroke will have a hard, sharp edge. It may take two or three glazes of the same wash to darken certain areas. Once it is dry, mix a more concentrated wash for the final dark bits, such as windows and doors.

Colored Pencils

When working with colored pencils, you will immediately notice the difference from graphite or any of the other mediums that we have explored. Colored pencils use a waxy pigment in the core of a wooden pencil. They are a dry, hard-edge medium, allowing you to jump around your work. There is no need to wait out drying times, and you don't have to worry about unintentionally smudging on contact.

The best way to get started with colored pencils is to get used to how they feel. Start drawing with just one pencil. Begin lightly, gradually adding more pressure to build up the dark tones. Notice how much pressure is required to fill the paper texture. Experiment with different sorts of paper to see which type you prefer.

STAY SHARP

I use a good electric pencil sharpener for this medium. The wax wears down fast and it would take forever to sharpen all the colors by hand or with a knife.

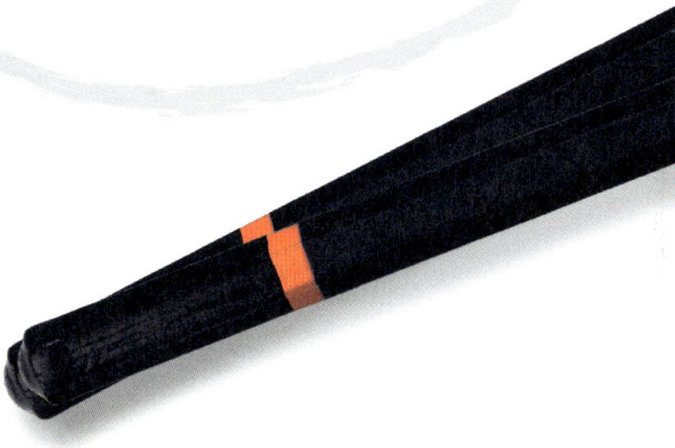

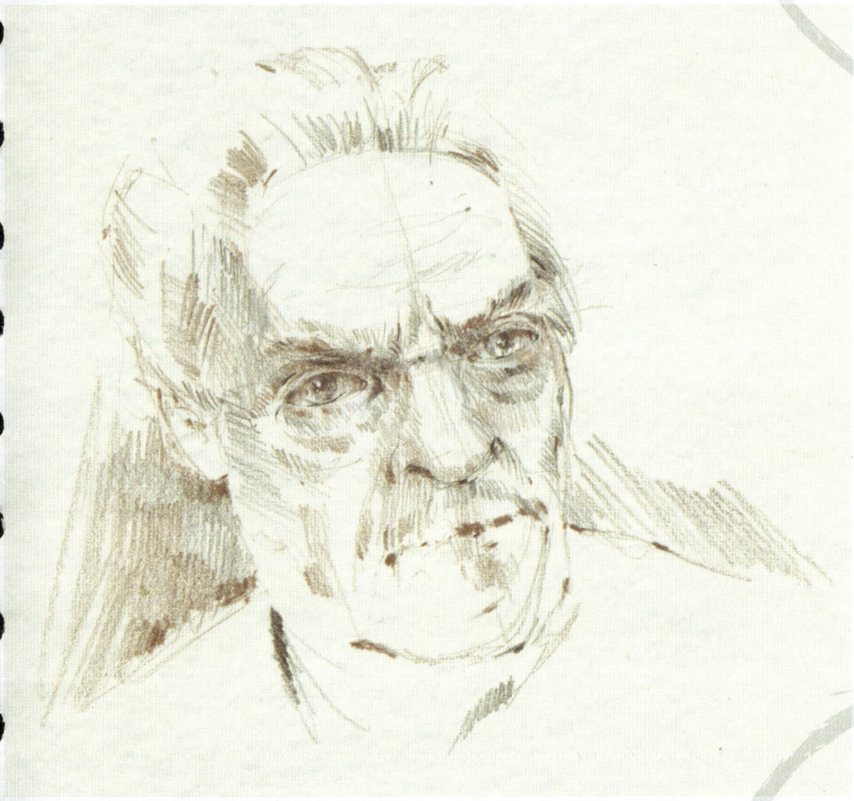

Self-Portrait

This self-portrait was rendered in dark brown pencil on off-white cartridge drawing paper. I blended a bit of white pencil into the brown to soften certain edges, but left it largely unfinished to show the building process. From this point, the drawing could be taken to whatever level of refinement I choose.

THE NAME GAME

Colored pencils are not always labelled with consistent names, and some may have no names at all. Ask your local art store to recommend a good quality brand of colored pencil.

Colored Pencil

Mix Colored Pencil Pigments

Let's get you mixing some color. Although I list specific color names in this series of steps, don't worry too much about using those exact colors. Anything similar will do. The purpose is simply to familiarize yourself with the behavior of this waxy medium. Because this wax does not dissolve in water or smudge easily, the preferred method for mixing colors is multi-layering.

MATERIALS

Surface
medium-texture illustration board
Colored pencil

Pigments
Burnt Sienna, Raw Sienna, White, Yellow Ochre

Other
electric pencil sharpener

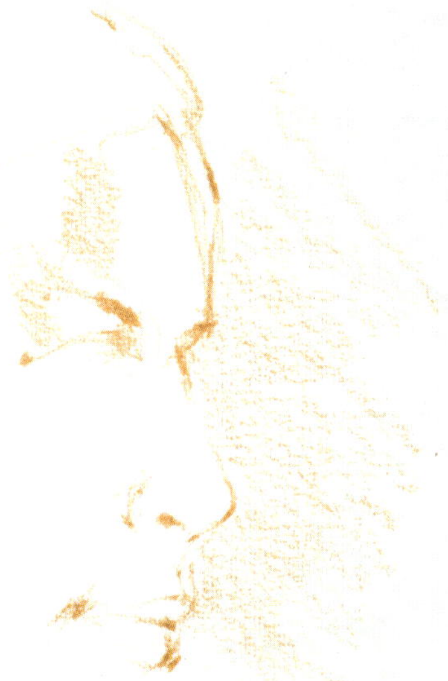

1 Sketch the Line Drawing

Start your line drawing with a Burnt Sienna pencil.

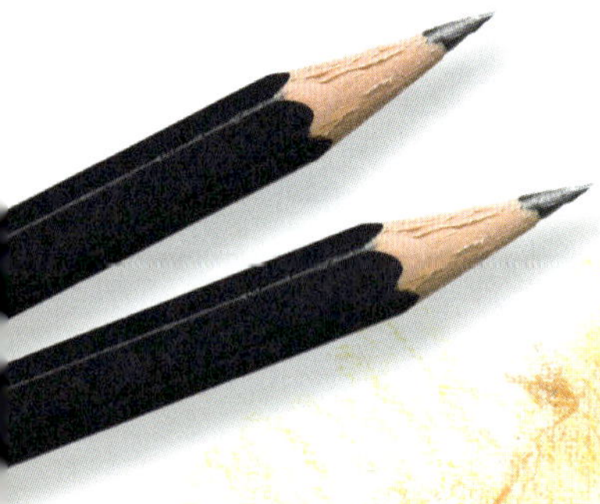

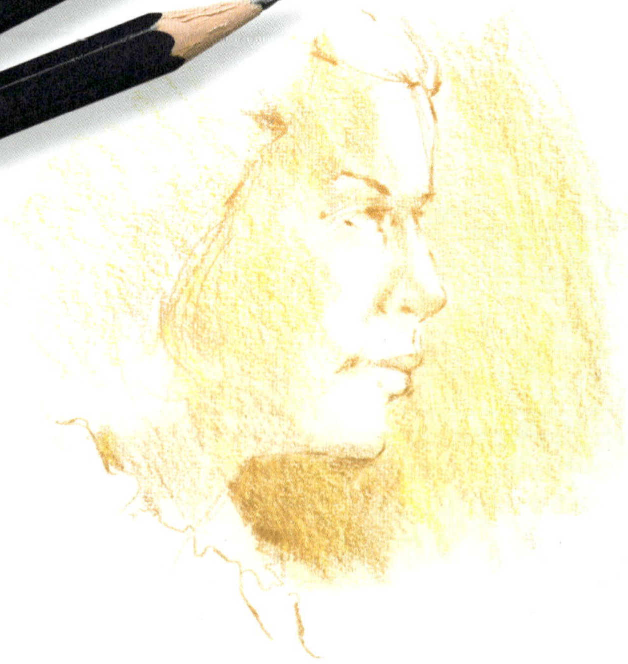

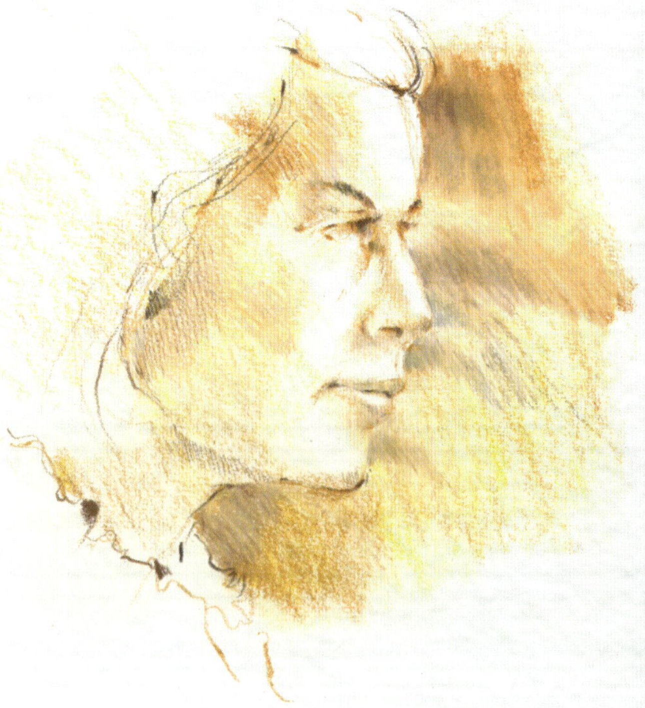

2 Add More Color

With a Raw Sienna pencil, press into the Burnt Sienna on the surface, causing the colors to mix. This can be done very lightly or very aggressively.

3 Continue Adding Color and Blend to Finish

Once you have enough pigment in an area, try putting a lighter color like Yellow Ochre over the darker colors. Blend it with a White pencil if you desire a softer blurry effect.

Colored Pencil

Draw Autumn Leaves

Now let's practice a more aggressive application of color using autumn leaves as the subject. The choice of color here is wide open. You'll want bright fall colors, so start with the obvious yellow, orange and red.

MATERIALS

Surface
medium-texture illustration board
Colored pencil

Pigments
black, blue, dark brown, green, medium brown, orange, red, yellow

Other
electric pencil sharpener

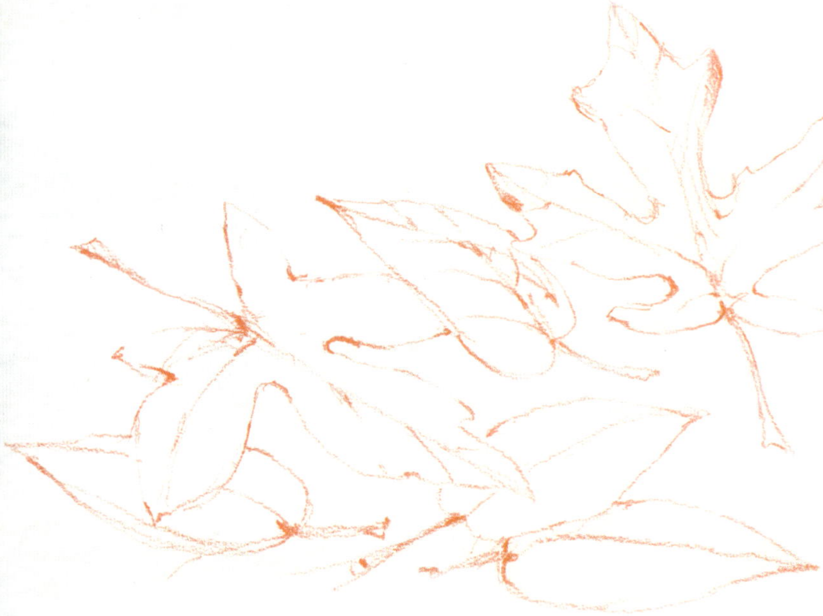

1 Sketch the Line Drawing

Sketch the contours with a neutral color. Any medium brown hue will work fine.

2 Add Color

Begin adding color, keeping the patches of pigment somewhat separate. Think about where you want the light and dark areas. Apply light and dark amounts of each color with the idea that you'll eventually layer other colors on top.

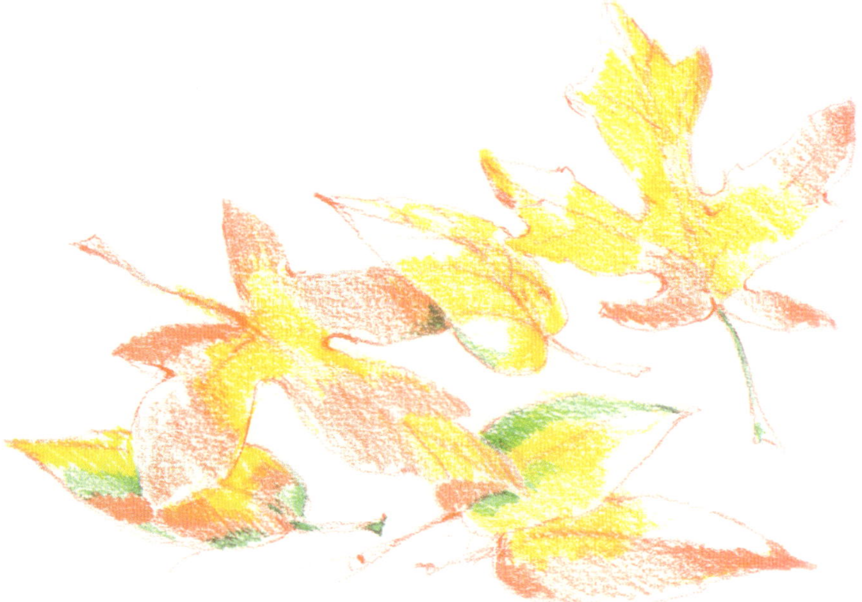

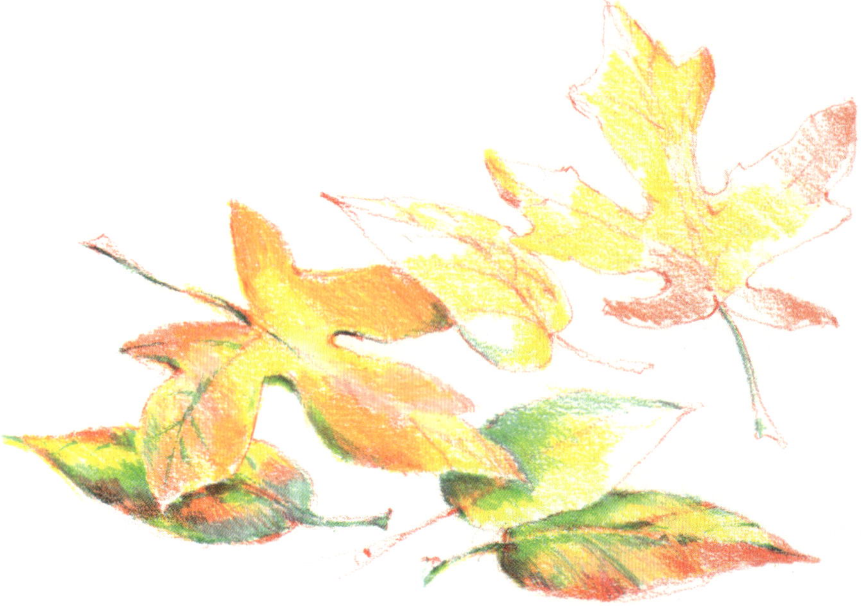

3 Play With Color Mixes

See what happens when you apply yellow over top of red. It usually requires a fair bit of pressure to get it to show, but it should mix right on the surface and begin to turn orange.

Add bits of green to suggest parts of the leaf that have not completely changed yet.

4 Continue Building Layers

As you continue building the layers, they'll begin to blend and the edges will become softer. The blending is not just with the color below but also with the adjacent colors, so the transitions become smoother.

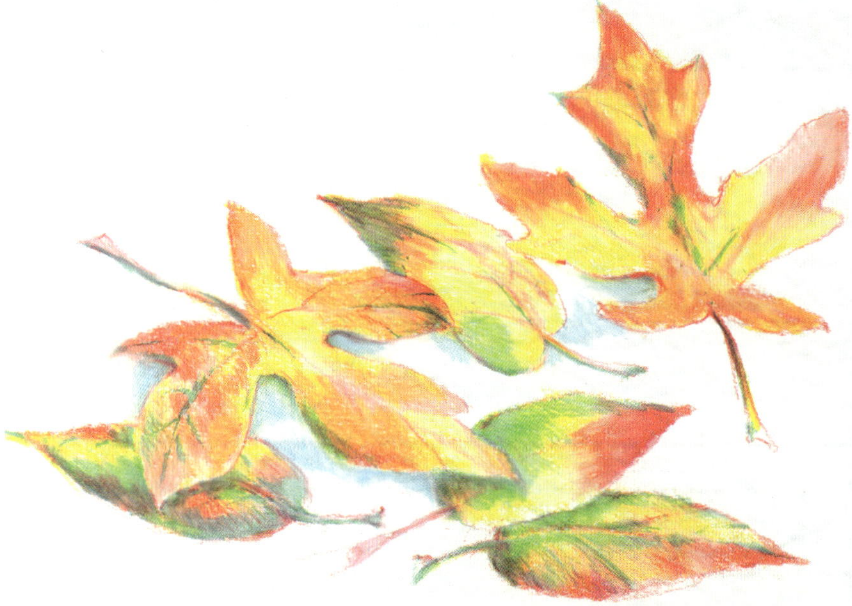

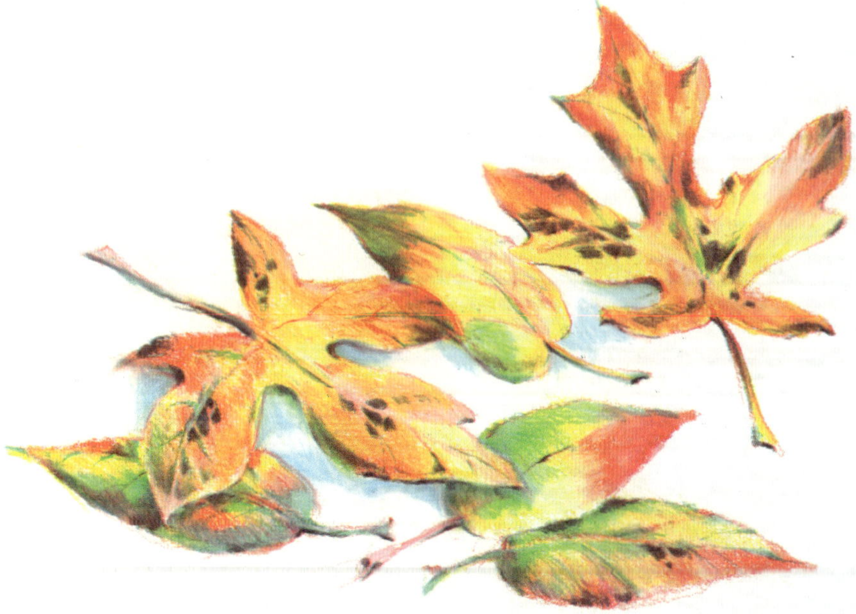

5 Add Final Tones

Add final dark tones with dark brown, green and black.

Colored Pencil

Draw Lily Pads

There are alternatives to working on a white surface. You can use colored paper or board such as pastel paper, or even acid-free mat board. Here I made my own by painting over illustration with watercolor and letting it dry thoroughly before starting the drawing. The gritty surface created from adding paint to the medium-textured board is interesting to work with.

MATERIALS

Surface
medium-texture illustration board
Colored Pencil

Pigments
black, blue, brown, green, orange, white, yellow
Watercolor
pigments
Burnt Umber

Other
electric pencil sharpener
water

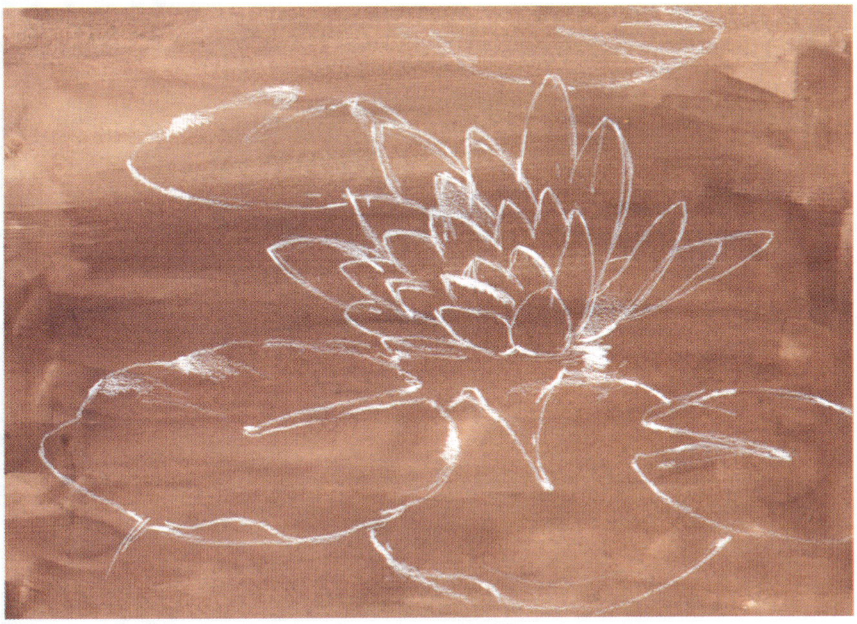

1 Apply the Wash and Sketch the Line Drawing

Apply a wash of Burnt Umber watercolor to the illustration board. Allow it to dry completely before proceeding. Sketch the line drawing in white pencil.

2 Rough In the Lily Pads

Start to rough in the lily pads with various shades of green, blue and even a bit of yellow. Mix the colors in some areas and leave them unmixed in others. It will make the drawing much more interesting if it is left to the viewer's eyes to mix the colors. So use green in the lily pads, but also use blue and yellow, the components of green.

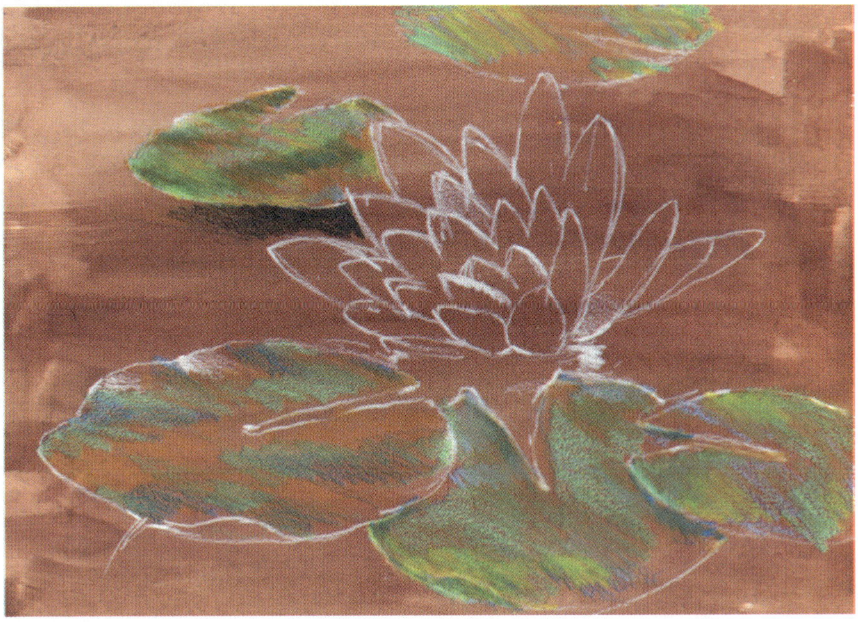

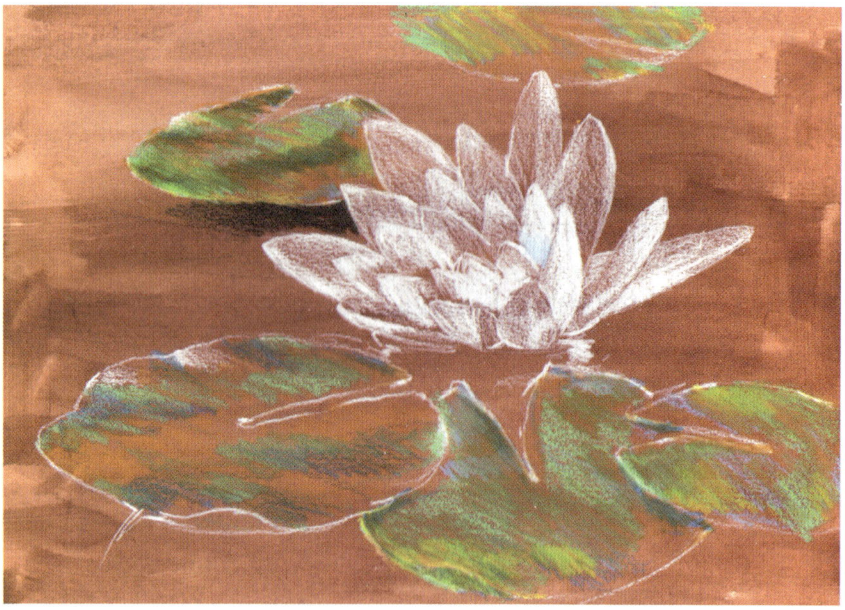

3 Fill In the Flower With Color

Apply the same color principle when working on the white flower. Start the flower with white and then suggest the shadow areas with a small amount of blue. White is made from a combination of all light waves, so bits of red, yellow and blue should all be evident in the final product.

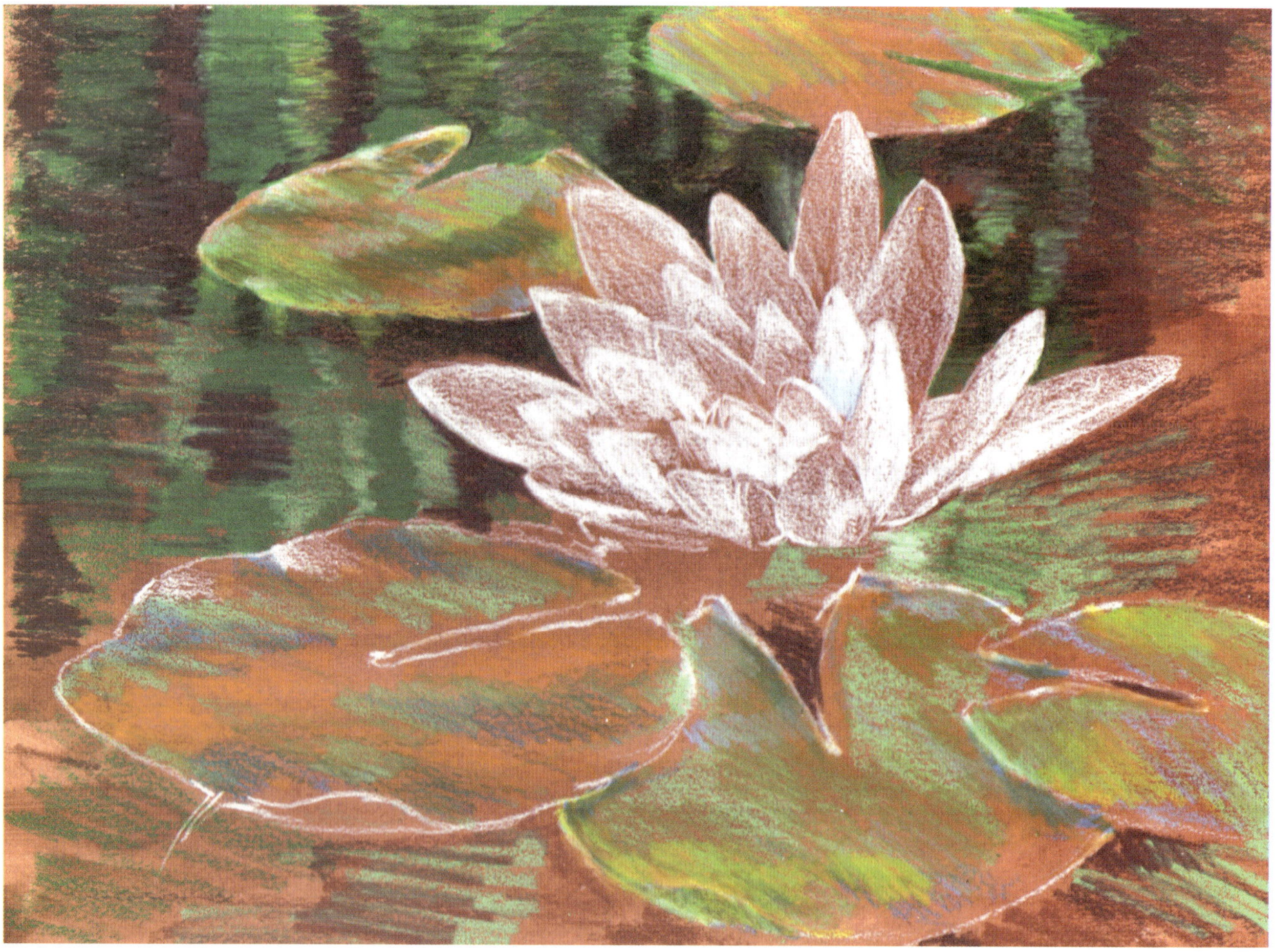

4 Develop the Background

Before going too far with detail on the flower, develop the background. Add in some black, but use it very sparingly. Black can have a tendency to kill color, and it works better with its surroundings if it has a bit of color personality. Work a bit of green and brown on top of the black. This will allow it to retain its dark value while helping it blend into the picture.

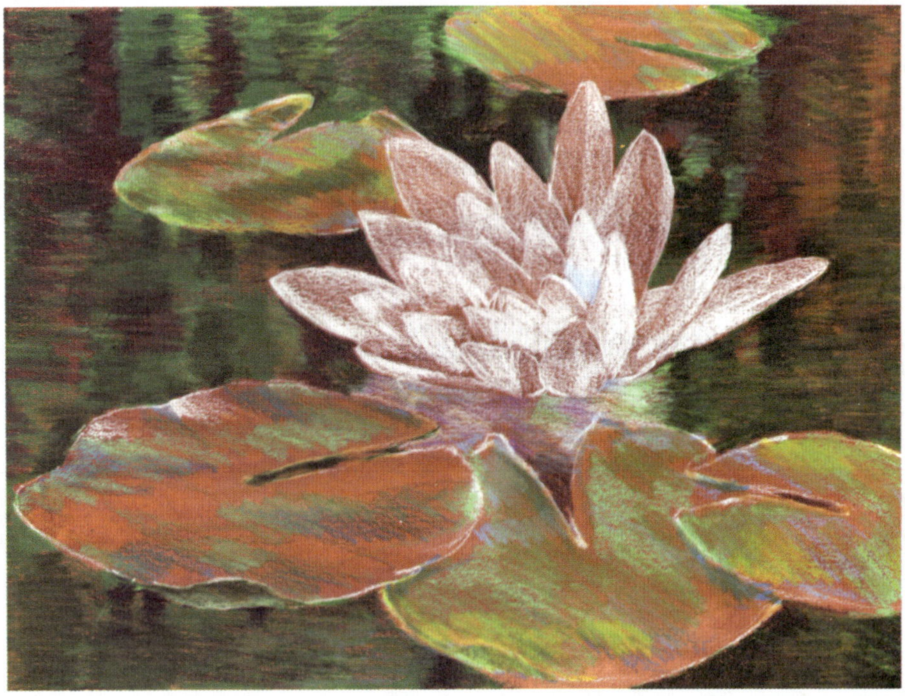

5 Add Reflections and Blend Colors

Reflections are usually darker than the objects they reflect, so add a bit of blue along with some orange to the white flower. This will neutralize the blue in its reflection. Blend the blue and orange with the white pencil, but do not over mix them or you'll end up with a muddy gray. All the colors in this piece should be slightly under mixed. It is all right to see the strokes of the pencils in the final work.

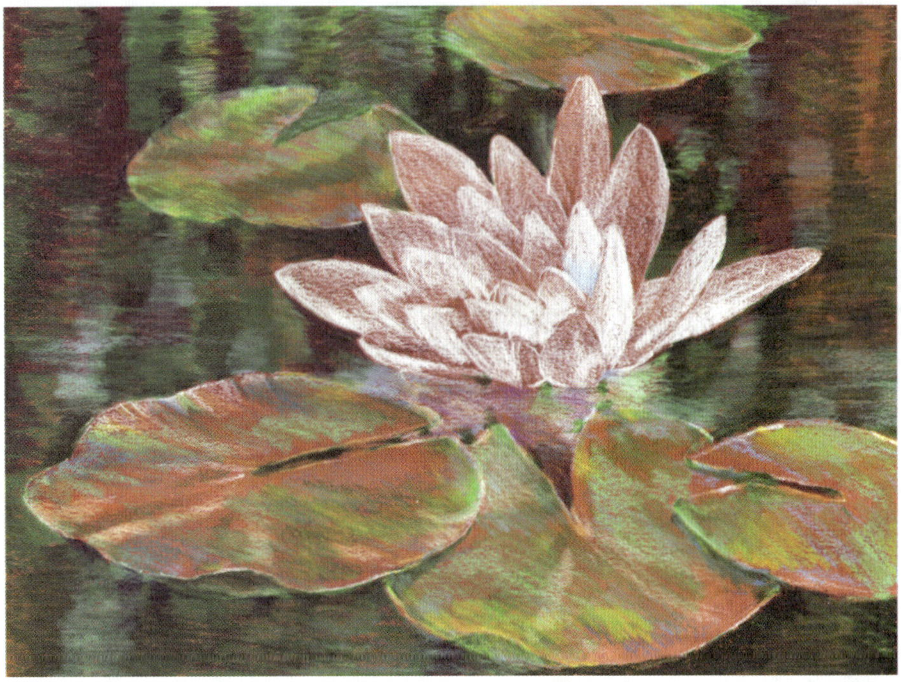

6 Refine the Lily Pads

A bit more work must be done on the lily pads to make them appear more flexible and not so flat and rigid. Add highlights and valleys. Lightly apply white pencil to areas of the lily pads, causing the surface to appear to bend upward. Darken the adjacent areas of the lily pads with green or a bit of blue, causing that part of the surface to appear lower, bending away from the light.

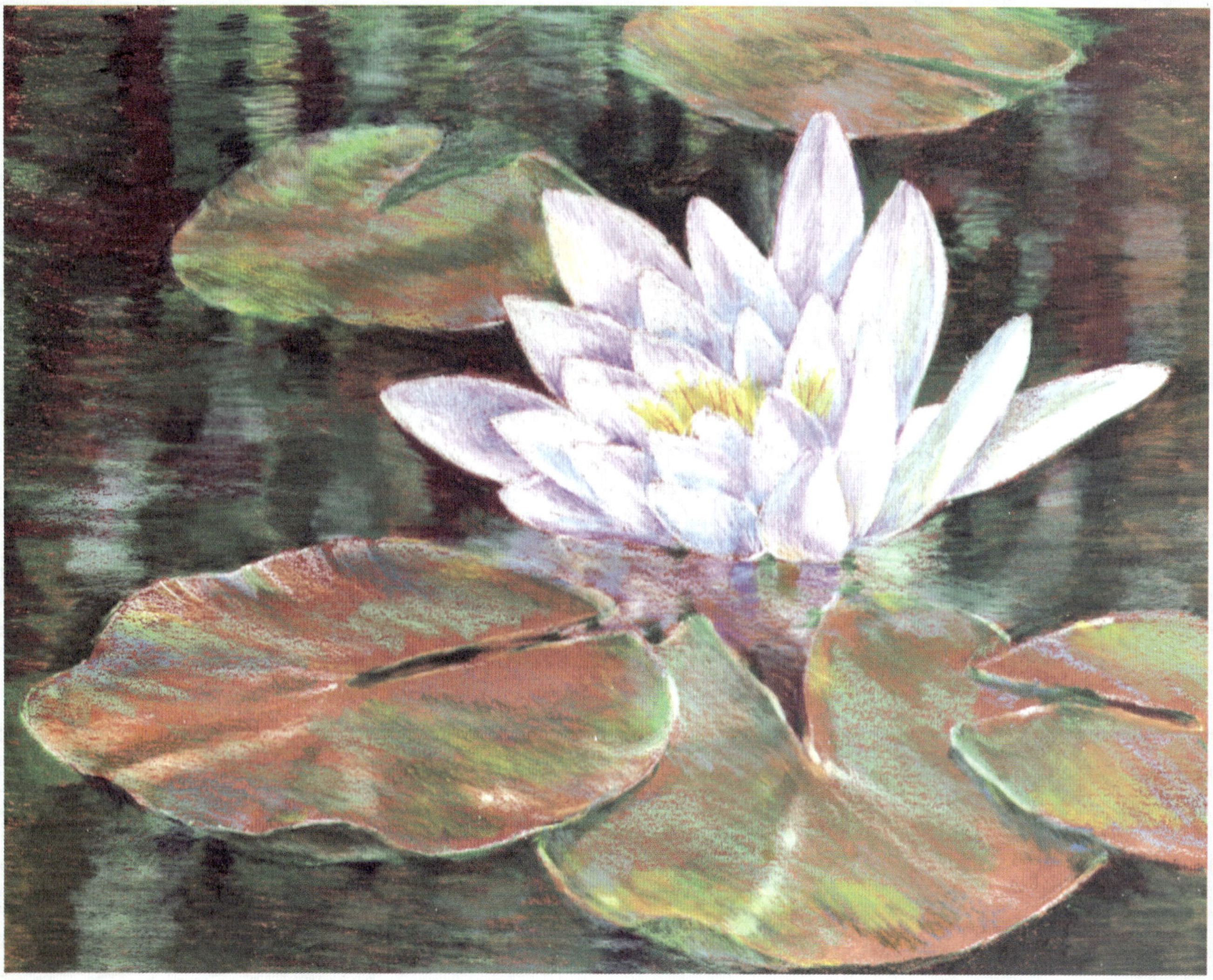

7 Add Finishing Details

Add some color on the shadow side of the flower petals to give them some dimension. Use a very light bit of orange in the shadow areas if the blue is too strong. You want the shadows to appear blue but not too blue. Add any other details you like to finish the piece.

Water Soluble

Wax Pastels

Water-soluble wax pastel is a fascinating medium. It is basically a water-soluble crayon. It feels exactly like a regular crayon when drawing, but if you wet it with a brush containing plain water, the wax dissolves. A bit of persistence with the brush is all it takes to remove nearly all the dry marks so there is no trace of the crayon line.

The wet brushwork does require some practice in order to get the desired effect, but you will soon see how a drawing can be transformed into a painting with this medium. It can be made to resemble pastel, oil or watercolor paint, depending on the amount of pigment applied and the nature of the brushwork.

Watercolor Pencils

Watercolor pencils are similar to wax pastels, but they are also distinct in a few ways. The core of the pencil is harder than a crayon and will sharpen to a fine point. This means it can be used to draw detailed subjects. It does not flow as easily, so it should be worked more with the brush to encourage blending. Like wax pastels, watercolor pencil pigments change when wet, though not in the same way. So try a few test samples on scrap paper before embarking on the real thing.

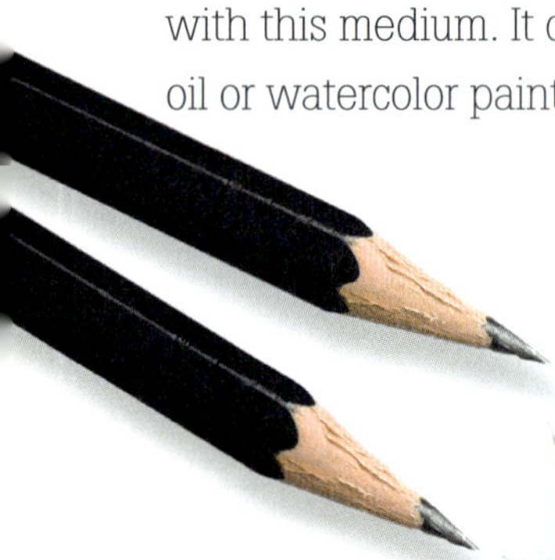

QUALITY IS KEY

When working with water-soluble media, use artist-quality pigments that retain a good resistance to fading. Also be sure to use good watercolor paper or illustration board because regular paper will not hold water.

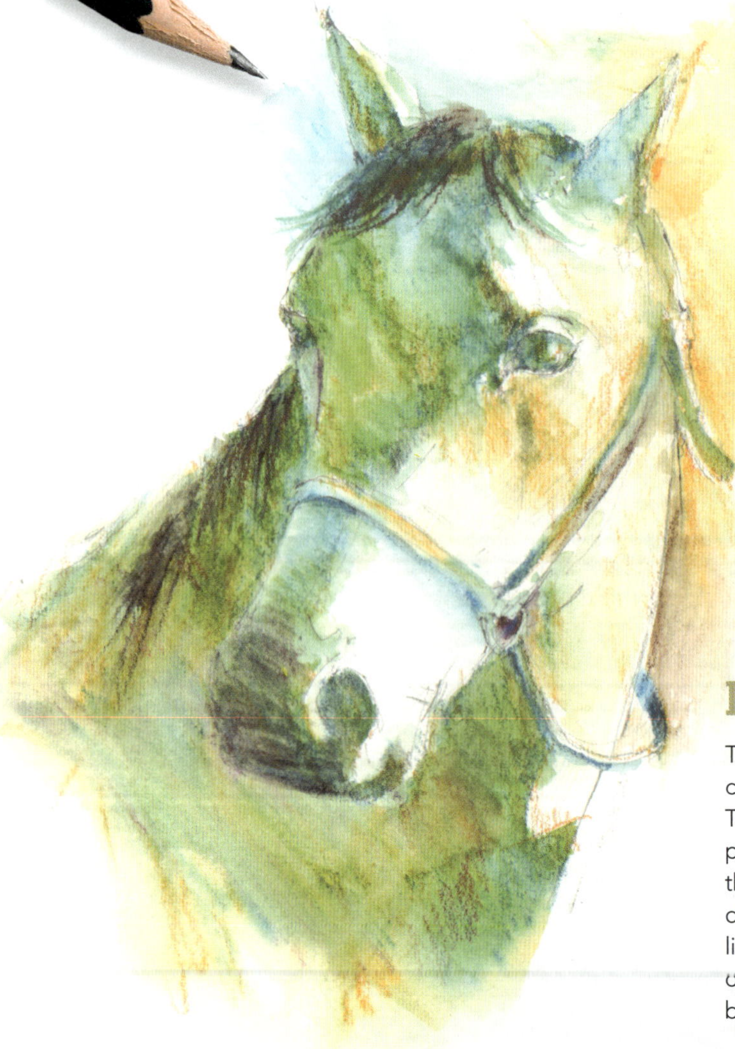

Is It a Drawing or a Painting?

This piece was sketched with a graphite pencil because pastel crayons do not have a high degree of precision for linework. The wax wears down quickly, so it is not easy to keep a sharp point. The color was filled in using the side of the crayon. When the water was applied, the pigment moved so willingly that the drawing took on a very relaxed quality and really became more like a painting. Most of the dry marks have dissolved, but some of the original graphite is still showing. It blends well enough to become part of the work.

Wax Pastels

Create Bold Sunflowers

The goal for this project is simply to explore how bold you can get with wax pastels. Have fun with it!

MATERIALS

Surface
medium-texture illustration board

Graphite
HB wooden pencil
no. 8 round
black, brown, dark brown, green, orange, yellow

Other
blow dryer
water

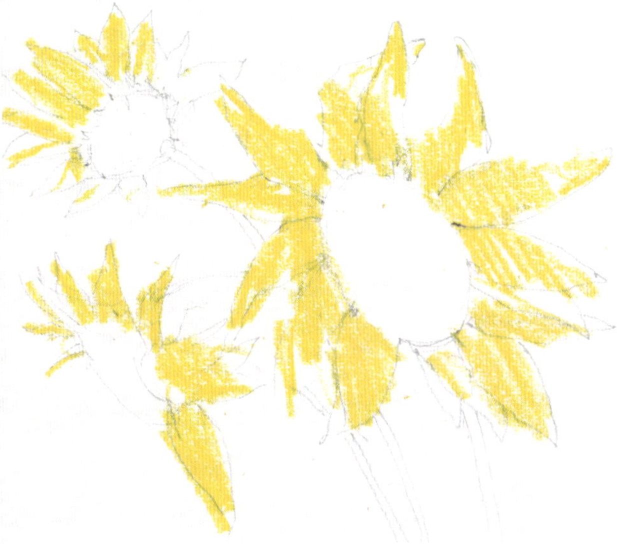

1 Sketch the Line Drawing and Begin Applying Color

Sketch the flowers with an HB pencil, taking care to keep the lines light so that they do not interfere with the color later on. Once your line drawing is complete, aggressively apply yellow to the petals.

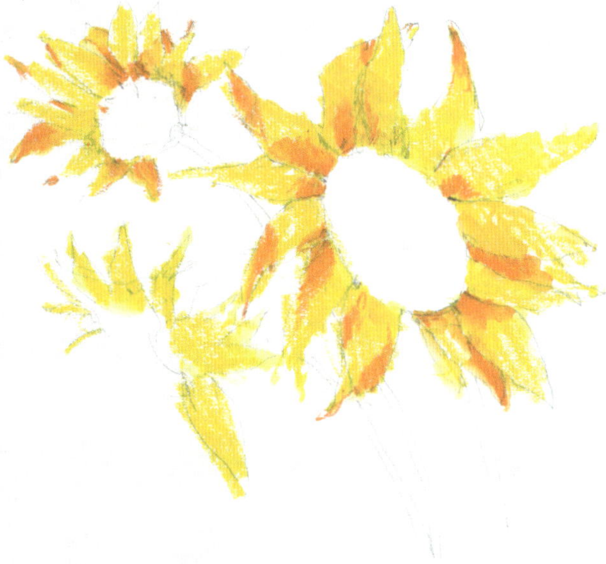

2 Add Shadows

Use orange to add shadow to the petals, as it seems to work best as a shadow color for yellow. High realism is not the main goal here though, so feel free to take some liberties with color if you wish.

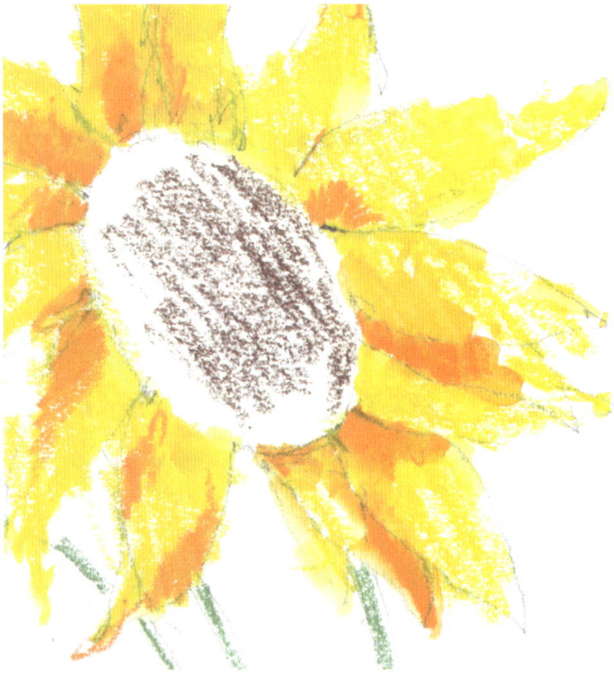

3 Continue Building Color

Hold off from applying water at this point and just focus on building up the pigment. Use dark brown for the centers of the sunflowers and green for the stems. These will be mixed with other colors later.

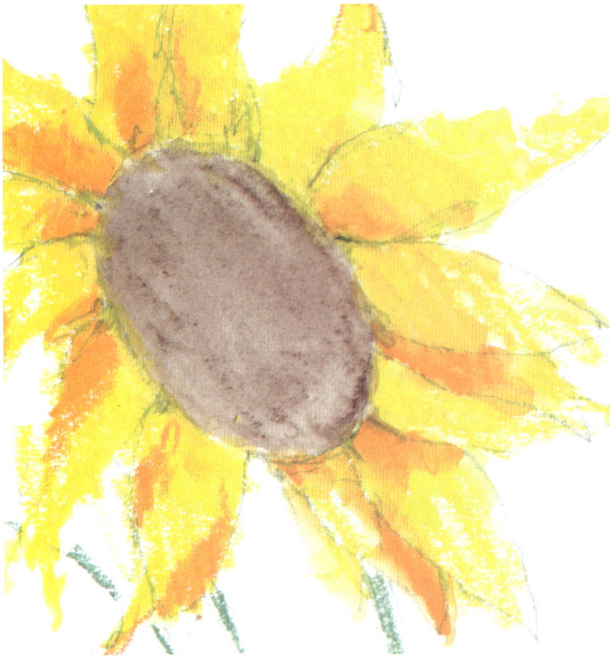

4 Test Water Application and Begin Blending Colors

Use a no. 8 round to apply a small amount of water to the center of the large flower in order to test how dark it will become. Wax pastel pigments change when wet, and each one behaves differently. Some fade and spread delicately while others become much more intense. Trial and error is the only method available.

Start with a small amount of water and add more to the pigment bit by bit until you get the value where you want it. Use your wet brush to lightly blend the color in the petals, but not so much that you remove the texture.

5 Develop the Background

Start with black and apply other colors such as brown and green on top to lighten it up as needed. (Plain black in color pieces can sometimes be too attention-getting.)

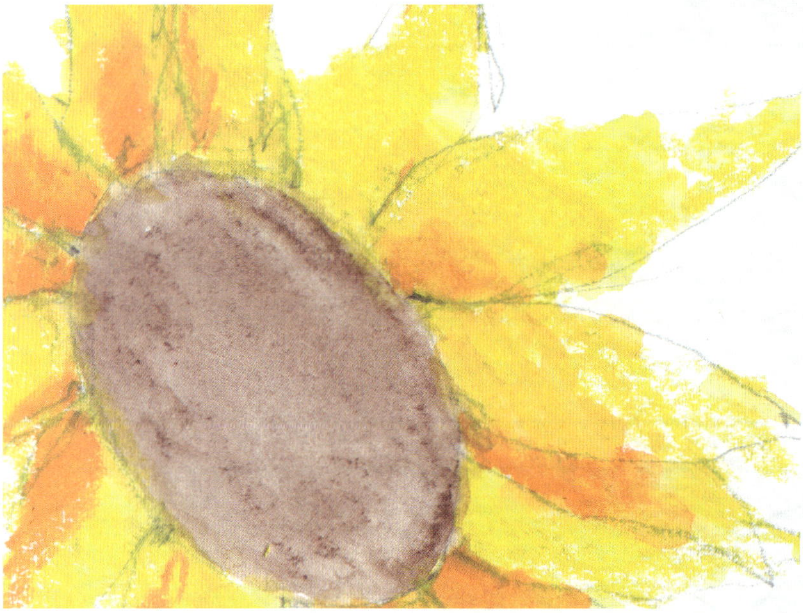

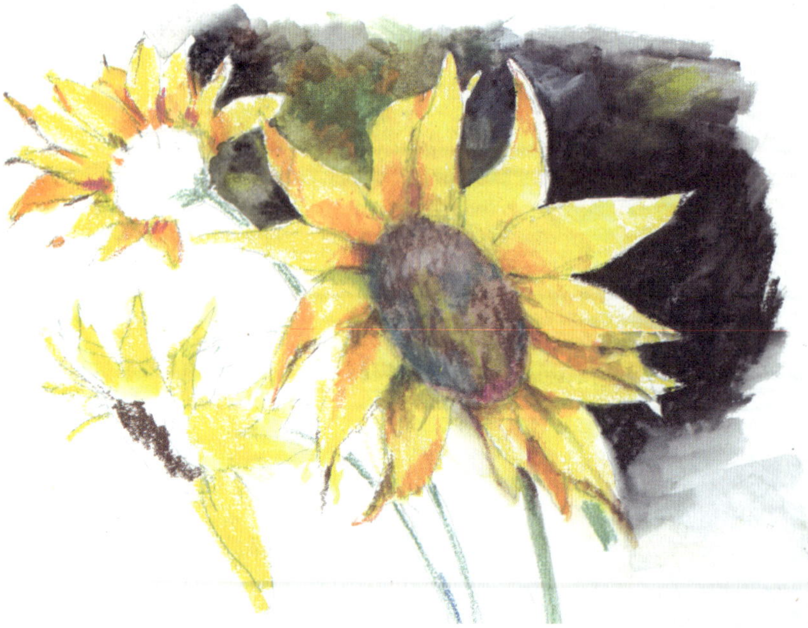

6 Blend the Background

Wet the pigment to dissolve it and let the paper dry. Continue to alternate applying with the wax pastel and spreading with the wet brush. This method is necessary to know how much pigment needs to be added in order to cover the area. Experiment to see what happens when the wax pastel goes on wet paper. It results in a different effect, but usually too much pigment is deposited. It is easier to control on dry paper and blend with the wet brush.

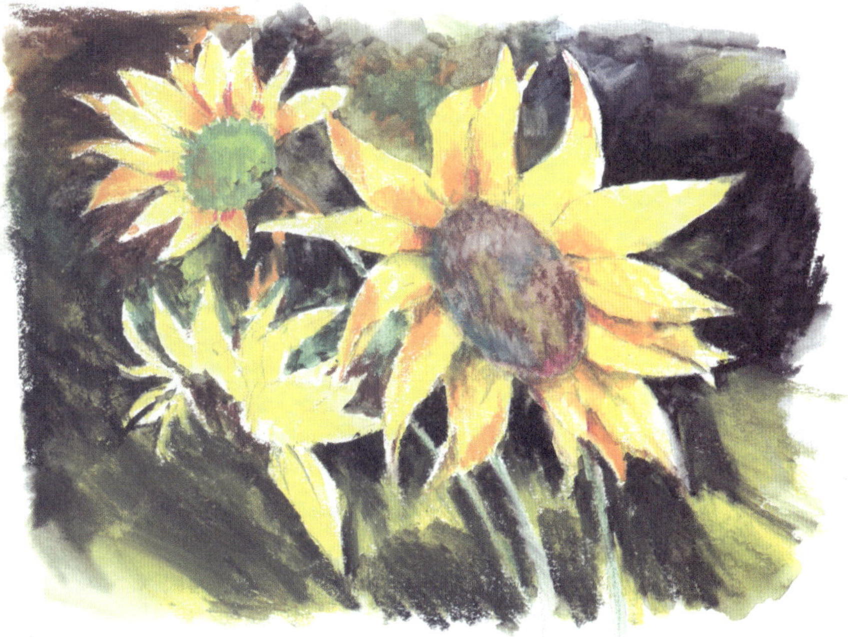

7 Add Finishing Details

Once the background has been blended and the colors of the subject are well established, add lighter values on top of the darks. This gives dimension to the background and offers a chance to blend some of the harsh edges. Do not apply too much water at this stage for fear of washing away your hard work. Get used to alternating between applying pigment with the wax pastel, then blending it with a wet or damp brush. You can choose to leave some of the pastel marks untouched and others well blended.

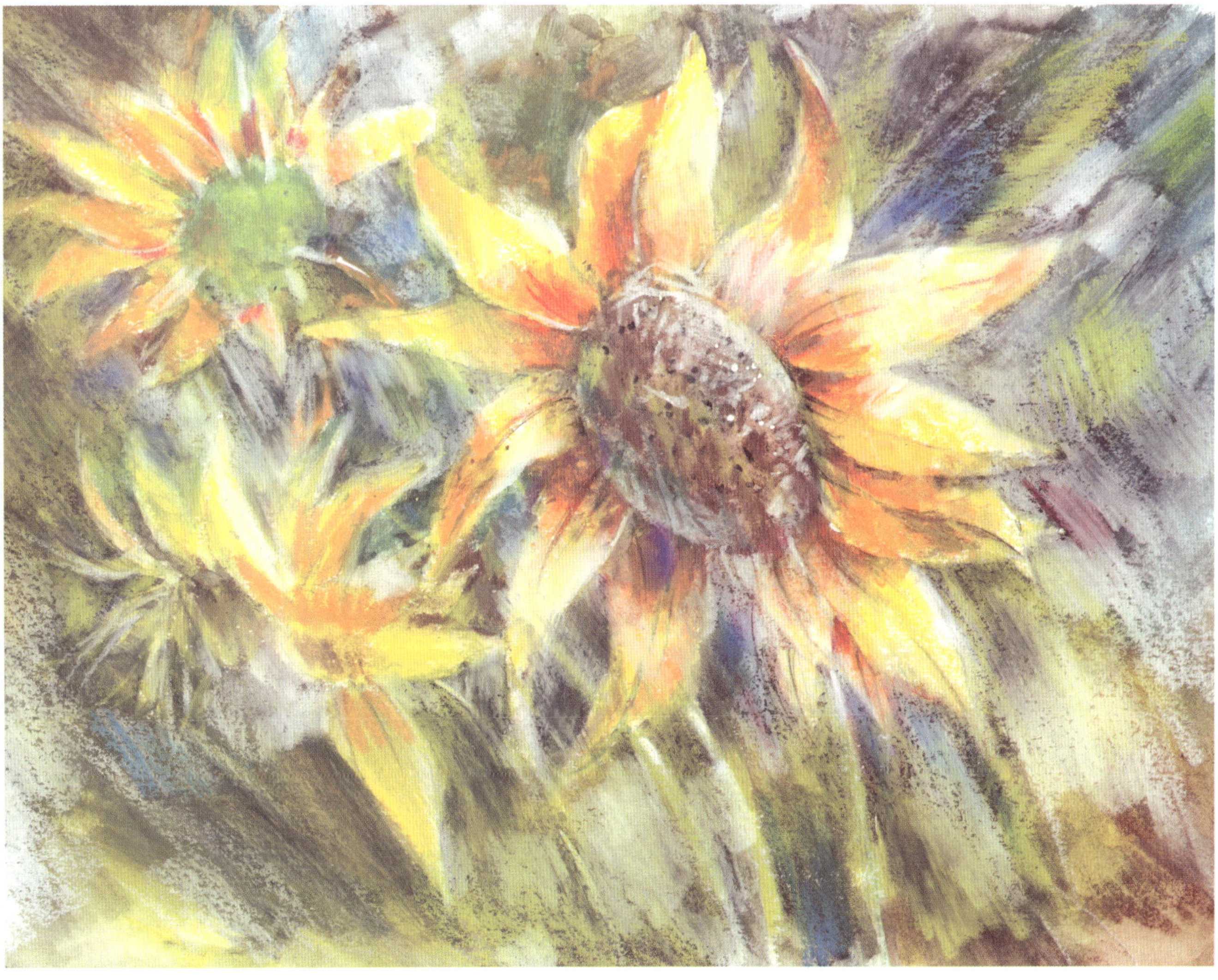

Wax Pastels

Get Watercolor Effects With Wax Pastels

Now let's practice using wax pastel to achieve the look of a watercolor painting.

MATERIALS

Surface
medium-texture illustration board

Graphite
HB wooden pencil
no. 8 round
blue, brown, green, orange, red, violet, yellow

Other
blow dryer
water

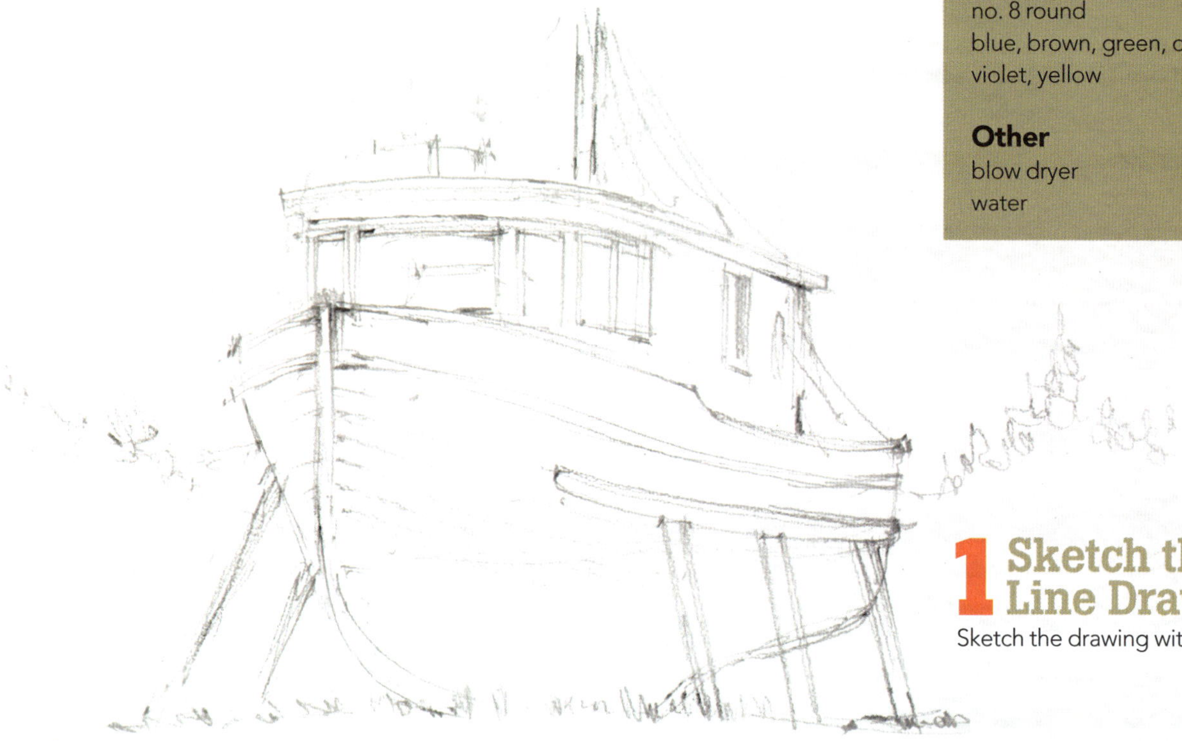

1 Sketch the Line Drawing

Sketch the drawing with an HB pencil.

2 Add Color

Add a light application of the various colors that will make up the objects. Fill in blue for the sky, and yellow, green and a bit of blue for the shrubs in the background.

Use a very light dusting of red or orange on the shadow side of the boat. Add some blue on top of that. This will give you a gray that will end up slightly on the purple side after the water is added later. Use brown and violet to make the dark color in the windows (avoid black).

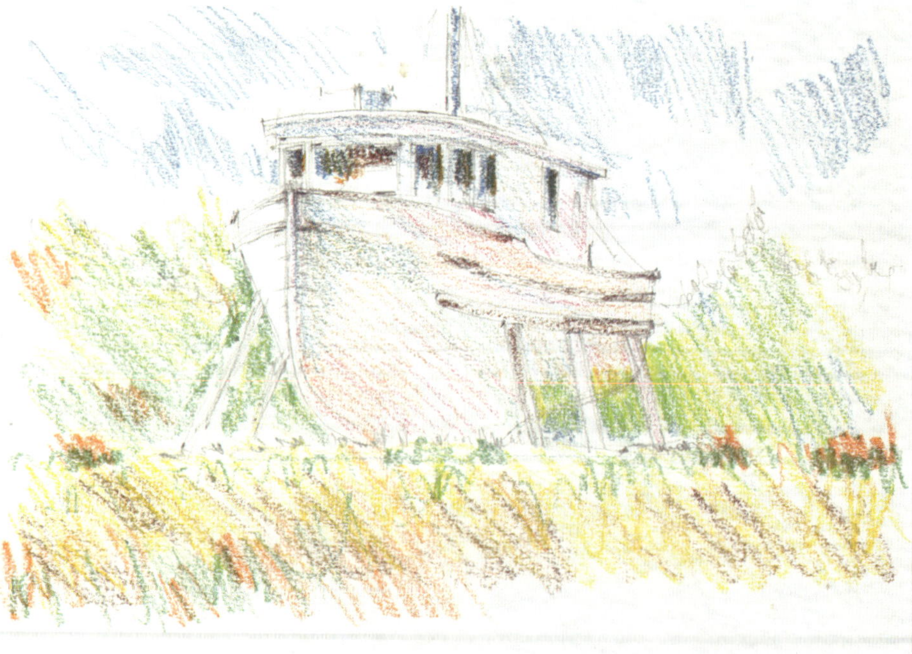

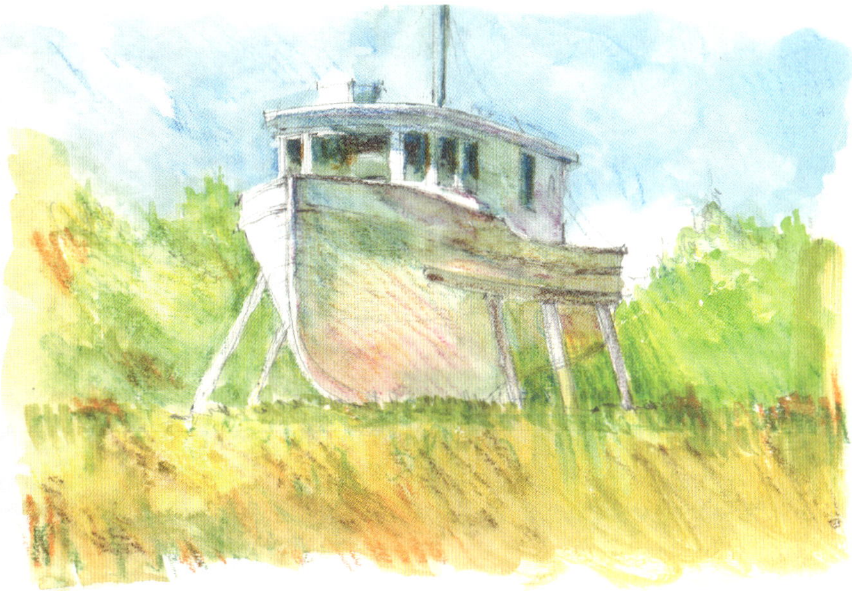

3 Apply Water

With a wet no. 8 round, gently dampen the wax and push it around a bit. If you find that you do not have enough color, allow the paper to dry, and then add more pigment.

AN ARSENAL OF BRUSHES

Sometimes you may need to use a flat watercolor brush or even an oil-painting bristle brush to blend the marks left by wax pastels.

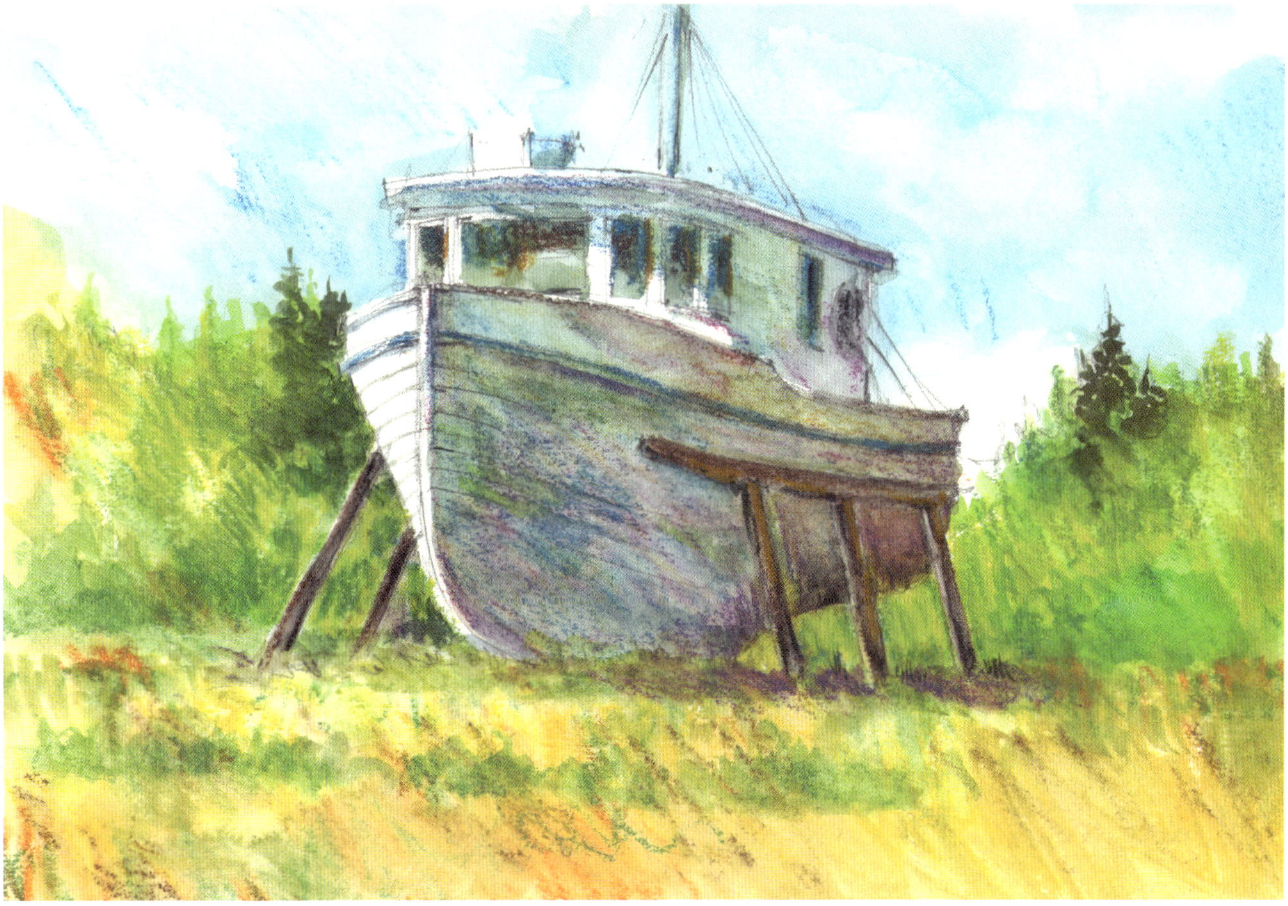

Watercolor Pencils

Create Painted China and Reflective Glass

Let's explore some of the effects that can be achieved with watercolor pencils. Follow along to create the look of reflective glass.

MATERIALS

Surface
medium-texture illustration board

Graphite
HB wooden pencil
no. 8 round
blue, brown, green, orange, red, violet

Other
blow dryer
tissue
water

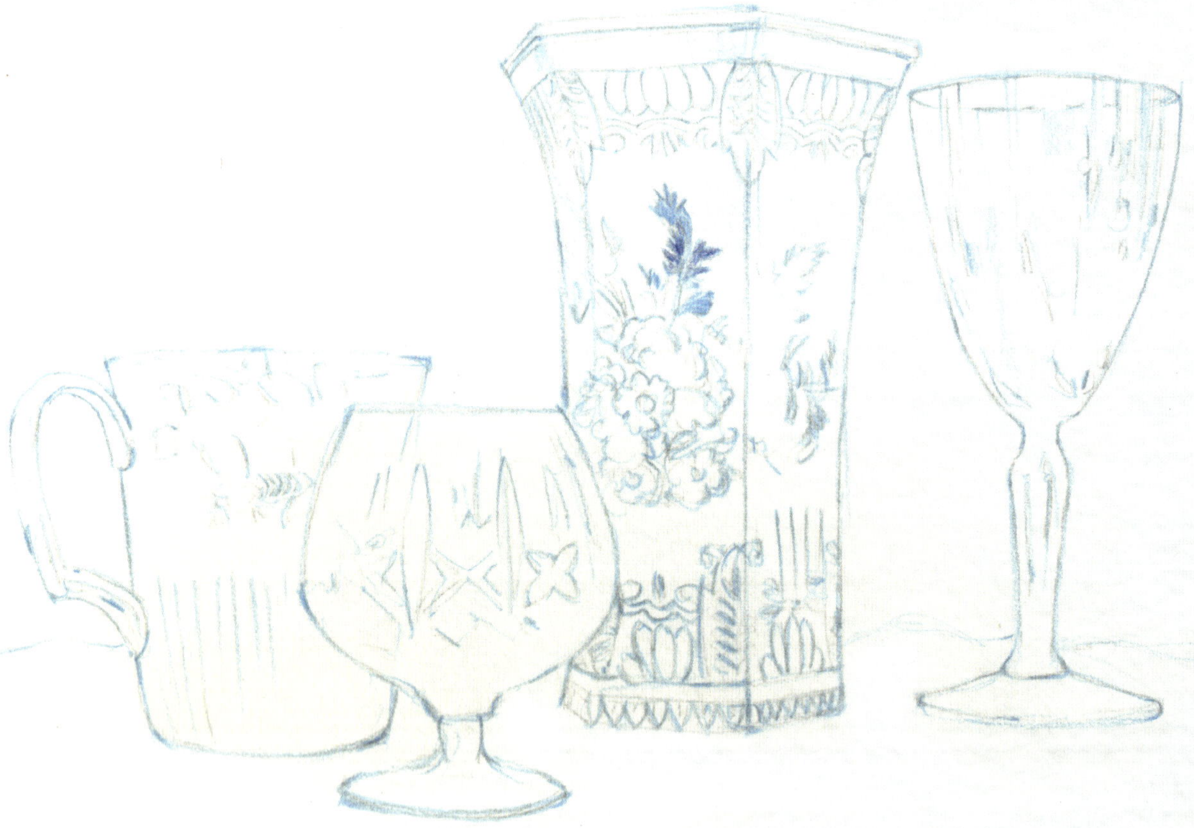

1 Sketch the Line Drawing

Sketch the line drawing with an HB wooden pencil. Go over the lines in blue watercolor pencil to reinforce the initial drawing. This can be lifted, but not easily erased.

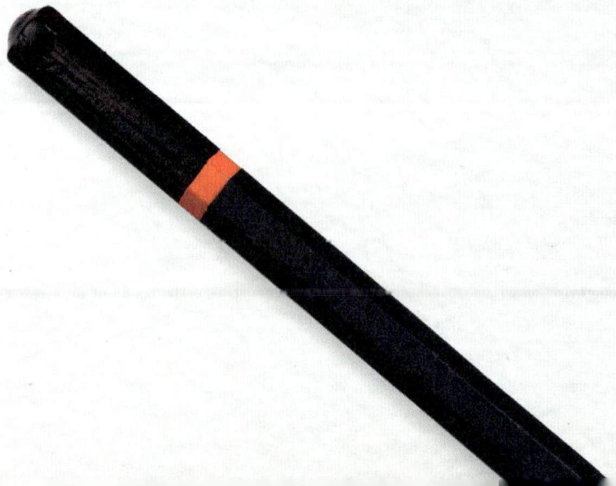

2 Add Color and Shadows

Fill in the painted designs of the pitcher and vase with color. Use a blue and orange complement for the shadow side of the figures. It's fine if the shadow goes a bit violet. This will happen if the orange is slightly red, or you intentionally put red in the shadow.

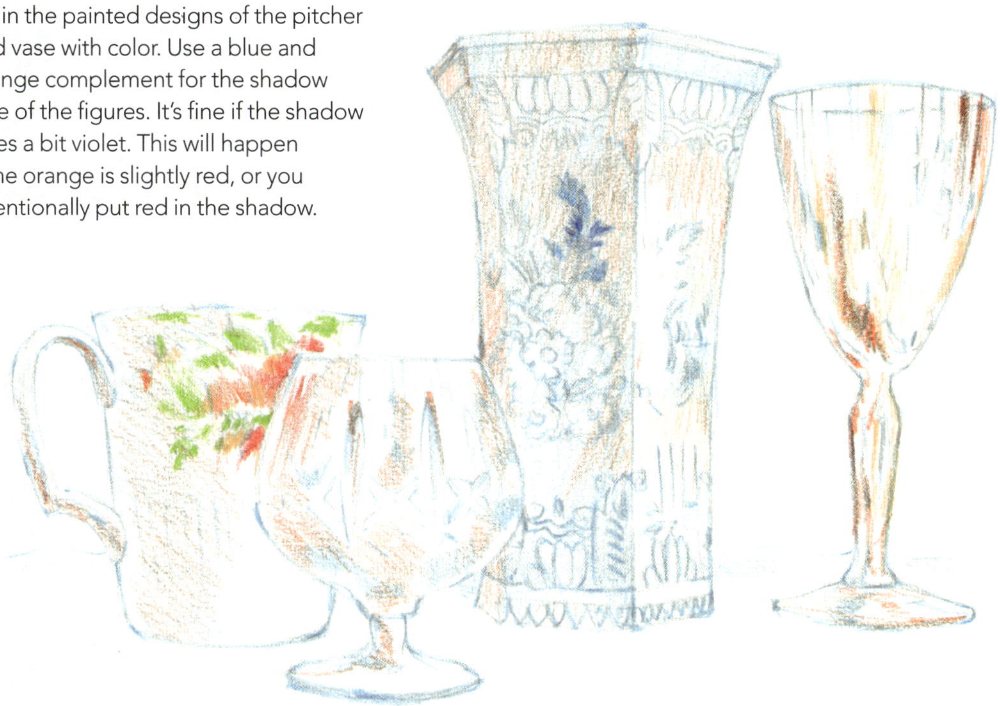

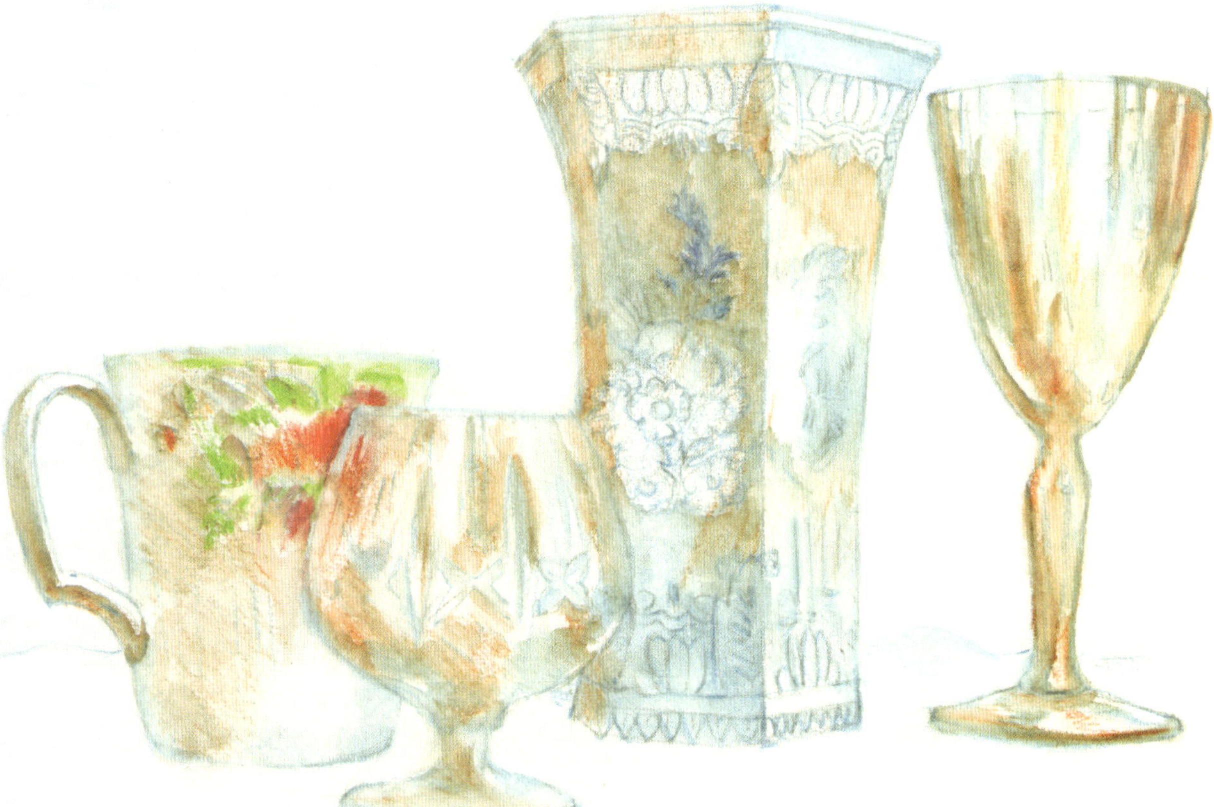

3 Apply Water

Apply the first coat of water with a no. 8 round. This example shows that there was too much red and brown for the effect I had wanted. If that happens, you can still blend the shapes. Just keep in mind that you will need to change the color later. The color is so much pure chance at this stage, so don't panic if you get a different result than you initially intended.

4 Adjust the Color

Use the no. 8 round to wet the areas of color you wish to change. Keep it small, about 1" (2.5cm) at a time, and quickly blot it with a tissue. This will mop up some of the pigment. Progress to the next area and do the same until the entire area has been lightened. Allow it to dry completely. Use the watercolor pencil of your choice (in this case I used blue) to add pigment to the desired area. Wet the area again with the brush and blend in the new color.

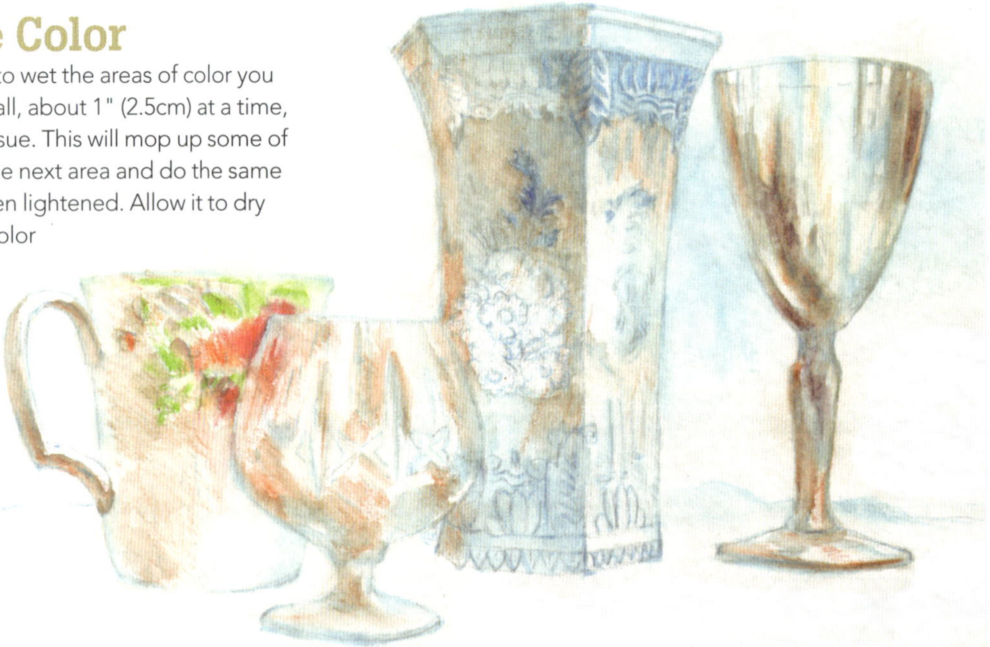

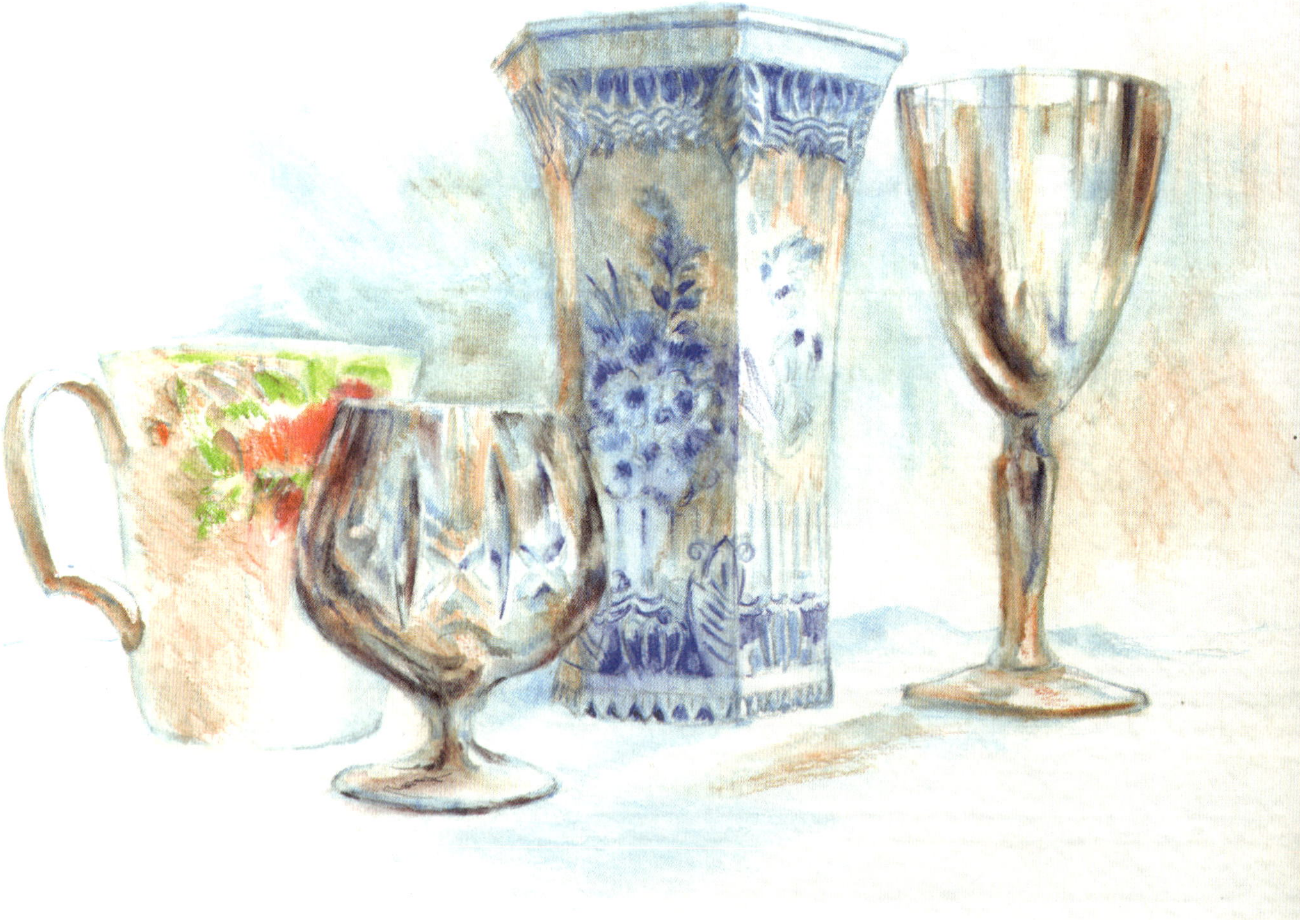

5 Continue Adding and Adjusting Color, Touch Up as Needed

Color adjustment may be required at several stages because the pigment mixing is so unpredictable. The advantage of this medium, though, is the precision with which the shapes can be controlled. Sometimes the color surprises are actually pleasant.

6 Develop the Background and Details

In order to develop the details you will need to draw wet and dry alternately. This will become quite routine, so it is very handy to keep a blow dryer nearby. Usually you would not wait this long to begin work on a background, but the uncertainty of color with this medium requires that you see the final results on the objects before deciding on the background. This still life needed some dark areas to contrast the light-colored objects. A blend of brown, blue, orange and violet was used where the darkest values were required.

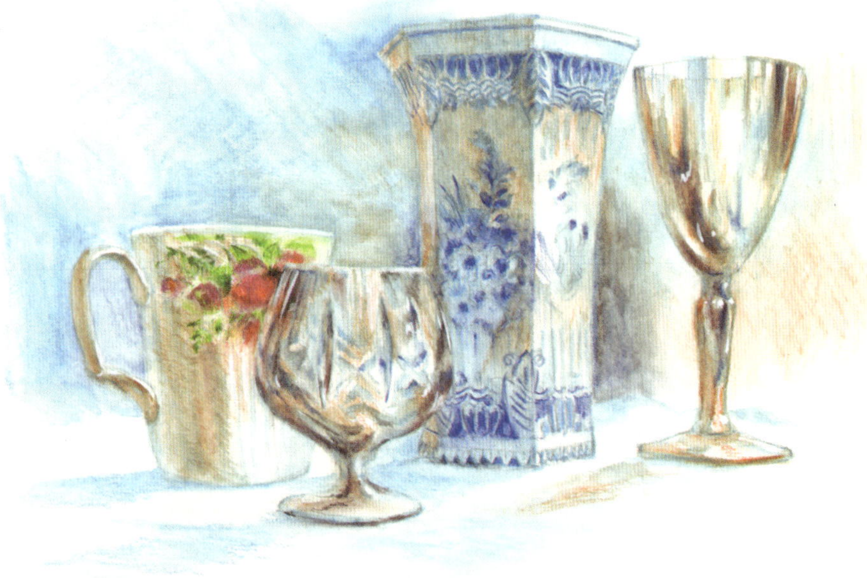

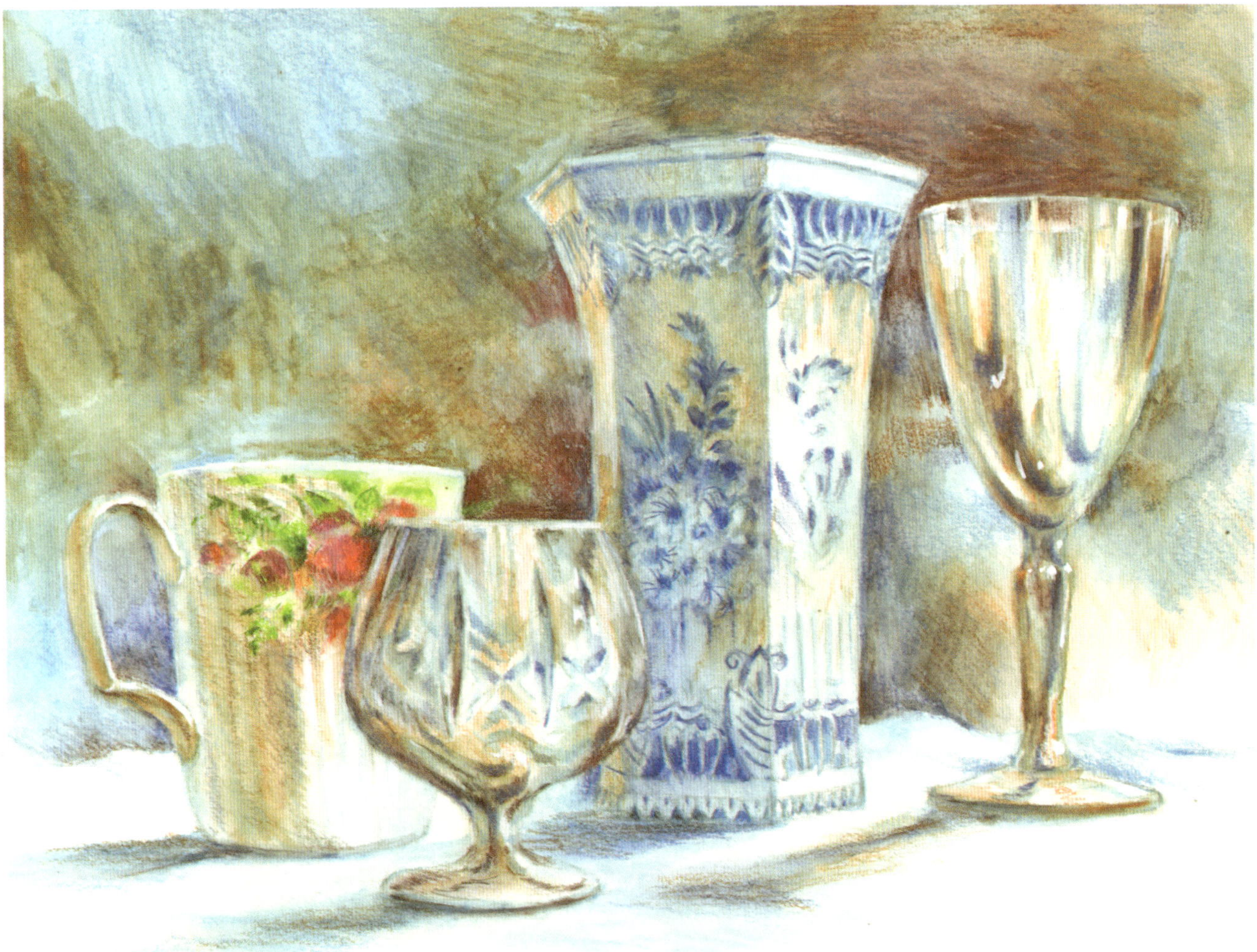

Watercolor Pencils

Blend Pigments in a Seascape

Let's explore just how smooth and well blended watercolor pencils can get. This is a relatively slow process but it offers the advantage of precise placement of color and value.

MATERIALS

Surface
200-lb. (425gsm) rag watercolor paper

Graphite
no. 8 round
black, blue, brown, orange, violet, white, yellow

Other
blow dryer
water

1 Start With the Sky

Begin with a light application of yellow and orange. Several passes with very light strokes work better than allowing the pencils to dig into the paper. Do the same with the blue. Wet the sky with a no. 8 round, but blend without over mixing.

2 Create the Trees and Rocks

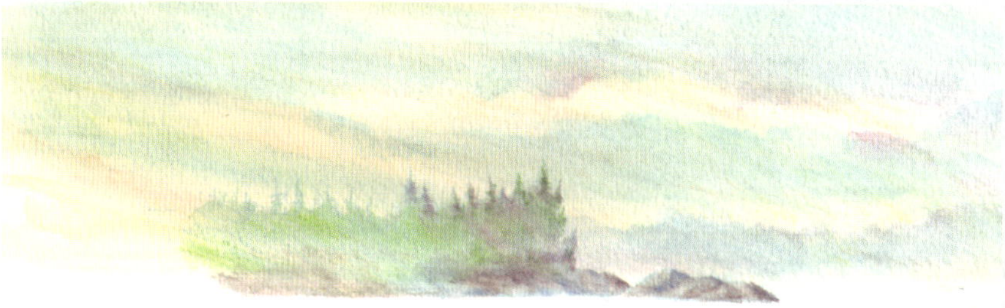

Create the distant trees with a mixture of blue, yellow, orange and violet. Keep the warm, light colors on the left. You want the light source in that area so that the shadows will be on the right side of the rocks.

Establish a routine of applying colored pencil on the dry paper, then blending with the damp brush. Dry the paper, then add more pigment. Alternate between applying and blending so you gradually build up the desired form.

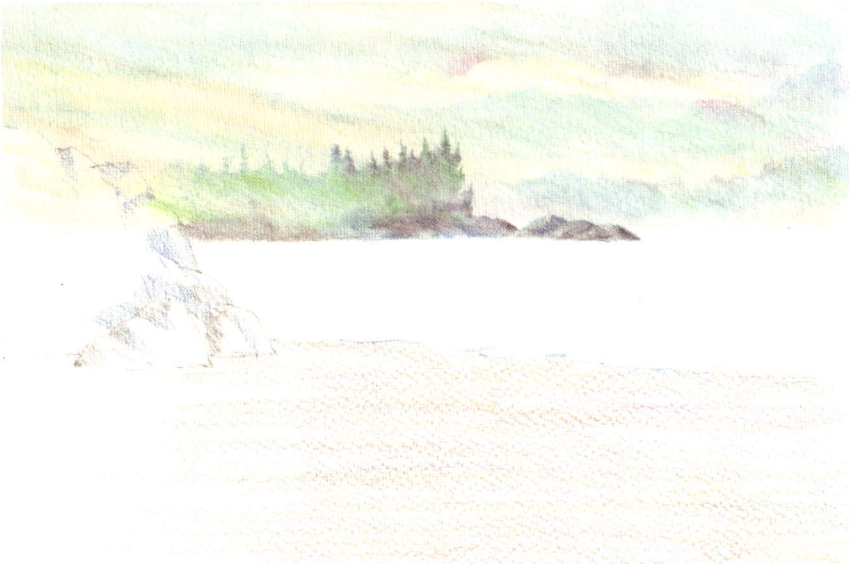

3 Lay In the Foreground

Jump to the foreground and use a combination of orange and blue for the wet sand at the bottom. If you have a Burnt Sienna pencil, it will work very well with blue to make a sandy gray color.

Use a bit of blue and violet to make the dark parts on the rocks, and brown or orange to tone them down.

4 Apply a Wet Brush

Use the wet brush horizontally, in the same direction as the patterns in the sand. This will cause them to blend nicely in a horizontal direction but retain a variation of value.

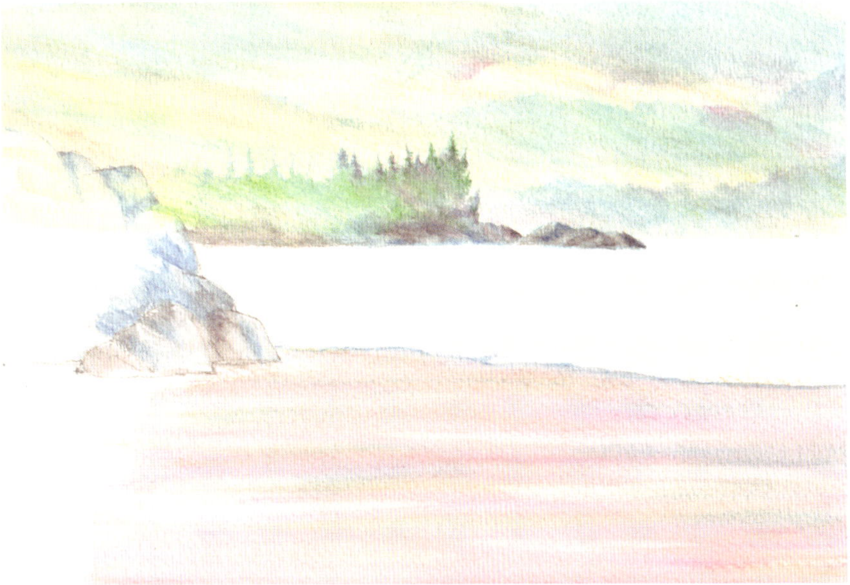

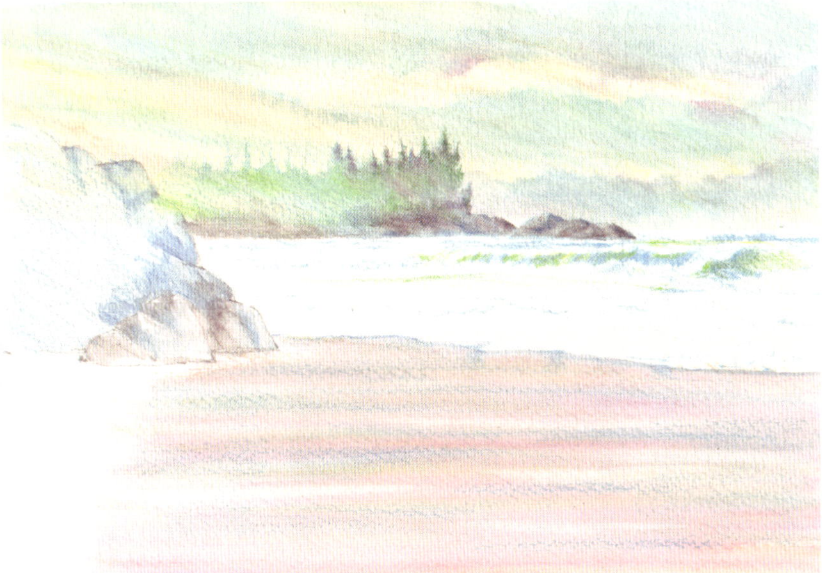

5 Create Foam and Waves

Use a combination of blue, yellow and orange to work around and shape the white caps of the waves. Add some light blue to the foreground rock because it will be in shadow.

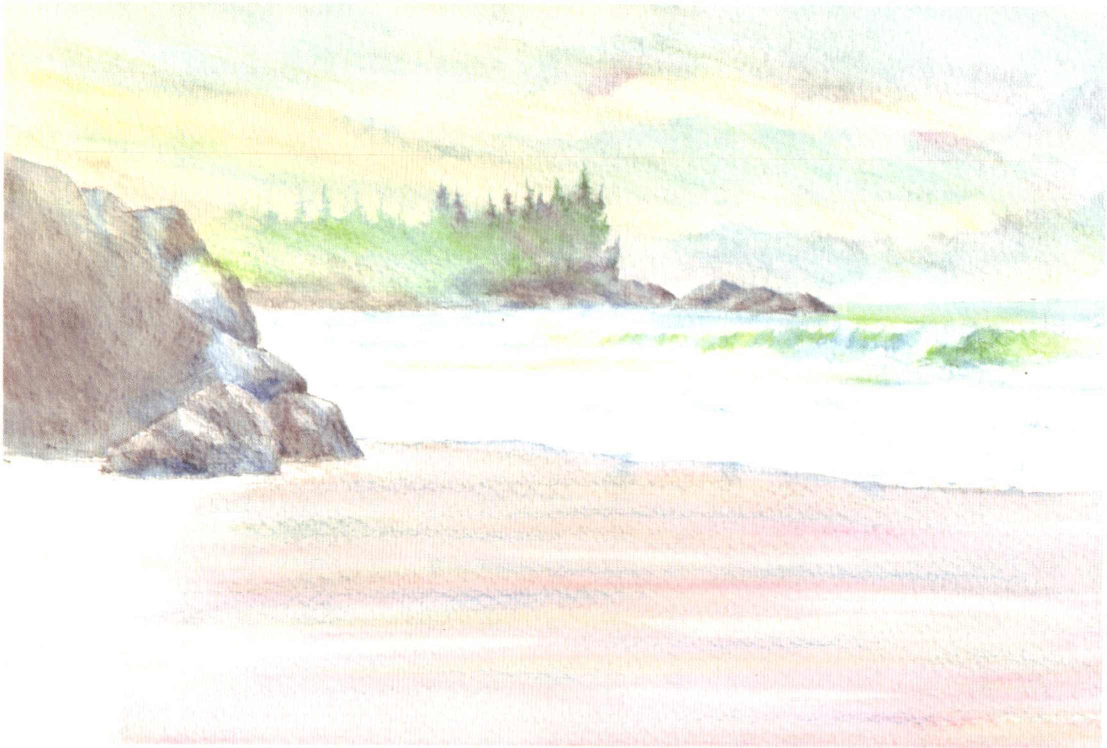

6 Continue Drawing and Refine the Rocks

Continue drawing small areas and wetting them as you go. Add some brown over the blue in the rocks. Some darks such as violet and brown work well to describe shape and details.

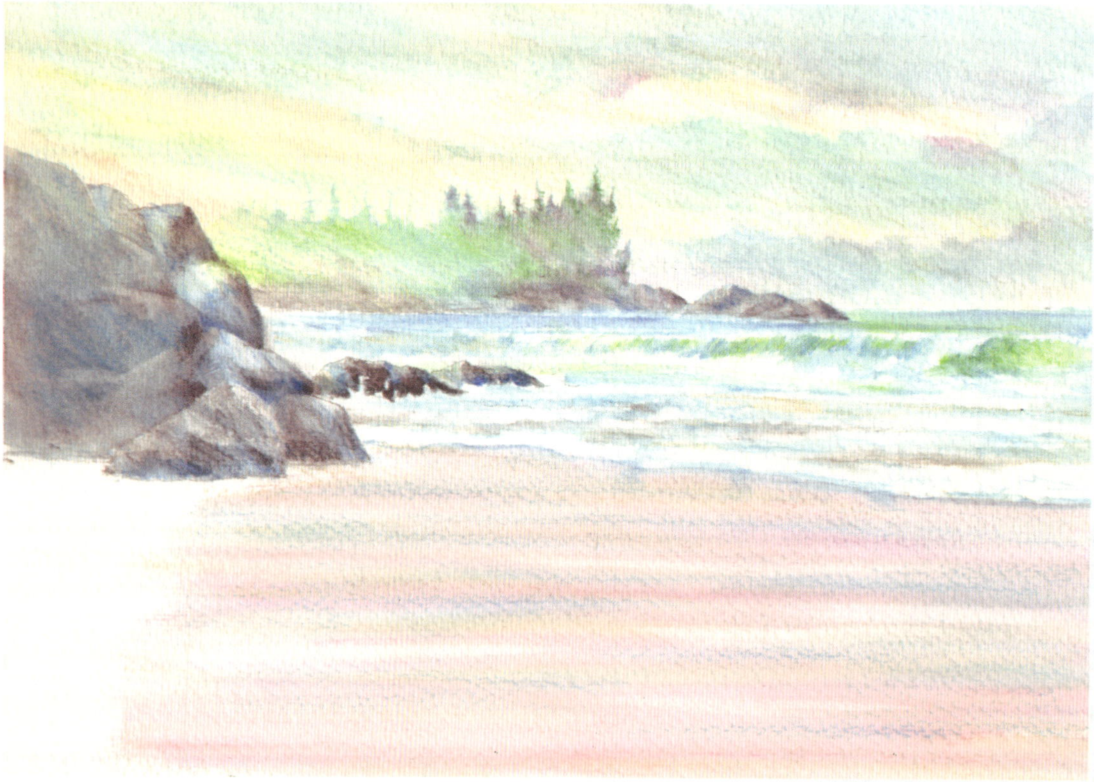

7 Add More Rocks

Add a couple of smaller rocks jutting out into the foam. Use a bit of blue to make a wet rock reflect the sky, along with brown and violet. Avoid black for now – it is too abrupt.

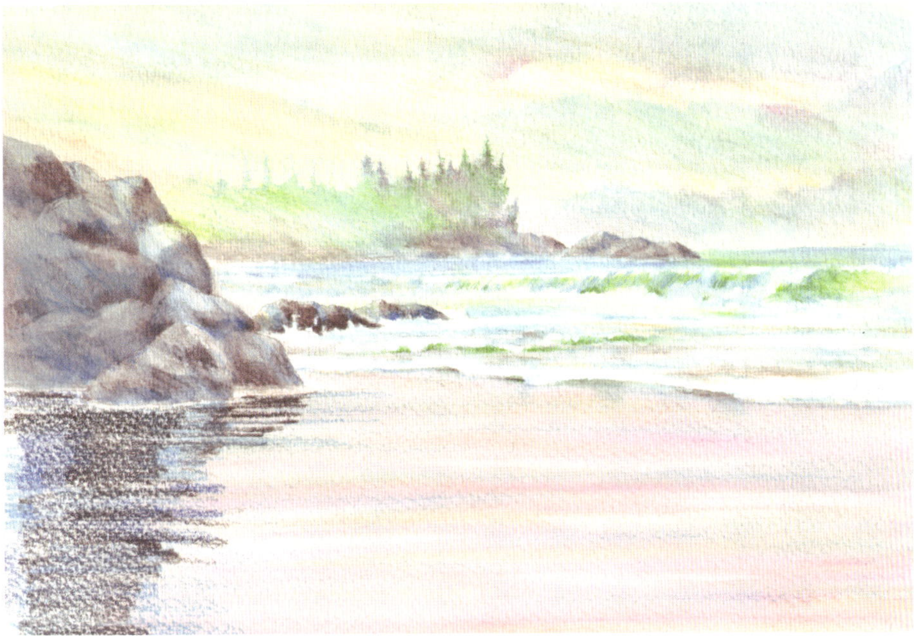

8 Add Reflections

Add a large, dark reflection of the rock in the wet sand. Build up this dark area with blue, violet, brown and a bit of orange in stages of dry and wet. Use horizontal brushstrokes to avoid mixing the pattern vertically and to keep the wet sand looking flat and shiny.

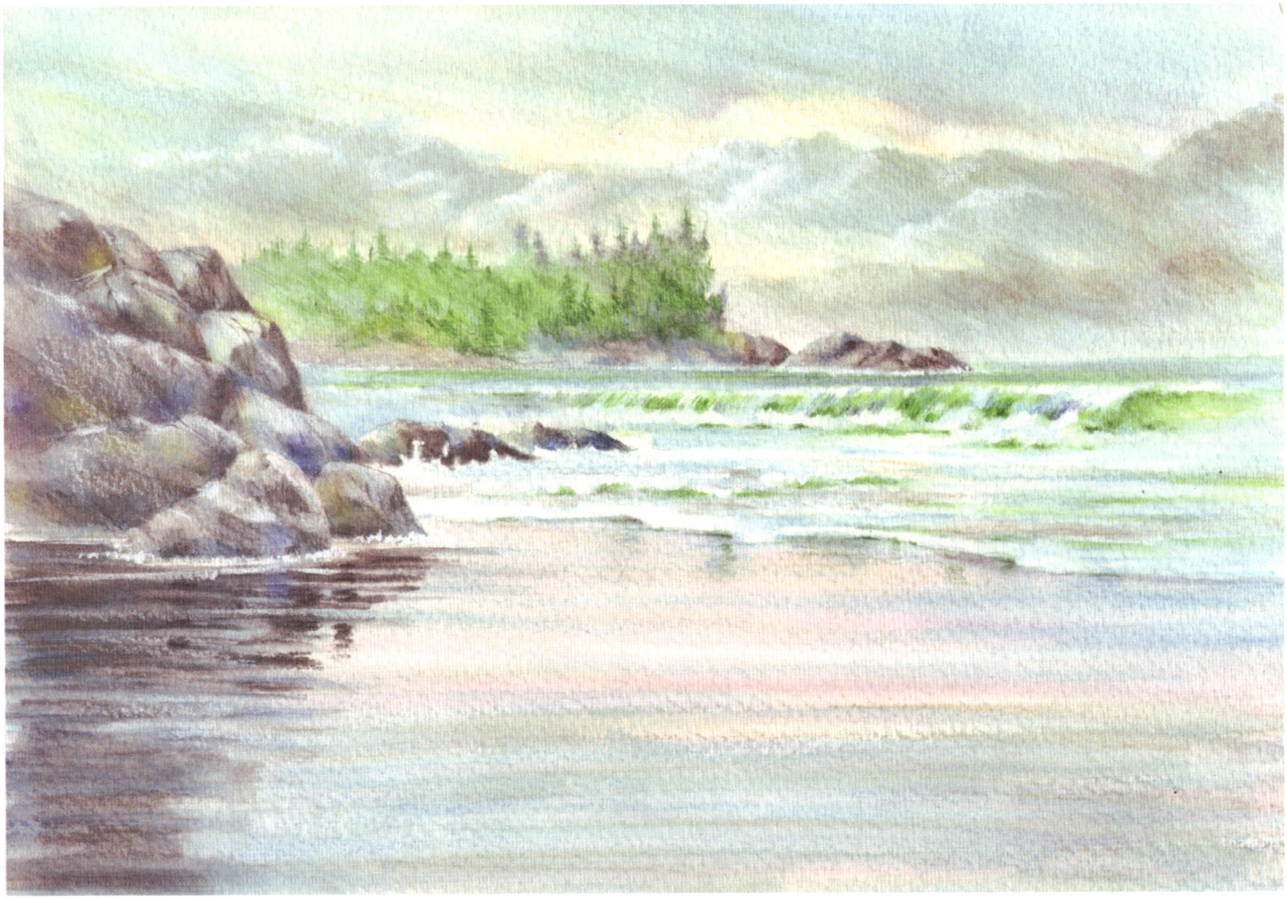

9 Add Finishing Touches

Work in a small amount of black and white. Use black to sharpen some of the edges of the rock, and white to catch the white foam on the base of the rock.

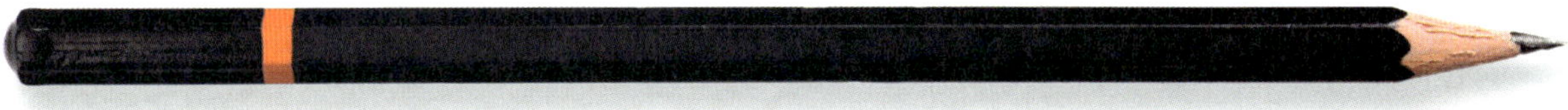

CHAPTER

9

Conclusion

I have always believed that drawing is the foundation of any visual art form. Whether the end result is an oil, acrylic, watercolor painting or sculpture in clay or stone, there must be a plan. The drawing is the plan, and if it is a good drawing, it may become a finished work of art in its own right.

Study the work of renowned sculptors such as Michelangelo and Henry Moore. Find books containing their drawings. You will soon see the direct relation between drawing and sculpture. Study the paintings of Picasso and then find examples of his drawings, especially the early ones before his venture into abstraction. His drawing skill as a young artist was amazing.

If drawing is looked upon as fun, an exploration, a study for a future work, then the stress is removed and progress will begin to show. What was once difficult and uncertain will become confident and spontaneous. Learning to draw requires practice but being shown what to practice can save many hours of trial and error. Everything I have recorded in this book is what was taught to me by other brilliant artists. It is only right to pass it along to those anxious to learn.

Grant Fuller

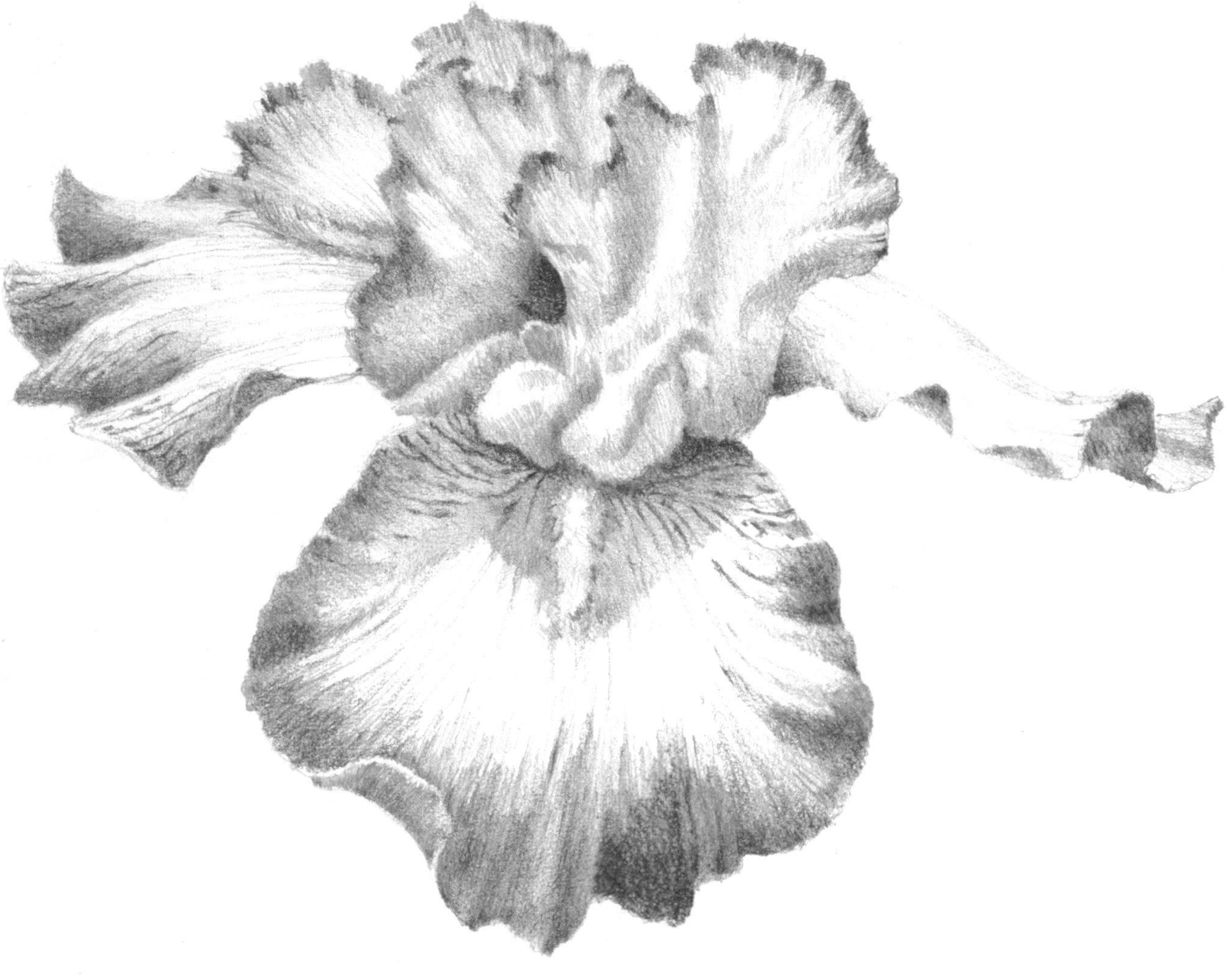

Index

A

Angle, 17, 25, 40

B

Back lighting, 52
Background, 87, 105
Blending tone, 29, 31, 34–35
Blind contour drawing, 14, 81.
Bristol board, 11
Brushes for watercolor, 113

C

Carbon paper, 23
Cartridge paper, 11
Center lighting, 52
Charcoal, 92, 95–97
Colored pencils, 100–107
Contour
- aiding direction, 41
- blind contour drawing, 14, 81
- faces, 80–83
- sketching, 30, 45, 66

Contrast, 15
Crosshatching, 93

D

Drawing on site, 61

E

Erasers, 10, 29

F

Faces, 78–87
Faking 3-D, 25–27
Figures, 88–89
Flat plane in perspective, 53
Foreshortening, 39–41
Freehand hard-line subjects, 16

G

Gesture drawing, 62, 90–91
Graphite, 5, 8
Graphite techniques, 12–23
Grid, 48–49

H

Hard lines, 15–16, 70–71
Hatching, 93
Horizon perspectives, 51, 54, 56

I

Illustration board, 11
Irregular surface shadows, 52

L

Lead shaping, 42
Light
- angle, 25
- back lighting, 52
- center lighting, 52
- front angled, 52
- reflected light, 26

Lines
- describing shape, 41
- freehand lines, 56
- hard lines, 15–16, 70–71
- quality, 13
- shadows. See Shadows
- soft lines, 17, 70–71

M

Memory, learning to "see," 18–21
- draw what you see, 20
- drawing figures, 89
- force yourself to see, 20
- practice, 20–21
- really see things, 19
- as roadblock, 19
- upgrade memory, 19

O

One-point perspective, 51, 58–59
Organic shapes, 14
On-site drawing, 61–77, 118–119
Outdoors, 60–77

P

Paper, 11, 92
Paper towels, 10
Pen and ink, 92, 93–94
Pencils. See also Graphite; Graphite techniques
- carpenter's pencil, 8
- colored, 100–107
- as a ruler, 37
- sharpened, 8
- sharpeners, 9, 100
- varying weights, 69

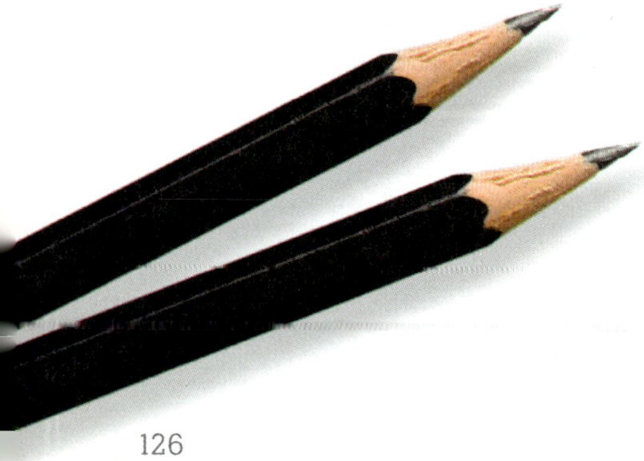

watercolor pencils, 108, 114–123
People
faces, 78–87
figures, 88–89
gesture drawing, 90–91
self-portrait, 100
Perspective, 50–59
Plein air, 60
Plotting proportion, 37–38
Portrait, 86–87
Professional instruction for drawing, 6
Proportion, 36–49
Props, 86

R

Reflections
on glass, 114–117
reflected light, 26
on water, 67, 68–69, 106, 123
Reversed proportions, 39
Ruler
pencil as, 37
scrap paper as, 38

S

Scale drawing with a grid, 48–49
Sepia drawings, 99
Shadows
faking 3-D, 26, 27
perspective, 52
Shapes
distant shapes, 66
faking 3-D, 25
lines describe, 41
perspective, 53
Shaping, lead, 42
Sharpeners, 9, 100
Simple perspective. See Perspective
Sketchbooks, 11
Smudging
applying tone with, 32–33
blending tones, 29
charcoal, 92, 95
unwanted, 75
Soft lines, 17, 70–71
Stumps, 10, 29, 31
Supplies and materials, 5, 8–10, 11
Surfaces, 5

T

Texture
cat fur, 42
outdoor drawing, 64–67
3-D, 25–27, 30, 39
Tone, 24–35
Tools
carpenter's pencil, 8
erasers, 10, 29
graphite, 5, 8
paper towels, 10
sharpeners, 9, 100
stumps, 10, 29, 31
utility knife, 10
Tracing, 22
Transfer a drawing, 22–23
Two-point perspective, 51, 54–57

U

Utility knife, 10

V

Value, 45
Vanishing points
estimating, 76–77
multiple, 74–75
two-point perspective, 54, 56

W

Wash drawing, 92, 98–99
Water
blending with pencil, 29, 34–35
blending with stump and eraser, 29
drawing on site, 62
reflections, 67, 68–69, 106, 123
seascape, 120–123
soft lines, 17
Watercolor pencils, 108, 114–123
Waterfront, outdoor drawing, 66–67
Wax pastels, 92, 108, 109–113
Work light to dark, 58

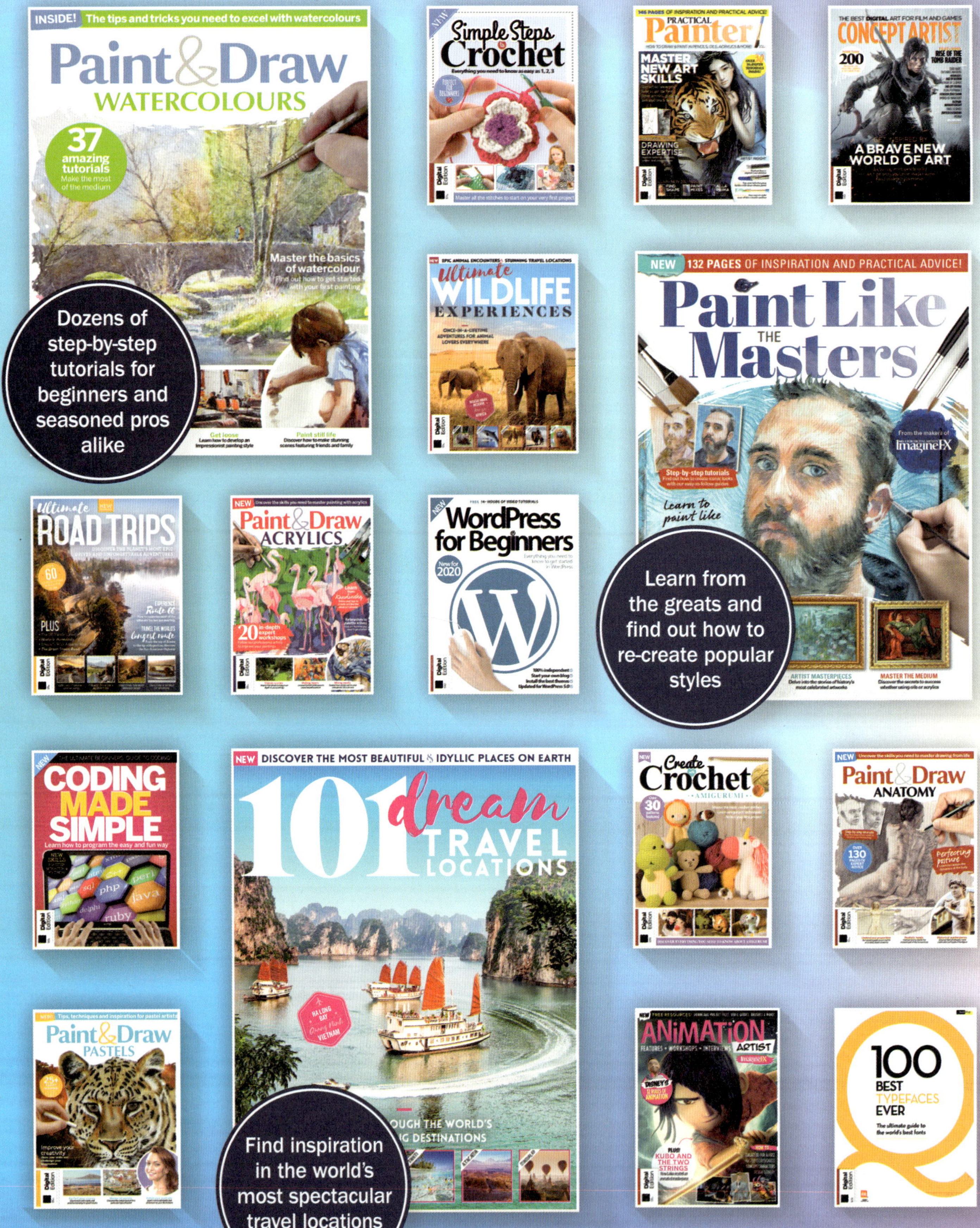
INSIDE! The tips and tricks you need to excel with watercolours
Paint & Draw WATERCOLOURS
37 amazing tutorials
Dozens of step-by-step tutorials for beginners and seasoned pros alike
Simple Steps to Crochet
PRACTICAL Painter
CONCEPT ARTIST
A BRAVE NEW WORLD OF ART
Ultimate WILDLIFE EXPERIENCES
NEW 132 PAGES OF INSPIRATION AND PRACTICAL ADVICE!
Paint Like THE Masters
Learn from the greats and find out how to re-create popular styles
Ultimate ROAD TRIPS
Paint & Draw ACRYLICS
WordPress for Beginners
CODING MADE SIMPLE
NEW DISCOVER THE MOST BEAUTIFUL & IDYLLIC PLACES ON EARTH
101 dream TRAVEL LOCATIONS
Find inspiration in the world's most spectacular travel locations
Create Crochet AMIGURUMI
Paint & Draw ANATOMY
Paint & Draw PASTELS
ANIMATION ARTIST
100 BEST TYPEFACES EVER

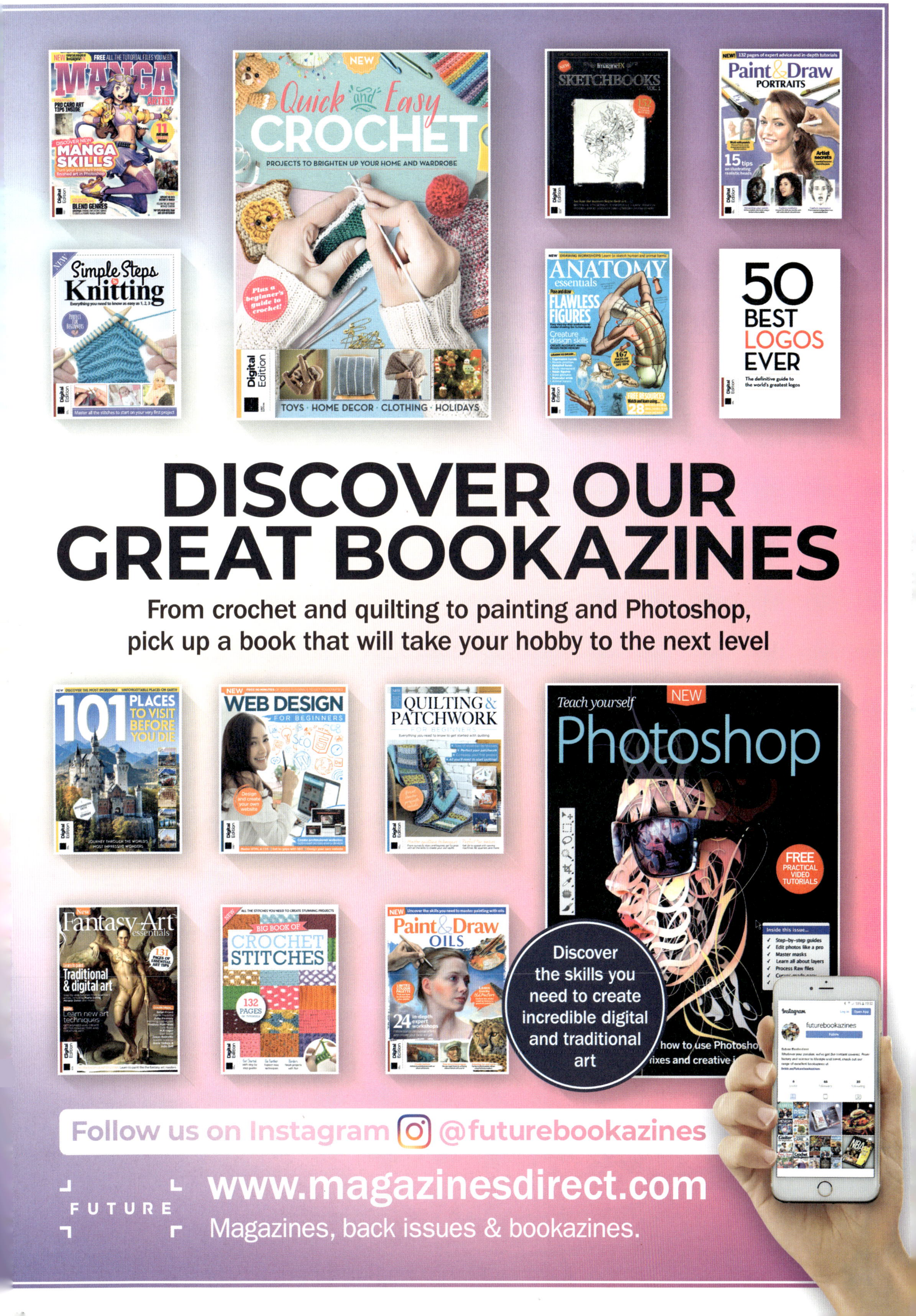
DISCOVER OUR GREAT BOOKAZINES
From crochet and quilting to painting and Photoshop, pick up a book that will take your hobby to the next level
Quick and Easy CROCHET
PROJECTS TO BRIGHTEN UP YOUR HOME AND WARDROBE
TOYS · HOME DECOR · CLOTHING · HOLIDAYS
MANGA ARTIST
SKETCHBOOKS
Paint & Draw PORTRAITS
Simple Steps to Knitting
ANATOMY essentials
50 BEST LOGOS EVER
101 PLACES TO VISIT BEFORE YOU DIE
WEB DESIGN FOR BEGINNERS
QUILTING & PATCHWORK FOR BEGINNERS
Teach yourself Photoshop
NEW
FREE PRACTICAL VIDEO TUTORIALS
Fantasy Art essentials
BIG BOOK OF CROCHET STITCHES
Paint & Draw OILS
Discover the skills you need to create incredible digital and traditional art
Follow us on Instagram @futurebookazines
FUTURE
www.magazinesdirect.com
Magazines, back issues & bookazines.